## Early Praise for *Core Data, Second Edition*

I learned Core Data reading the first edition of this book. It has long been my go-to reference, but a lot has changed since the first edition hit the shelves. The coverage of iOS and iCloud is a welcome addition, and the updated chapters on versioning and threading are a must-read. Those getting started with Core Data and those already using it owe it to themselves to read this fantastic book.

➤ **Kirby Turner, Chief Code Monkey, White Peak Software, Inc.**

If you need to know Core Data inside and out, you need this book. Marcus not only communicates what you need to know but has deep experience in making Core Data applications. That experience shines through in every chapter and example.

➤ **Bill Dudney, Gala Factory Software, LLC**

This book has information for beginners and experts alike, particularly around new features such as iCloud syncing. It's a must-have if you're going to be doing anything with Core Data.

➤ **Patrick Burleson, Owner, BitBQ, LLC**

If you're using Core Data and haven't read this book, you're doing yourself and your customers a disservice. Marcus Zarra explains the fundamental components of the Core Data framework and shows how the framework is used in real-world programming. This book is a must-read for anyone new to Core Data, but there's plenty of great information even for seasoned veterans.

➤ **Jeff LaMarche, Author and Co-Founder of MartianCraft, LLC**

# Core Data, 2nd Edition

Data Storage and Management for iOS, OS X, and iCloud

Marcus S. Zarra

The Pragmatic Bookshelf

Dallas, Texas • Raleigh, North Carolina

Many of the designations used by manufacturers and sellers to distinguish their products are claimed as trademarks. Where those designations appear in this book, and The Pragmatic Programmers, LLC was aware of a trademark claim, the designations have been printed in initial capital letters or in all capitals. The Pragmatic Starter Kit, The Pragmatic Programmer, Pragmatic Programming, Pragmatic Bookshelf, PragProg and the linking *g* device are trademarks of The Pragmatic Programmers, LLC.

Every precaution was taken in the preparation of this book. However, the publisher assumes no responsibility for errors or omissions, or for damages that may result from the use of information (including program listings) contained herein.

Our Pragmatic courses, workshops, and other products can help you and your team create better software and have more fun. For more information, as well as the latest Pragmatic titles, please visit us at *http://pragprog.com*.

The team that produced this book includes:

Colleen Toporek (editor)
Potomac Indexing, LLC (indexer)
Kim Wimpsett (copyeditor)
David J Kelly (typesetter)
Janet Furlow (producer)
Juliet Benda (rights)
Ellie Callahan (support)

Printed in the United States of America.
ISBN-13: 978-1-937785-08-6
Printed on acid-free paper.
Book version: P1.0—January 2013

# Contents

Introduction  .    .    .    .    .    .    .    .    .    .    ix

1.   **Under the Hood of Core Data**  .    .    .    .    .    .    .    1
    1.1   NSManagedObjectModel    1
    1.2   NSPersistentStoreCoordinator    5
    1.3   NSManagedObjectContext    8
    1.4   NSManagedObject    10
    1.5   NSFetchRequest    17
    1.6   NSSortDescriptor    20
    1.7   Fetched Properties    21
    1.8   Wrapping Up    21

2.   **iOS: NSFetchedResultsController**    .    .    .    .    23
    2.1   How to Use the NSFetchedResultsController    23
    2.2   Under the Hood of the NSFetchedResultsController    31
    2.3   Building Our Own: ZSContextWatcher    32
    2.4   Wrapping Up    36

3.   **Versioning and Migration**    .    .    .    .    .    37
    3.1   Some Maintenance Before We Migrate    38
    3.2   A Simple Migration    39
    3.3   The Difference Between Light and Heavy Migrations    42
    3.4   A Heavy/Manual Migration    44
    3.5   Fundamentals of Core Data Versioning    51
    3.6   Progressive Data Migration (An Academic Exercise)    54
    3.7   Wrapping Up    59

4.   **Performance Tuning** .    .    .    .    .    .    .    61
    4.1   Persistent Store Types    61
    4.2   Optimizing Your Data Model    63
    4.3   Fetching    67
    4.4   Faulting    71

|     | 4.5 | Access Patterns | 75 |
|     | 4.6 | Wrapping Up | 76 |
| **5.** | **Threading** | | **77** |
|     | 5.1 | Why Isn't Core Data Thread-Safe? | 77 |
|     | 5.2 | Creating Multiple Contexts | 78 |
|     | 5.3 | Exporting Recipes | 81 |
|     | 5.4 | Importing Recipes | 87 |
|     | 5.5 | Parent-Child NSManagedObjectContext Instances | 92 |
|     | 5.6 | Wrapping Up | 98 |
| **6.** | **Using iCloud** | | **99** |
|     | 6.1 | Introducing the UIManagedDocument | 100 |
|     | 6.2 | Direct NSManagedObjectContext to iCloud | 106 |
|     | 6.3 | Consuming Changes from iCloud | 109 |
|     | 6.4 | Under the Hood | 110 |
|     | 6.5 | Migrating an Existing Application | 113 |
|     | 6.6 | Desktop iCloud Integration | 116 |
|     | 6.7 | Data Quantities | 118 |
|     | 6.8 | Sharing Data Between iOS and OS X | 119 |
|     | 6.9 | Wrapping Up | 120 |
| **7.** | **Adding a Desktop Foundation** | | **121** |
|     | 7.1 | Our Application | 121 |
|     | 7.2 | Our Application Design | 122 |
|     | 7.3 | Sharing the Data Model | 122 |
|     | 7.4 | Building the Controller Layer | 123 |
|     | 7.5 | Building the User Interface | 126 |
|     | 7.6 | Adding a Splash of Code | 132 |
|     | 7.7 | Wrapping Up | 135 |
| **8.** | **OS X: Bindings, KVC, and KVO** | | **137** |
|     | 8.1 | Key Value Coding | 137 |
|     | 8.2 | Key Value Observing | 142 |
|     | 8.3 | Cocoa Bindings and Core Data | 143 |
|     | 8.4 | Other Interface Elements That Use KVO, KVC, and Core Data | 147 |
|     | 8.5 | Wrapping Up | 151 |
| **9.** | **Spotlight, Quick Look, and Core Data** | | **153** |
|     | 9.1 | Integrating with Spotlight | 154 |
|     | 9.2 | Integrating with Quick Look | 168 |

9.3    Putting It All Together                                    176
9.4    Wrapping Up                                                176

10.  **Dynamic Parameters**      .      .      .      .      .      .      .      .      .    **179**
10.1  Building the Xcode Example Project                          181
10.2  The DocumentPreferences Object                             181
10.3  Wrapping Up                                                186

11.  **Distributed Core Data**   .      .      .      .      .      .      .      .      .    **189**
11.1  Building the Server                                        190
11.2  Building the Client                                        199
11.3  Testing the Networking Code                                202
11.4  Wrapping Up                                                206

A1.  **Building a Foundation**   .      .      .      .      .      .      .      .      .    **209**
A1.1  The Storyboard                                             209
A1.2  The Recipe List                                            211
A1.3  The Recipe Detail                                          213
A1.4  The Edit Workflow                                          214
A1.5  Ready for Core Data                                        219

A2.  **Macros in the Precompiled Header**   .      .      .      .      .      .    **221**
A2.1  Where Are the Macros?                                      221
A2.2  What Do They Do?                                           222

    **Bibliography**   .      .      .      .      .      .      .      .      .      .    **225**

    **Index**   .      .      .      .      .      .      .      .      .      .      .    **227**

# Introduction

It is truly amazing how much has changed since the last time I sat down to write an introductory chapter for *Core Data*. The last time, in 2009, the iPhone had just been released, and Core Data was not available for it yet; in fact, the SDK had been released only that year. Of course, by the time we were finished with the production of the book, we did have Core Data on the iPhone, but it was in its infancy.

When I began putting together this second edition of the book, Core Data had just received a major update to its API, the first major update to its core API since its initial release for Mac OS X 10.4 Tiger. Now, that update has been out for more than a year, and we are settling into those changes and how they impact our development of applications.

## Is This Book for You?

If you plan on writing an application that saves data to disk, then you should take a very long look at Core Data. Whether you are focusing on the desktop or the iPhone, Core Data is the most efficient solution to data persistence.

A good way to confirm that you know enough Cocoa to benefit from this book is to take a look at Appendix 1, *Building a Foundation*, on page 209. You should find it dense, but every step should be familiar to you.

## What Is Core Data?

In the simplest terms, Core Data is an object graph that can be persisted to disk. But just like describing a man as a "bag of mostly water," that description hardly does Core Data justice. If you have worked with Interface Builder (specifically on OS X), you know that it effectively removes a third of the coding from the Model View Controller (MVC) design pattern. With Interface Builder, developers do not need to spend countless hours writing and rewriting their user interface to make sure that it is pixel perfect. Instead, they simply drag and drop the elements in the IDE, bind them together, and call it done.

Of course, the problem with Interface Builder is that we still need to code the other two parts! Both the controller and the model need to be developed in code and made to work with the interface we just designed. That is where Core Data comes in. In a nutshell, Core Data deals with a third of that MVC design: Core Data is the model.

It is a common misconception that Core Data is a database API for Cocoa that allows a Cocoa application to store its data in a database. Although that description is factually accurate, Core Data does a lot more. It serves as the entire model layer. It is not just the persistence on disk; it is also all the objects in memory that we normally consider to be data objects. If you have experience working with Java, C#, or some other object-oriented language, the data objects take a lot of time to write, and they are generally very repetitive in nature. Core Data eliminates most, if not all, of that boilerplate code for us and lets us focus on the business logic, or the controller layer, of our application. It does this with an interface that is as easy to use as Interface Builder.

In addition to ease of use, Core Data is also highly flexible. If we need to step in and change the functionality of some portion of the data model, we can. From how a value is handled when it is being accessed to how data is migrated from one persistent store to another, we can choose how little or how much we want to code ourselves and how much we want Core Data to do for us.

When you start to learn Core Data, it is best to think in terms of objects. Core Data is a framework designed to manage your data and data object graph. As a secondary function, it will persist that data to disk. However, its primary function is to manage the objects.

## Core Data and iOS 5.0

If you have started to flip through this book, you probably noticed that I refer to iOS 6.0 and OS X 10.8 frequently, and I rarely mention iOS 5.0 or OS X 10.7, although the API changes that impacted Core Data the most were introduced in iOS 5.0 and OS X 10.7. There is a reason for this. There are significant, unavoidable issues with these new APIs in their first release. These issues are so significant that I cannot recommend using the new APIs in their first release.

It took me a long time to come to this conclusion, and even now I truly wish I had a better answer. I kept hoping that a new point release would come out for iOS 5 that would address some of these issues; unfortunately, it never did. Now that iOS 6.0 has been released to the public, I do not believe we will ever see another release for 5.0.

It is possible to use the new features in iOS 5.0 and get them to work, but that's the exception, not the rule. It is far too easy to get into a threading deadlock or cause some of the new features to spin wildly out of control and have no way to correct the behavior.

I am not going to start this book by bashing Core Data; I love the API. However, iOS 5.0 (and Mac OS X 10.7) was a stumble, a misstep. It is far better to skip it and move on to iOS 6.0. But what about when your client/boss/customer requires you to be compatible with iOS 5.0? My advice is to use only the Core Data APIs that were available in iOS 4.x. They are well-tested and mature, and they work fine in iOS 5.0.

## Sample Code

In the first edition of this book, we spent a full chapter creating an application so that we could then walk through Core Data. This book follows the same path as the first: we will be working with one application throughout the book, and we will update it chapter by chapter, learning more about Core Data as we go. However, that application's construction is no longer at the front of the book. Instead, the walk-through of its construction is included in Appendix 1, *Building a Foundation*, on page 209, and it is available for your reference. The sample application in this second edition focuses on the iPhone instead of the desktop. The largest number of Objective-C developers develop only for iOS, and therefore we will keep our focus there. With that shift of focus does come a cost with regard to our sample application. The application itself has a significantly more complex user interface when compared to our previous desktop version.

If you are comfortable working with iOS applications already, you most likely will be able to dive into Chapter 1, *Under the Hood of Core Data*, on page 1. However, if you are relatively new to iOS or storyboards, following along with the walk-through of the application creation will do no harm. The code is also available online; if you want to dive right into Core Data, you can grab it directly instead of creating it anew.

Having said that, the focus of this book is Core Data. If you are not comfortable with the fundamentals of Objective-C or developing applications for iOS, then I highly recommend you review Tim Isted's *Beginning Mac Programming [Ist10]* and Bill Dudney and Chris Adamson's *iOS SDK Development [AD12]*, both published by the Pragmatic Bookshelf.

## Macros

Over the years, I have developed many coding habits while working with Objective-C code. I tend to avoid most of those habits when I am writing or explaining code to someone else because they are shortcuts...distractions from the true journey of learning and becoming truly proficient with the language. However, there are a few exceptions. In Appendix 2, *Macros in the Precompiled Header*, on page 221, I discuss a few macros that have become so much part of my daily development life that I would feel remiss if I did not include them in this work. They are not shortcuts so much as enhancements. They help make the code easier to read and consume. I strongly suggest you at least skim over them before reading the code in this book so that you understand their purpose when used.

## In This Book

In this book, we build a single application that utilizes Core Data. We will use that application as the foundation through our journey with Core Data. While the application is actually written in Appendix 1, *Building a Foundation*, on page 209, we will start our journey with the fundamentals of Core Data. In Chapter 1, *Under the Hood of Core Data*, on page 1, we explore the building blocks of Core Data and how they fit together.

Once we have an understanding of the building blocks of Core Data, we are going to dive into NSFetchedResultsController, one of the most useful classes on iOS. In Chapter 2, *iOS: NSFetchedResultsController*, on page 23, we walk through how to use the NSFetchedResultsController and discuss *how* it works, and we wrap up with our own version that can be used not only on iOS (which the NSFetchedResultsController is limited to) but also on OS X.

Our next step will be into the realm of versioning and migration. In Chapter 3, *Versioning and Migration*, on page 37, we examine the very common situation of changes to our data model. How does Core Data deal with changing application requirements and changes to the structure of our data? We'll learn how Core Data determines version changes and how we can migrate our data from one version to another.

No application is complete until it performs well. In Chapter 4, *Performance Tuning*, on page 61, we look through the tools provided and how they can be used with our Core Data application to find hot, slow, or expensive parts of code in our application and address them. We also discuss some of the most common performance problems with Core Data applications and provide some solutions.

In Chapter 5, *Threading*, on page 77, we delve into the complex world of threading. Threading is often treated as a magic sauce to add to any application to make it automatically faster. With some experience (and more than a few hard knocks), we'll see that life is rarely that easy. In this chapter, we explore the best practices when working with Core Data in a threaded application. We take a look at a few examples of how we can get more performance out of our application in a threaded environment without adding to the complexity.

Once we are done with threading, it is time to explore iCloud. In Chapter 6, *Using iCloud*, on page 99, we look into how iCloud works with Core Data, what its limitations are, and how to integrate it into our application. At the time of the writing of this book, iCloud is still very much in its infancy, but I expect great things from it.

After we have explored iCloud, we'll turn our attention to the desktop. While most of our focus is on iOS, OS X is still very much alive and well. With the creation of iCloud, it is more important than ever to provide our users with the choice and ability to use our application either on the go or on the desktop. In Chapter 7, *Adding a Desktop Foundation*, on page 121, we build a desktop version of our iOS application so we can explore some of the features of Core Data that are available only on the desktop.

With our desktop version built, it is time to explore KVO and KVC. While these frameworks are available on both iOS and OS X, they are most heavily used on OS X. In Chapter 8, *OS X: Bindings, KVC, and KVO*, on page 137, we discuss what these frameworks are, how to use them, and why they are so extremely important to Core Data.

In Chapter 9, *Spotlight, Quick Look, and Core Data*, on page 153, we examine two features that are available only on OS X: Spotlight and Quick Look. We will add these desktop features to our application so that our users can enjoy a fully integrated experience.

To wrap up this book, we end with a couple of chapters designed to help you think outside the box. In Chapter 10, *Dynamic Parameters*, on page 179, we examine using the power of KVC combined with Core Data to give us the ability to store parameters in Core Data with a minimum amount of overhead.

In our final chapter, Chapter 11, *Distributed Core Data*, on page 189, we look at an academic exercise of integrating Core Data with distributed objects. Could we use Core Data on a server in the place of a traditional database design? We explore that question in this chapter.

## Acknowledgments

When I first started working with Core Data, I enjoyed it so much that I wanted to share all the discoveries that I had made with it. I soon continued sharing discoveries with other technologies as my enjoyment of the sharing became addictive. A while back I had the pleasure of meeting a fellow developer by the name of Matt Long and helped him become more proficient with Cocoa and its related technologies. During that time, we continued to share what we were learning and teaching in the form of the blog "Cocoa Is My Girlfriend." All of that led to this book. What started out with a simple altruistic gesture has turned into the text you are about to enjoy. Along the way, I have been helped by a number of fantastic developers.

First, I would like to thank Matt Long for convincing me to share what we learned in a broader space than just one on one. I think that discussion has changed both of our lives forever.

Second, thanks go to Tom Harrington for turning me on to Core Data in the first place. Being pointed at this technology at that particular time had a drastic, positive change on my development efforts at the time.

I would also like to thank one man who tends to remain behind the scenes: Brent Simmons. A quote from Mark Twain comes to mind when I think of Brent: "Keep away from people who try to belittle your ambitions. Small people always do that, but the really great make you feel that you, too, can become great." Thank you, Brent, for making me feel that I, too, can become great.

I would also like to thank the reviewers of this book who have caught, corrected, and pointed out my many mistakes while writing. In addition to a general thank-you to everyone who has been a part of the beta, I would like to especially call out and thank the following reviewers: Matt Blackmon, Michael Bordas, Patrick Burleson, Bill Dudney, Michael Fey, Dave Klein, and Robert Miller. Gentlemen, I know how busy your schedules are, and I appreciate you making time for me. Included in that list is Daniel Steinberg, who was the editor on the first edition of this book and of course Colleen Toporek who made this second edition possible.

As every developer knows, it is nearly impossible to test your own code, and the same goes for your own writing. Without the people who read this book and tested the code while it was being written, this would be a far inferior work than the one you have in front of you. The testers and reviewers of this book have gone further than I ever expected to help make sure this work is accurate.

# CHAPTER 1

# Under the Hood of Core Data

Part of the barrier to entering the world of Core Data is that it is perceived as having a very steep learning curve. Looking at the code samples that Apple provides for developers, you might at first glance agree with that evaluation.

In my experience of working with and writing persistence layers for various languages, I am constantly amazed at how simple and elegant the Core Data API is. There is very little overlap in functionality between the individual pieces of Core Data—no wasted space or unnecessary redundancy. Because Core Data is built on the infrastructure of Objective-C and Core Foundation, it does not seek to duplicate functionality that already exists in other parts of the overall API but instead uses that functionality to its full extent.

In this chapter, we go through the key pieces of Core Data and remove some of the mysticism that surrounds them. We will also rewrite the sample code from Apple in order to present it in a much smaller and easier-to-maintain package. By the end of this chapter, you'll have a much higher comfort level and will be able to understand what all of that sample code does.

The Core Data API, or *stack* as it is commonly called, consists of three primary pieces: the NSManagedObjectModel, the NSPersistentStoreCoordinator, and the NSManagedObjectContext. All of these work together to allow a program to retrieve and store NSManagedObject instances. In most situations, the program will access the NSManagedObjectContext only once the stack has been created. It is possible to access the other components of the stack, but it is rarely necessary.

## 1.1 NSManagedObjectModel

The first part of our exploration of the components of Core Data is the portion of the framework that is the least-accessed: the NSManagedObjectModel. The NSManagedObjectModel can be considered a compiled, binary version of the data model that we create in Xcode. When we say that we are manipulating the object model, we mean we are editing the source file in Xcode that will get compiled and used by the NSManagedObjectModel. From a database perspective, this file represents the schema of the database. In Xcode, this file is shown in two different styles; the easiest to recognize is shown in Figure 1, *The data model*, on page 2.

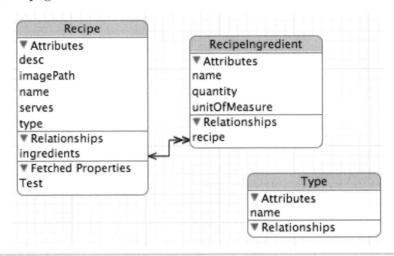

**Figure 1—The data model**

While this view is great for conceptualizing the data and the objects, it is not great for editing. Therefore, the style can be changed using a control in the lower-right corner called Editor Style. The second style is shown in Figure 2, *The data model in grid view*, on page 3.

At its most basic level, Core Data is an object graph designed to manage data objects. It is common when you are first approaching Core Data to think of it as an object-relational mapping framework—and in truth, it can be used as such. However, that is not the best approach. My elevator pitch for Core Data goes like this: "Core Data is an object graph that *can* persist to a database." The primary function of Core Data is to *manage* the object graph. Persisting the data to disk is a secondary, although vital, function.

With that in mind, the NSManagedObjectModel—and, by extension, the associated source file in the object model—is what we think of when we need to change the object model. The source file is saved as an .xcdatamodel file. In Xcode 4, this file is actually a bundle with an XML document stored inside. In prior versions of Xcode or in older project files, it's a bundle containing two binary files. In either version, it is best to edit this file only from within Xcode.

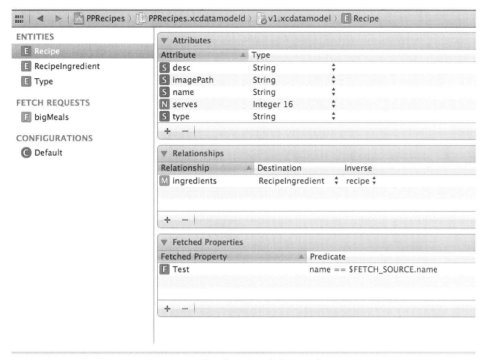

Figure 2—The data model in grid view

Xcode understands how to compile this file. When Xcode encounters this file during the compile process of a project, it compiles it into a binary form ending with the extension .mom. We can also build this file from the command line using the momc tool.

### Editing the Data Model

In Appendix 1, *Building a Foundation*, on page 209, we started with a sample project that already has a data model included. How did we create that data model? To begin with, we told Xcode to create a new file (File > New > File...), and we selected Data Model from the template, as shown in Figure 3, *Creating a new data model*, on page 4.

This presents us with a blank data model ready to be edited. From here, in grid view, we added the three entities being used in the project: Recipe, RecipeIngredient, and Type. We then added the attributes and relationships for each of those entities. For a discussion of entities, attributes, and relationships, take a look at Section 1.4, *NSManagedObject*, on page 10.

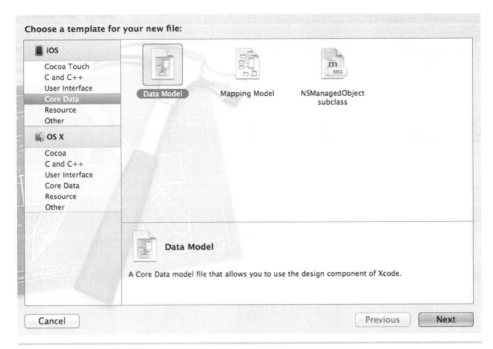

**Figure 3—Creating a new data model**

## Loading the Data Model

Once we have created the source file for the data model, we need to instantiate it within our application. In the Xcode sample projects, this is generally done in its own method in the application's AppDelegate. However, this process is unnecessary and tends to add to code bloat in the AppDelegate. My preference is to construct the entire Core Data stack in a single method because it is a single action from the perspective of the application. Further, I prefer to kick off the initialization of the Core Data stack as soon as the application launches so that it is available, in some form, immediately. Therefore, in our sample application, we have a method named -initializeCoreDataStack that starts off with constructing the data model.

```
RecipesV1/PPRecipes/PPRAppDelegate.m
- (void)initializeCoreDataStack
{
  NSURL *modelURL = [[NSBundle mainBundle] URLForResource:@"PPRecipes"
                                         withExtension:@"momd"];
  ZAssert(modelURL, @"Failed to find model URL");

  NSManagedObjectModel *mom = nil;
  mom = [[NSManagedObjectModel alloc] initWithContentsOfURL:modelURL];
  ZAssert(mom, @"Failed to initialize model");
```

To initialize the NSManagedObjectModel, we first need to locate it within the application bundle. We call upon the NSBundle and retrieve the -mainBundle, which represents the application bundle. From there, we call -URLForResource: withExtension: using the name of our data model—in this case PPRecipes—and the extension .momd. We use one of the macros discussed in Appendix 2, *Macros in the Precompiled Header*, on page 221, and we verify that we did receive a NSURL. We then initialize the NSManagedObjectModel with that NSURL. We again verify that everything worked correctly by checking the new instance against nil.

And that's all that is involved in constructing the NSManagedObjectModel. Our next step is to construct the NSPersistentStoreCoordinator, which uses the NSManagedObjectModel we just initialized.

## 1.2    NSPersistentStoreCoordinator

The NSPersistentStoreCoordinator is the true maestro of Core Data. The NSPersistentStoreCoordinator is responsible for persisting, loading, and caching data. Think of the NSPersistentStoreCoordinator as the heart of Core Data. Having said this, we do very little work with the NSPersistentStoreCoordinator directly. We work with it upon initialization, but we almost never touch it again over the life of the application.

As part of our initialization, we perform two steps with the NSPersistentStoreCoordinator. First, we initialize it, which requires a valid NSManagedObjectModel. Once it is initialized, we add one or more NSPersistentStore instances. An NSPersistentStore is a representation of a location in which the data is saved/persisted. Typically, this persistence is done to disk. However, that step is not required; it could be in memory or even over the network. For now, let's focus on disk persistence. The NSPersistentStore is responsible for describing the file format used. This file format can be one of several: SQLite, binary, or atomic. (There's also an XML store for OS X, but I do not recommend using it because it is not available on iOS, nor does it perform very well.) To keep our focus, we will use the SQLite format in this first iteration of our application and explore the other formats later in the book.

In previous versions of Core Data and the sample projects, the initialization of the NSPersistentStoreCoordinator and the addition of the NSPersistentStore were done in a single method. This example tended to lead to a number of issues for developers because they did not fully understand the impact of the example. Therefore, we are going to do this initialization in a more complex way, but it will be a way that will not paint us into a corner.

RecipesV1/PPRecipes/PPRAppDelegate.m

```
NSPersistentStoreCoordinator *psc = nil;
psc = [[NSPersistentStoreCoordinator alloc] initWithManagedObjectModel:mom];
ZAssert(psc, @"Failed to initialize persistent store coordinator");
```

In this first bit of code, we initialize the NSPersistentStoreCoordinator and pass it
the NSManagedObjectModel that we previously initialized. This call returns immediately, and therefore we can do it inline as part of the start-up of the
application.

Adding one or more NSPersistentStore instances to the NSPersistentStoreCoordinator,
however, can take an unknown amount of time. The reason for the unpre-
dictability is that we could be performing a migration during the call (as
discussed in Chapter 3, *Versioning and Migration*, on page 37), or we could
be linking and updating with iCloud (as discussed in Chapter 6, *Using iCloud*,
on page 99). If either of those situations occurs, the addition of the NSPersistentStore can delay the launch of the application to the point of providing a
poor user experience or, worse, being terminated by the operating system.
To avoid either of these situations, we want to add the NSPersistentStore on a
background queue so that the application can finish launching while we
perform our start-up.

RecipesV1/PPRecipes/PPRAppDelegate.m

```
dispatch_queue_t queue = NULL;
queue = dispatch_get_global_queue(DISPATCH_QUEUE_PRIORITY_DEFAULT, 0);
dispatch_async(queue, ^{
  NSFileManager *fileManager = [NSFileManager defaultManager];
  NSArray *directoryArray = [fileManager URLsForDirectory:NSDocumentDirectory
                                      inDomains:NSUserDomainMask];

  NSURL *storeURL = nil;
  storeURL = [directoryArray lastObject];
  storeURL = [storeURL URLByAppendingPathComponent:@"PPRecipes.sqlite"];

  NSError *error = nil;
  NSPersistentStore *store = nil;

  store = [psc addPersistentStoreWithType:NSSQLiteStoreType
                        configuration:nil
                                URL:storeURL
                            options:nil
                              error:&error];
  if (!store) {
    ALog(@"Error adding persistent store to coordinator %@\n%@",
        [error localizedDescription], [error userInfo]);
    //Present a user facing error
  }
```

In this portion of the code, we grab a reference to a global queue with a default priority. Then we add a block to be executed on that queue that will handle the addition of the NSPersistentStore to the NSPersistentStoreCoordinator.

Inside of that block, we first determine where we want to store the file associated with our NSPersistentStore. In this example, we are going to put it into the Documents directory that is part of the application sandbox. If we were working on OS X, we could put it in the Application Support folder or anywhere else that was appropriate. We resolve this path using the NSFileManager and call its -URLsForDirectory: inDomains: method, which will return an array of NSURL instances. We call -lastObject on that array to retrieve the last NSURL. We then append the filename for our NSPersistentStore to the end of that NSURL.

With the location of the store now resolved, we can add the NSPersistentStore to the NSPersistentStoreCoordinator. We do this with a call to -addPersistentStoreWithType: configuration: URL: options: error:. This is a complex method call, so let's break it down by parameter. There are five in all.

- The first parameter is Type. This tells the NSPersistentStoreCoordinator what type of store we want initialized. In this case, we are passing NSSQLiteStoreType to indicate we want a SQLite store. This is the parameter to change if we want to use another store type.

- The second parameter is configuration. This is an advanced setting that allows us to partition our data model into different configurations for different uses. Since we are not partitioning our data model at this time, we will pass nil, which tells the NSPersistentStoreCoordinator that we want to use the default configuration.

- The third parameter, URL, accepts the NSURL for the store. We pass in the NSURL that we resolved earlier.

- The fourth parameter, options, allows us to change the behavior of the NSPersistentStore. This parameter is used during versioning, during iCloud configuration, and for on-disk encryption. We are not using any of these features at this time, so we pass nil here as well.

- The last parameter, error, is used when something goes wrong with the addition of the NSPersistentStore. It is tempting to pass nil here as well, but I strongly advise against it. This is the only indicator when something goes wrong. I recommend passing a pointer to an NSError variable so that we can interrogate the error if something goes wrong.

This call will either return a NSPersistentStore or return nil. If it returns nil, that means something failed, and we need to interrogate the error. Since we do not normally need to have a reference to the NSPersistentStore after its creation, let's just check the return for nil and continue.

Once this call is completed, our NSPersistentStoreCoordinator is fully initialized and ready to be used. Since we have completed this step on a background queue, it is helpful to notify the UI that it is ready to be used. Therefore, we end the block with a call back onto the main queue and allow the UI to complete its initialization. This completion could include removing a modal dialog or even just telling the view controllers to reload themselves. The exact experience is left up to the developer.

RecipesV1/PPRecipes/PPRAppDelegate.m
```
  dispatch_sync(dispatch_get_main_queue(), ^{
    [self contextInitialized];
  });
});
```

Once we initialize the NSPersistentStoreCoordinator, we rarely, if ever, access it directly again. It silently works in the background, persisting the data. Because of this, we do not need to keep a reference to it directly in my AppDelegate; instead, we can rely on the NSManagedObjectContext to do that for us.

## 1.3  NSManagedObjectContext

Next to NSManagedObject, NSManagedObjectContext is the object in the Core Data stack that we'll most often access. The NSManagedObjectContext is the object we access when we want to save to disk, when we want to read data into memory, and when we want to create new objects. As shown in Figure 4, *The Core Data stack*, on page 9, the NSManagedObjectContext is at the top of the Core Data "stack" in that it is accessed directly by our code frequently. It is much less common for us to need to go deeper into the stack.

NSManagedObjectContext isn't thread-safe. Each thread that needs access to the data should have its own NSManagedObjectContext. This is generally not an issue, since most applications are not multithreaded or their multithreaded portions do not need to interact with NSManagedObjectContext on any thread other than the main thread. However, it is important to keep in mind that, like the UI, NSManagedObjectContext should be accessed only on the thread that created it, which is generally the main thread.

RecipesV1/PPRecipes/PPRAppDelegate.m
```
NSManagedObjectContext *moc = nil;
NSManagedObjectContextConcurrencyType ccType = NSMainQueueConcurrencyType;
moc = [[NSManagedObjectContext alloc] initWithConcurrencyType:ccType];
[moc setPersistentStoreCoordinator:psc];
[self setManagedObjectContext:moc];
```

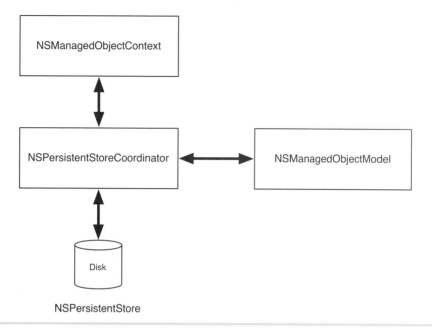

**Figure 4—The Core Data stack**

The NSManagedObjectContext itself is fairly straightforward to initialize. As of iOS 5 and Mac OS X 10.7, the initialization accepts a parameter to define what type of context we are constructing. The different types of contexts are discussed in detail in Chapter 5, *Threading*, on page 77. For now, we will be constructing an NSMainQueueConcurrencyType NSManagedObjectContext. That parameter tells Core Data that the NSManagedObjectContext we are initializing can be used only from the main (UI) queue of our application.

Once the NSManagedObjectContext has been initialized, we only need to set the NSPersistentStoreCoordinator that it is going to access. From there, it is ready to be used. Therefore, we hand off the reference to it to our AppDelegate so that the rest of the application can access it.

If you look at our sample application, you will notice that the order in which I described these events is different from the order they appear in the code. In the code, I actually initialize the NSManagedObjectContext prior to kicking off the block to add the NSPersistentStore to the NSPersistentStoreCoordinator. The reason for this is one of potential order. I want to guarantee that the @property for the NSManagedObjectContext is set before the NSPersistentStore is added and before the -contextInitialized method is called. While it is highly unlikely that the block on the queue would complete before the method we are in, there is no reason to risk it.

## 1.4 NSManagedObject

The NSManagedObject is the object we work with the most in a Core Data application. Each instance of the NSManagedObject represents one entity in our Core Data repository. By combining Core Data with KVO and KVC (discussed in great detail in Chapter 8, *OS X: Bindings, KVC, and KVO*, on page 137), this one object can dynamically represent any object that we need and that can be defined in our data model.

All of the properties and relationships defined in our data model are available and are easy to access directly from the NSManagedObject. Without subclassing it, we can access values associated with an NSManagedObject in the following ways.

### Accessing Attributes

Attributes are the easiest to access. By utilizing KVC, we can get or set any attribute on the NSManagedObject directly. If you have reviewed our sample app in Appendix 1, *Building a Foundation*, on page 209, you may have noticed that we did not write a Recipe class. At this point in our application, the NSManagedObject provides all of the functionality that we require. For example, we could get the name as follows:

```
NSManagedObject *recipe = ...;
NSString *name = [recipe valueForKey:@"name"];
```

Likewise, we can set the name in a similar fashion, as follows:

```
NSManagedObject *recipe = ...;
[recipe setValue:@"New Name" forKey:@"name"];
```

When we want to subclass NSManagedObject, we can also define properties for the attributes (and relationships discussed in a moment) so that we can access them directly. In the header of our subclass, we would define the properties normally.

RecipesV2/PPRecipes/PPRRecipeMO.h
```
@interface PPRRecipeMO : NSManagedObject

@property (strong) NSString *desc;
@property (strong) NSString *imagePath;
@property (strong) NSString *lastUsed;
@property (strong) NSString *name;
@property (strong) NSString *serves;
@property (strong) NSString *type;
```

As you can see, we are defining the property like normal, but there are no ivars associated with those properties. Since these properties are created dynamically at runtime, we do not need to declare them in the header. However, we do need to flag them as dynamic so that the compiler will not issue a warning. This is done in the implementation file.

```
RecipesV2/PPRecipes/PPRRecipeMO.m
#import "PPRRecipeMO.h"
@implementation PPRRecipeMO
@dynamic desc;
@dynamic imagePath;
@dynamic lastUsed;
@dynamic name;
@dynamic serves;
@dynamic type;
```

By declaring them as @dynamic, we are telling the compiler to ignore any warnings associated with these properties because we "promise" to generate them at runtime. Naturally, if they turn up missing at runtime, our application is going to crash. However, when we are working with NSManagedObject objects, the attributes will be looked up for us, and we do not need to implement anything. By adding that code, we can access the attribute directly, as shown in the following example:

```
PPRecipe *myRecipe = ...;
NSString *recipeName = [myRecipe name];
//Do something with the name
[myRecipe setName:recipeName];
```

## Primitive Access

It should be noted that accessing the attribute via KVC or properties will trigger KVO notifications that the attribute has changed. There are situations where we do not want this to occur or where we prefer it to occur later. In those situations, we can access the attribute using the -primitiveValueForKey: and -setPrimitiveValue:forKey: methods. Both of these methods work the same as the -valueForKey: and -setValue:forKey methods that we are used to working with, but they do not cause KVO notifications to fire. This means the rest of our application will be unaware of any changes we make until and unless we notify it.

Where is this useful? I find it quite useful when I am loading in data from an external source and the data is going to impact several attributes at once. Imagine we wrote a recipe importer that accepted a comma-separated value (CSV) file from another recipe application. In that situation, we might not want the UI or other parts of our application making decisions based on the data in the middle of the import. Therefore, we would want to update the values without notifications, and once all of them are done, we let the notifications go out. The code to handle this situation would look like this:

```
- (void)importData:(NSDictionary*)values //CSV translated into a dictionary
{
  [self willChangeValueForKey:@"name"];
  [self willChangeValueForKey:@"desc"];
  [self willChangeValueForKey:@"serves"];
  [self willChangeValueForKey:@"type"];
  [self setPrimitiveValue:[values valueForKey:@"name"] forKey:@"name"];
  [self setPrimitiveValue:[values valueForKey:@"desc"] forKey:@"desc"];
  [self setPrimitiveValue:[values valueForKey:@"serves"] forKey:@"serves"];
  [self setPrimitiveValue:[values valueForKey:@"type"] forKey:@"type"];
  [self didChangeValueForKey:@"type"];
  [self didChangeValueForKey:@"serves"];
  [self didChangeValueForKey:@"desc"];
  [self didChangeValueForKey:@"name"];
}
```

In this example code, we are handling all the change notifications ourselves and setting the values into our NSManagedObject directly using the -setPrimitiveValue:forKey: method. This will cause all the values to be updated prior to the notifications being fired.

## Accessing Relationships

Accessing relationships on an NSManagedObject is nearly as easy as accessing attributes. There is a bit of a difference between working with a to-one relationship and a to-many relationship, though.

### Accessing a To-One Relationship

When we are accessing a to-one relationship, we can treat it the same as we do an attribute. Since Core Data is first and foremost an object graph, a to-one relationship can be treated exactly like a property that contains any other object. For example, the relationship between RecipeIngredient and its Recipe is a to-one relationship from the RecipeIngredient side. Therefore, if we were accessing this relationship from that point of view, the code would be as follows:

```
NSManagedObject *ingredient = ...;
NSManagedObject *recipe = [ingredient valueForKey:@"recipe"];
```

In this example, we are using the -valueForKey: KVC method to access the relationship, and the NSManagedObject returns the object on the other side of the relationship, which is the entity. Likewise, to set the recipe for an ingredient, we would use the following code:

```
NSManagedObject *ingredient = ...;
NSManagedObject *recipe = ...;
[ingredient setValue:recipe forKey:@"recipe"];
```

### Accessing a To-Many Relationship

The many side of a relationship is stored unordered. This means each time we fetch the objects on the many side of a relationship, the order is not guaranteed, and it is probable that the order will change between fetches. However, we are guaranteed that each object will be included only once. In other words, when we access a to-many relationship using KVC, we will get an NSSet back. For example, if we want to access the ingredients of a recipe, we would use code similar to the following:

```
NSManagedObject *recipe = ...;
NSSet *ingredients = [recipe valueForKey:@"ingredients"];
```

Likewise, setting the ingredients into a recipe is as follows:

```
NSManagedObject *recipe = ...;
NSSet *someIngredients = ...;
[recipe setValue:someIngredients forKey:@"ingredients"];
```

### Mutable Access of To-Many Relationships

You might notice that the NSSet we get back when accessing a to-many relationship is immutable. Adding an object to a to-many relationship with an immutable NSSet requires creating a mutable copy of the NSSet, adding the new object to the NSMutableSet, and setting the NSMutableSet back onto the parent object. It's a painful process and, fortunately, unnecessary. When we want to add an object to a to-many relationship, we can use -mutableSetValueForKey: in the place of -valueForKey:. This returns an NSMutableSet for us that is already associated with the parent object and reduces our code to the following:

```
NSManagedObject *newIngredient = ...;
NSManagedObject *recipe = ...;
NSMutableSet *ingredients = [recipe mutableSetValueForKey:@"ingredients"];
[ingredients addObject:newIngredient];
```

Note that we did not need to set the NSMutableSet back into the entity, and therefore the code to add an object to a to-many relationship is quite short.

One important thing to notice in these relationship examples is that when we update the relationship, we are updating only one side of it. Because we defined these relationships as double-sided (that is, they include an inverse relationship that we defined in Section 1.1, *NSManagedObjectModel*, on page 1), Core Data handles keeping the integrity of the relationships intact. When we update one side of a relationship, Core Data automatically goes in and sets the other side for us.

## Primitive Access

Similar to the process of accessing attributes discussed earlier, changes to a relationship will fire KVO notifications. Since there are situations in which we do not want this to occur or in which we want a finer-grained control over the notifications, there are primitive accessors for relationships as well. However, there is no primitive method for retrieving an NSMutableSet for a to-many relationship. Therefore, if the code requires changes to a relationship with either delayed or no observations being fired, we must use -primitiveValue-ForKey: to get back an NSSet, call -mutableCopy on the NSSet, add our new object to the NSMutableSet, and finally use -setPrimitiveValue:forKey: to apply the changes.

## Property Accessors

Relationships can use properties, just like the attributes discussed earlier. In the code in *Mutable Access of To-Many Relationships*, on page 13, if we want to add a property to retrieve the relationship, we declare the following property:

```
@property (strong) NSSet *recipeIngredients;
```

And then we flag it as dynamic in the implementation file.

## Subclassing NSManagedObject

Although NSManagedObject provides a tremendous amount of flexibility and handles the majority of the work a data object normally does, it does not cover every possibility, and there are occasions where we might want to sub-class it. Subclassing to gain @property access to attributes and relationships is one common situation, but we may also want to add other convenience methods or additional functionality to the object. When such a situation arises, there are some general rules to remember.

### Methods That Are Not Safe to Override

In Apple's documentation, the methods shown in Table 1, *Methods never to override*, on page 15 should never be overridden.

It's quite a list. Most, if not all, of these methods are common sense, and experience with Objective-C explains why they should not be overridden. Even though this is a fairly long list, I'm going to add a few more.

### -initXXX

The first is -initXXX. There is really no reason or benefit to overriding the -init methods of an NSManagedObject, and there are situations in which doing so has unpredictable results. Although it is not specifically against the documentation

| -primitiveValueForKey: | -setPrimitiveValue:forKey: | -isEqual: |
|---|---|---|
| -hash | -superclass | -class |
| -self | -zone | -isProxy: |
| -isKindOfClass: | -isMemberOfClass: | -conformsToProtocol: |
| -respondsToSelector: | -retain | -release |
| -autorelease | -retainCount | -managedObjectContext |
| -entity | -objectID | -isInserted |
| -isUpdated | -isDeleted | -isFault |
| -alloc | -allocWithZone: | +new |
| +instancesRespondToSelector: | +instanceMethodForSelector: | -methodForSelector: |
| -methodSignatureForSelector: | -isSubclassOfClass: | |

**Table 1—Methods never to override**

to override the -init methods, I recommend strongly against it. The -awakeFromInsert and -awakeFromFetch methods provide sufficient access that overriding -init is unnecessary. (Both -awakeFromInsert and -awakeFromFetch are discussed in more depth later in this chapter.)

### KVO Methods

I'd also add all of the KVO methods. The documentation flags these methods as "discouraged," but I'd put them right in the "do not subclass" list. There is no reason to override these methods, and any logic that you would want to put into them can probably be put somewhere else with fewer issues.

### -description

In addition, there's the -description method, used fairly often in logging. It is a great way to dump the contents of an object out to the logs during debugging. However, when we are dealing with faults (discussed in Chapter 4, *Performance Tuning*, on page 61), we do not want to fire a fault in the -description method. Since the default implementation of -description does the right thing with regard to faults, it is best that we not try to override its behavior.

### -dealloc

-dealloc is normally the place that we release memory before the object is being freed. However, when we are dealing with NSManagedObject objects, it is possible that the object will not actually be released from memory when we think it will. In fact, the -dealloc method may never get called in the life cycle of our application! Instead of releasing objects in the -dealloc method, I recommend using -didTurnIntoFault as the point of releasing transient resources. -didTurnIntoFault

> ### Joe asks:
> ## What Is a Fault?
>
> Core Data faults are similar to virtual memory page faults. Faulted objects are scoped objects that may or may not actually be in memory, or "realized," until you actually use them. Although there is no guarantee for when a faulted NSManagedObject will be loaded into memory, it is guaranteed to be loaded when accessed. However, the object will be an instance of the appropriate class (either an NSManagedObject or the designated subclass), but its attributes are not initialized.

will be called whenever the NSManagedObject is "faulted," which occurs far more often than the object actually being removed from memory.

### -finalize

-finalize is on the list for the same reason as -dealloc. When dealing with NSManagedObject objects, -finalize is not the proper point to be releasing resources.

### Methods to Override

With the long list of methods that we should not override, what methods should we consider overriding? There are a few methods we will commonly override.

### -didTurnIntoFault

This method is called after the NSManagedObject has been turned into a fault. It is a good place to release transient resources. One important thing to note is that when this method is called, all the stored values/relationships in the NSManagedObject are already out of memory. If you access any of them, it will fire the fault and pull them all back into memory again.

### -willTurnIntoFault

Similar to -didTurnIntoFault, this method is called just before the NSManagedObject is turned into a fault. If your code needs to access attributes or relationships on the NSManagedObject before it is turned into a fault, then this is the entry point to use. Transient resources that impact attributes and relationships should be released here.

### -awakeFromInsert

As mentioned, overriding any of the -init methods is risky and unnecessary. However, it is very useful to be able to prepare an NSManagedObject before it starts accepting data. Perhaps we want to set up some logical defaults or assign some relationships before handing the object to the user. In these situations, we use -awakeFromInsert. As the name implies, this method is called right after the NSManagedObject is created from an insert call. This method is called before any values are set and is a perfect opportunity to set default values, initialize transient properties, and perform other tasks that we would normally handle in the -init method. This method is called exactly once in the entire lifetime of an object. It will not be called on the next execution of the application, and it will not be called when an object is read in from the persistent store. Therefore, we do not need to worry about overriding values that have been set previously. When we override this method, we should be sure to call [super awakeFromInsert] at the very beginning of our implementation to allow the NSManagedObject to finish anything it needs to before we begin our code.

### -awakeFromFetch

-awakeFromFetch is the counterpart to -awakeFromInsert. The -awakeFromFetch method will be called every time the object is retrieved from the persistent store (that is, loaded from disk). This method is highly useful for setting up transient objects or connections that the NSManagedObject will use during its life cycle. At this point in the creation of the NSManagedObject, the observation of changes to the object (or other objects) is turned off, and Core Data will not be aware of any changes made. Ideally, we should avoid making any changes to relationships during this method because the inverse will not be set. However, if we explicitly set both sides of the relationship, it is possible to make changes here. Like the -awakeFromInsert method, when we override this method, we should call [super awakeFromFetch]; before any of our own code is called.

## 1.5   NSFetchRequest

NSFetchRequest is the part of Core Data that causes people to think it is a database API instead of an object hierarchy. When we want to retrieve objects from Core Data, we normally use an NSFetchRequest to do the retrieval. It is best to view an NSFetchRequest as a way to retrieve *all* instances of an entity from the object hierarchy, with the option to filter the results with an NSPredicate. There are two parts to the creation of an NSFetchRequest: setting the entity to be retrieved and optionally defining an NSPredicate to filter the objects we want retrieved.

### Setting the Entity

One thing that we must do as part of every NSFetchRequest is define the entity we want returned from the fetch. We do this by passing the appropriate NSEntityDescription to the NSFetchRequest. For example, if we want retrieve Recipe entities, we construct the NSFetchRequest as follows:

```
NSManagedObjectContext *moc = [self managedObjectContext];
NSFetchRequest *request = [[NSFetchRequest alloc] init];
[request setEntity:[NSEntityDescription entityForName:@"Recipe"
                            inManagedObjectContext:moc]];
```

In this example code, we construct a new NSFetchRequest and call -setEntity: on it. We use the class method +entityForName:inManagedObjectContext: on the NSEntity-Description class to get the appropriate instance of NSEntityDescription back for the setter.

## Executing a Fetch Request

Once we have constructed our NSFetchRequest, we need to execute it against the NSManagedObjectContext to get the results. Like a result set when accessing a database, an executed NSFetchRequest will return an NSArray of entities matching our search criteria. Since it is possible that a search might fail, the execution of an NSFetchRequest accepts a pointer to an NSError to describe any problems that resulted from the execution. For example, if we want to execute the fetch from the previous example, we use the following code:

```
NSManagedObjectContext *moc = [self managedObjectContext];
NSFetchRequest *request = [[NSFetchRequest alloc] init];
[request setEntity:[NSEntityDescription entityForName:@"Recipe"
                            inManagedObjectContext:moc]];
NSError *error = nil;
NSArray *results = [moc executeFetchRequest:request error:&error];
if (error) {
  NSLog(@"Error: %@\n%@", [error localizedDescription], [error userInfo]);
  return;
}
```

In this example, we call -executeFetchRequest:error: on the NSManagedObjectContext, passing in the NSFetchRequest and a pointer to a local NSError. If the fetch failed with an error, the pointer will be directed to an instance of NSError that describes the problem, and the NSArray will be assigned to nil. In that situation, we dump the error to the console and return. If there is no error, we can proceed with our code. Note that the NSArray is guaranteed to not be nil at this point, but it could be empty if no results are returned.

## NSPredicate

When we don't want every instance of an entity returned, we use an NSPredicate to narrow the search or filter the results. The NSPredicate class is quite complex and powerful and can be used for more things than just Core Data. It is frequently used to filter the results of collection classes by acting on the KVC API and doing logic checks on the objects contained in the NSArray or NSSet.

One of the most common ways to use an NSPredicate is to construct a SQL-like query, such as the following example:

```
NSManagedObjectContext *moc = [self managedObjectContext];
NSFetchRequest *request = [[NSFetchRequest alloc] init];
[request setEntity:[NSEntityDescription entityForName:@"Recipe"
                                inManagedObjectContext:moc]];
NSPredicate *predicate = [NSPredicate predicateWithFormat:@"serves > 10"];
[request setPredicate:predicate];
```

There are many different ways to build an NSPredicate. The one shown in the previous example accepts a SQL-like NSString and can accept any number of parameters after the NSString. For example, if we were going to pass in the number of servings, we would rewrite the NSPredicate as follows:

```
NSUInteger numberOfServings = 10;
NSManagedObjectContext *moc = [self managedObjectContext];
NSFetchRequest *request = [[NSFetchRequest alloc] init];
[request setEntity:[NSEntityDescription entityForName:@"Recipe"
                                inManagedObjectContext:moc]];
NSPredicate *predicate = nil;
predicate = [NSPredicate predicateWithFormat:@"serves > %i", numberOfServings];
[request setPredicate:predicate];
```

It is possible to add as many parameters to the NSPredicate as needed.

The NSPredicate class is quite flexible and can be used in a large number of ways. For further reading on how to use the class to its full potential, I recommend Apple's *Predicate Programming Guide*.[1]

## Stored Fetch Requests

In addition to constructing the NSFetchRequest directly in code, it is possible to build them within the data model and store them for later use. By storing the fetch requests within the model itself, it is possible for us to change them as needed without having to go through all the code looking for every place that it is used. Simply changing it in the model will automatically update wherever it is being used. To store an NSFetchRequest within the data model, we select the entity that we want to run the request against and choose Design > Data Model > Add Fetch Request from the main menu. From there we will be able to set the name of the fetch request and define its predicate, as shown in Figure 5, *Stored fetch request*, on page 20.

Once we have the fetch request in our data model, we can request a reference to it by asking the NSManagedObjectModel. Once we have a reference to the

---

1.  http://developer.apple.com/documentation/Cocoa/Conceptual/Predicates/Articles/pUsing.html

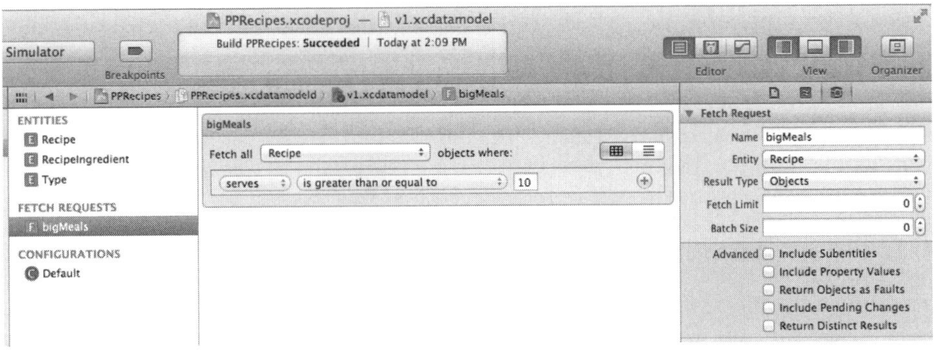

**Figure 5—Stored fetch request**

NSFetchRequest, we can execute it in the same manner as we do with an NSFetch-Request that has been constructed in code.

**RecipesV1/PPRecipes/PPRSelectIngredientTypeViewController.m**
```
NSManagedObjectContext *moc = [self managedObjectContext];
NSPersistentStoreCoordinator *psc = [moc persistentStoreCoordinator];
NSManagedObjectModel *model = [psc managedObjectModel];
NSFetchRequest *request = [model fetchRequestTemplateForName:@"allIngredients"];

NSMutableArray *sortArray = [NSMutableArray array];
[sortArray addObject:[[NSSortDescriptor alloc] initWithKey:@"name"
                                              ascending:YES]];
[request setSortDescriptors:sortArray];
```

As shown, we call the -fetchRequestTemplateForName: method on the NSManagedObjectModel, which returns a fully formed NSFetchRequest to us. This NSFetchRequest will already have the NSEntityDescription and NSPredicate set, so we can execute the NSFetchRequest immediately. We can also update this NSFetchRequest to include sort descriptors if needed.

## 1.6 NSSortDescriptor

NSSortDescriptor has been around longer than Core Data, and it is still quite useful for ordering data. As mentioned previously, data that comes from a to-many relationship is unordered by default, and it is up to us to order it. For example, if we wanted to retrieve all the recipes and sort them by their name property in alphabetical order, we would require an additional step as part of the fetch.

**RecipesV1/PPRecipes/PPRMasterViewController.m**
```
NSFetchRequest *fetchRequest = nil;
fetchRequest = [NSFetchRequest fetchRequestWithEntityName:@"Recipe"];
```

```
NSSortDescriptor *sort = [[NSSortDescriptor alloc] initWithKey:@"name"
                                                     ascending:YES];
[fetchRequest setSortDescriptors:[NSArray arrayWithObject:sort]];
```

In this example, we are retrieving all the Recipe entities by creating an NSFetchRequest with the NSEntityDescription set to our entity and no predicate. However, in addition to fetching the Recipe entities, we also want them sorted. We accomplish the sorting by adding an NSArray of NSSortDescriptor instances directly to the NSFetchRequest, which cause the returned NSArray to be properly sorted.

The NSSortDescriptor takes two parameters as part of its -init: a key and a BOOL denoting whether the sort is ascending or descending. We can have as many NSSortDescriptor objects as we want as part of the sort, and therefore they are placed within an NSArray prior to the sort being performed.

Adding an NSSortDescriptor is especially useful on Cocoa Touch because the NSFetchedResultsController continues to keep its results sorted without any intervention on our part. The NSFetchedResultsController is discussed in more depth in Chapter 2, *iOS: NSFetchedResultsController*, on page 23.

## 1.7 Fetched Properties

In addition to NSFetchRequest objects, we have the ability to define a lazy relationship between objects. Fetched properties are kind of a cross between relationships and the NSFetchRequest. A fetched property is not a relationship in the strictest sense and is not realized until the property is requested. When the property is accessed, Core Data performs the underlying NSFetchRequest and returns the result. Unlike a normal relationship, a fetched property is returned as an NSArray as opposed to an NSSet.

In practice, I have found fetched properties to be less useful and less flexible than either creating a stored fetch request or building the fetch request in code. Usually when a situation calls for a fetched property, it tends to be easier to subclass the entity in question, perform an NSFetchRequest in code, and return the results.

## 1.8 Wrapping Up

We covered a large number of the important pieces of Core Data in this chapter. As we continue to explore Core Data in depth, please use this chapter as a reference point for the aspects of Core Data and how they all fit together. By the end of the book, each of these elements should be very familiar to you.

# iOS: NSFetchedResultsController

The NSFetchedResultsController was introduced alongside Core Data when the framework was added to iOS with version 3.0. Since its introduction, developers have settled into a love–hate relationship with this class. When it is used in the way it was intended, it works extremely well. The hate part comes in when developers attempt to use the NSFetchedResultsController outside of its intended niche—that is when things start to fall apart quickly.

In this chapter, we discuss what the NSFetchedResultsController is designed to do and how it works. Once we have a handle on how it works, we'll explore alternatives so you know what to use when NSFetchedResultsController is not the correct fit.

## 2.1  How to Use the NSFetchedResultsController

When Core Data was added to iOS, it was clear to the Core Data team that Core Data and the UITableView would be used together extensively. They also realized that getting these two pieces to work together smoothly would require a fair amount of code that could be abstracted away; that abstraction is the NSFetchedResultsController. The NSFetchedResultsController is the glue that binds a UITableView to Core Data so that we need to write very little code.

The purpose of the NSFetchedResultsController is twofold. First, the NSFetched-ResultsController is designed to retrieve data from Core Data and store that data for access. It does this with an internal NSFetchRequest that it uses for the retrieval. It then stores the data and makes it available for use. As part of the storage and retrieval, the NSFetchedResultsController organizes the returned data into sections, in the process making the data more useful to a UITableView.

The NSFetchedResultsController's second purpose is to monitor changes in the data. Without the ability to be notified when the data has changed, the NSFetched-ResultsController would not be much more use than an NSArray. When the

NSManagedObjectContext associated with the NSFetchedResultsController changes, the NSFetchedResultsController checks to see whether any of the objects it is referencing are impacted. Further, it also watches inserts to determine whether any newly inserted objects should be included in what is being referenced. If any changes occur, the NSFetchedResultsController notifies its delegate of the changes. The delegate is normally its associated UITableView.

## Standing Up an NSFetchedResultsController

The creation of a NSFetchedResultsController takes a number of steps and uses several of the classes that we discussed in Chapter 1, *Under the Hood of Core Data*, on page 1.

RecipesV1/PPRecipes/PPRMasterViewController.m

```
- (NSFetchedResultsController *)fetchedResultsController
{
  if (fetchedResultsController) return fetchedResultsController;
  NSManagedObjectContext *moc = [self managedObjectContext];

  NSFetchRequest *fetchRequest = nil;
  fetchRequest = [NSFetchRequest fetchRequestWithEntityName:@"Recipe"];

  NSSortDescriptor *sort = [[NSSortDescriptor alloc] initWithKey:@"name"
                                                       ascending:YES];
  [fetchRequest setSortDescriptors:[NSArray arrayWithObject:sort]];

  NSFetchedResultsController *frc = nil;
  frc = [[NSFetchedResultsController alloc] initWithFetchRequest:fetchRequest
                                        managedObjectContext:moc
                                          sectionNameKeyPath:nil
                                                   cacheName:@"Master"];

  [self setFetchedResultsController:frc];
  [[self fetchedResultsController] setDelegate:self];

  NSError *error = nil;
  ZAssert([[self fetchedResultsController] performFetch:&error],
          @"Unresolved error %@\n%@", [error localizedDescription],
          [error userInfo]);

  return fetchedResultsController;
}
```

The NSFetchedResultsController is effectively a wrapper around an NSFetchRequest. Therefore, we first need to construct the NSFetchRequest that will be used. In this example, we are building an NSFetchRequest that retrieves all of the available recipes. Further, we are going to sort the Recipe entities based on their name attribute.

Once we have built the NSFetchRequest, we construct the NSFetchedResultsController. In its initialization, it accepts an NSFetchRequest, an NSManagedObjectContext, an NSString for its sectionNameKeyPath, and another NSString for its cacheName. Let's explore each of these in turn.

### NSFetchRequest

The NSFetchRequest retrieves the data from Core Data and makes it available for use. This is the NSFetchRequest we just defined in code.

### NSManagedObjectContext

The NSFetchedResultsController requires an NSManagedObjectContext to perform the fetch against. This is also the NSManagedObjectContext that the NSFetchedResults-Controller will be monitoring for changes. Note that the NSFetchedResultsController is designed to work against user interface elements, and therefore, it works best when it is pointed at an NSManagedObjectContext that is running on the main/UI thread. Threading is discussed in more depth in Chapter 5, *Threading*, on page 77.

### sectionNameKeyPath

The sectionNameKeyPath is what the NSFetchedResultsController uses to break the retrieved data into sections. Once the data is retrieved, the NSFetched-ResultsController calls for a property on each entity using KVC (more on this in Chapter 8, *OS X: Bindings, KVC, and KVO*, on page 137). The value of that property will be used to break the data into sections. In our current example, we have this set to nil, which means our data will not be broken into sections. However, we could easily add it, as follows:

RecipesV1/PPRecipes/PPRMasterViewController.m

```
if (fetchedResultsController) return fetchedResultsController;
NSManagedObjectContext *moc = [self managedObjectContext];

NSFetchRequest *fetchRequest = nil;
fetchRequest = [NSFetchRequest fetchRequestWithEntityName:@"Recipe"];
NSMutableArray *sortArray = [NSMutableArray array];
[sortArray addObject:[[NSSortDescriptor alloc] initWithKey:@"type"
                                               ascending:YES]];
[sortArray addObject:[[NSSortDescriptor alloc] initWithKey:@"name"
                                               ascending:YES]];
[fetchRequest setSortDescriptors:sortArray];

NSFetchedResultsController *frc = nil;
frc = [[NSFetchedResultsController alloc] initWithFetchRequest:fetchRequest
                                    managedObjectContext:moc
                                      sectionNameKeyPath:@"type"
                                               cacheName:@"Master"];
```

Something to note here is that along with passing in @"type" to the initialization of the NSFetchedResultsController, we also added a second NSSortDescriptor to the NSFetchRequest. The NSFetchedResultsController requires the data to be returned in the same order as it will appear in the sections. As a result, we must sort the data first by type and then by name.

### cacheName

The last property of the initialization of the NSFetchedResultsController is the cacheName. This value is used by the NSFetchedResultsController to build up a small data cache on disk. That cache will allow the NSFetchedResultsController to skip the NSPersistentStore entirely when its associated UITableView is reconstructed. This cache can dramatically improve the launch performance of any associated UITableView.

However, this cache is extremely sensitive to changes in the data and the NSFetchRequest. Therefore, this cache name cannot be reused from one UITableView to another, nor can it be reused if the NSPredicate changes.

Once the NSFetchedResultsController has been initialized, we need to populate it with data. This can be done immediately upon initialization, as in our current example, or it can be done later. When to populate the NSFetchedResultsController is more of a performance question. If the associated UITableView is constructed very early, we may want to wait to populate the NSFetchedResultsController until the UITableView is about to be used. For now and until we can determine there is a performance issue, we will populate it upon initialization. This is done with a call to -performFetch:, which takes a pointer to an NSError variable. If there is an error in the fetch, the NSError will be populated, and the call will return NO. This is a perfect place to use our ZAssert macro, which is discussed in depth in Appendix 2, *Macros in the Precompiled Header*, on page 221.

### Wiring the NSFetchedResultsController to a UITableView

Now that we have our NSFetchedResultsController initialized, we need to wire it into its associated UITableView. We do this within the various UITableViewDatasource methods.

RecipesV1/PPRecipes/PPRMasterViewController.m
```
- (NSInteger)numberOfSectionsInTableView:(UITableView *)tableView
{
  return [[[self fetchedResultsController] sections] count];
}
```

The first one is -numberOfSectionsInTableView:. Here we ask the NSFetchedResultsController to return its array of sections, and we return the count of them. If we don't have a sectionNameKeyPath set on the NSFetchedResultsController, there will be either zero or one section in that array. In previous versions of iOS (prior to iOS 4.*x*), the UITableView did not like being told there were zero sections. You may run across older code that checks the section count and always returns a minimum of one section (with zero rows). That issue has been addressed, and the associated check is no longer needed.

**RecipesV1/PPRecipes/PPRMasterViewController.m**
```
- (NSInteger)tableView:(UITableView *)tableView
 numberOfRowsInSection:(NSInteger)section
{
  NSArray *sections = [[self fetchedResultsController] sections];
  id <NSFetchedResultsSectionInfo> sectionInfo = nil;
  sectionInfo = [sections objectAtIndex:section];
  return [sectionInfo numberOfObjects];
}
```

The tableView: numberOfRowsInSection: method is slightly more complex. Here, we grab the array of sections, but we also grab the object within the array that is at the index being passed into the method. There is no need to check to see whether the index is valid since the -numberOfSectionsInTableView: method is the basis for this index. The object that is in the NSArray is undetermined but guaranteed to respond to the NSFetchedResultsSectionInfo protocol. One of the methods on that protocol is numberOfObjects, which we use to return the number of rows in the section.

**RecipesV1/PPRecipes/PPRMasterViewController.m**
```
- (UITableViewCell *)tableView:(UITableView *)tableView
        cellForRowAtIndexPath:(NSIndexPath *)indexPath
{
  UITableViewCell *cell = nil;
  NSManagedObject *object = nil;

  object = [[self fetchedResultsController] objectAtIndexPath:indexPath];

  cell = [tableView dequeueReusableCellWithIdentifier:@"Cell"];
  [[cell textLabel] setText:[object valueForKey:@"name"]];

  return cell;
}
```

In the -tableView: cellForRowAtIndexPath: method, we use another very useful ability of the NSFetchedResultsController: the -objectAtIndexPath: method. With this method, we can retrieve the exact object we need to work with in a single call. This reduces the complexity of our -tableView: cellForRowAtIndexPath: method significantly.

There are many additional examples of how to wire in the NSFetchedResultsController to the UITableView, but these three highlight the most common usage. Even with just these three methods, we can see how the NSFetchedResultsController drastically reduces the amount of code we need to write (and thereby maintain) to access the data to be displayed.

## Listening to the NSFetchedResultsController

In addition to making it very easy for us to retrieve and display the data for a UITableView, the NSFetchedResultsController also makes it relatively painless to handle changes in that data. If the values within one of our recipes changes (perhaps through iCloud, as discussed in Chapter 6, *Using iCloud*, on page 99, or through an import), we want our UITableView to immediately reflect those changes. In addition, if a recipe is removed or added, we want our UITableView to be accurate. To make sure these updates happen, we need to add the delegate methods for the NSFetchedResultsControllerDelegate protocol. As mentioned, it is common for the UIViewController to also be the delegate for the NSFetched-ResultsController. There are five methods in this protocol; let's take a look at each of them.

### -controllerWillChangeContent:

The first method, -controllerWillChangeContent:, tells us that changes are about to start. This method is our opportunity to instruct the UITableView that changes are coming. Typically this is where we tell the UITableView to stop updating the user interface so that all of the changes can be displayed at once.

RecipesV1/PPRecipes/PPRMasterViewController.m
```
- (void)controllerWillChangeContent:(NSFetchedResultsController *)controller
{
  [[self tableView] beginUpdates];
}
```

### -controller: didChangeSection: atIndex: forChangeType:

This method is called when a section changes. The only valid change types are NSFetchedResultsChangeInsert and NSFetchedResultsChangeDelete. This is our opportunity to tell the UITableView that a section is being added or removed.

RecipesV1/PPRecipes/PPRMasterViewController.m
```
- (void)controller:(NSFetchedResultsController *)controller
  didChangeSection:(id <NSFetchedResultsSectionInfo>)sectionInfo
           atIndex:(NSUInteger)sectionIndex
     forChangeType:(NSFetchedResultsChangeType)type
{
  NSIndexSet *indexSet = [NSIndexSet indexSetWithIndex:sectionIndex];
  switch(type) {
```

```
  case NSFetchedResultsChangeInsert:
    [[self tableView] insertSections:indexSet
                    withRowAnimation:UITableViewRowAnimationFade];
    break;

  case NSFetchedResultsChangeDelete:
    [[self tableView] deleteSections:indexSet
                    withRowAnimation:UITableViewRowAnimationFade];
    break;
  }
}
```

Here we use a switch to determine what the change type is and pass it along to the UITableView.

### -controller: didChangeObject: atIndexPath: forChangeType: newIndexPath:

This is the most complex method in the NSFetchedResultsControllerDelegate protocol. In this method, we are notified of any changes to any data object. There are four types of changes that we need to react to, listed next.

RecipesV1/PPRecipes/PPRMasterViewController.m
```
- (void)controller:(NSFetchedResultsController *)controller
   didChangeObject:(id)anObject
       atIndexPath:(NSIndexPath *)indexPath
     forChangeType:(NSFetchedResultsChangeType)type
     newIndexPath:(NSIndexPath *)newIndexPath
{
  NSArray *newArray = [NSArray arrayWithObject:newIndexPath];
  NSArray *oldArray = [NSArray arrayWithObject:indexPath];
  switch(type) {
    case NSFetchedResultsChangeInsert:
      [[self tableView] insertRowsAtIndexPaths:newArray
                              withRowAnimation:UITableViewRowAnimationFade];
      break;

    case NSFetchedResultsChangeDelete:
      [[self tableView] deleteRowsAtIndexPaths:oldArray
                              withRowAnimation:UITableViewRowAnimationFade];
      break;

    case NSFetchedResultsChangeUpdate:
    {
      UITableViewCell *cell = nil;
      NSManagedObject *object = nil;
      cell = [[self tableView] cellForRowAtIndexPath:indexPath];
      object = [[self fetchedResultsController] objectAtIndexPath:indexPath];
      [[cell textLabel] setText:[object valueForKey:@"name"]];
      break;
    }
    case NSFetchedResultsChangeMove:
```

```
        [[self tableView] deleteRowsAtIndexPaths:oldArray
                            withRowAnimation:UITableViewRowAnimationFade];
        [[self tableView] insertRowsAtIndexPaths:newArray
                            withRowAnimation:UITableViewRowAnimationFade];
        break;
    }
}
```

An NSFetchedResultsChangeInsert is fired when a new object is inserted that we need to display in our UITableView. When we receive this call, we pass it along to the UITableView and tell the table view what type of animation to use.

An NSFetchedResultsChangeDelete is fired when an existing object is removed. Just as we do with an insert, we pass this information along to the UITableView and tell it what type of animation to use when removing the row.

An NSFetchedResultsChangeUpdate is fired when an existing object has changed internally, in other words, when one of its attributes has been updated. We do not know from this call if it is an attribute that we care about. Instead of spending time determining whether we *should* update the row, it is generally cheaper to just update the row.

An NSFetchedResultsChangeMove is fired when a row is moved. The move could be as a result of a number of factors but is generally caused by a data change resulting in the row being displayed in a different location. In our example, if the name or type of a recipe were altered, it would most likely cause this change type. It is quite possible—and common—to receive an NSFetchedResults-ChangeMove and an NSFetchedResultsChangeUpdate in the same batch of changes. When this change type is received, we make two calls to the UITableView: one to remove the row from its previous location and another to insert it into its new location.

### -controller: sectionIndexTitleForSectionName:

We use this method when we want to massage the data coming back from our NSFetchedResultsController before it is passed to the UITableView for display. One situation where this might be necessary is if we want to remove any extended characters from the title before it is displayed; another example is if we want to add something to the displayed title that is not in the data.

**RecipesV1/PPRecipes/PPRMasterViewController.m**
```
- (NSString*)controller:(NSFetchedResultsController*)controller
sectionIndexTitleForSectionName:(NSString*)sectionName
{
    return [NSString stringWithFormat:@"[%@]", sectionName];
}
```

### -controllerDidChangeContent:

The final method tells us that this round of changes is finished and we can tell the UITableView to update the user interface. We can also use this method to update any other parts of the user interface outside of the UITableView. For example, if we had a count of the number of recipes displayed, we would update that count here.

```
RecipesV1/PPRecipes/PPRMasterViewController.m
- (void)controllerDidChangeContent:(NSFetchedResultsController *)controller
{
  [[self tableView] endUpdates];
}
```

With the implementation of the five methods described earlier, our UITableView can now retrieve, display, and update its display without any further work from us. In fact, a large portion of the code in the NSFetchedResultsControllerDelegate methods is fairly boilerplate and can be moved from project to project, further reducing the amount of "new" code we need to maintain.

## 2.2 Under the Hood of the NSFetchedResultsController

We can see the value of an NSFetchedResultsController, but how does it actually work? When I started to explore the details, I was shocked to find out that I could duplicate much of the behavior of the NSFetchedResultsController using publicly available APIs.

At its core, the NSFetchedResultsController takes advantage of the notifications that an NSManagedObjectContext fires off. When we initialize the NSFetchedResultsController, it sets itself up as an observer and then reacts as the notifications come in.

### NSManagedObjectContextObjectsDidChangeNotification

One of the three notifications that the NSFetchedResultsController listens for is the NSManagedObjectContextObjectsDidChangeNotification. This very chatty notification tells the NSFetchedResultsController whenever one of the attributes of any object has changed. The NSFetchedResultsController uses this information, combined with its NSFetchRequest, to determine whether it needs to notify its delegate of the changes. Changes of this type often result in a call to -controller: didChangeObject: atIndexPath: forChangeType: newIndexPath:, with a change type of NSFetchedResultsChange-Update and/or NSFetchedResultsChangeMove.

### NSManagedObjectContextWillSaveNotification

Without access to the source code of the NSFetchedResultsController, I can't say with 100 percent certainty that this notification is used; however, it appears that NSManagedObjectContextWillSaveNotification is being used to catch when an object is deleted. When an object is deleted, the NSFetchedResultsController determines whether it is relevant to our NSFetchRequest and issues the appropriate delegate callbacks. This would typically result in a call to -controller: didChangeSection: atIndex: forChangeType: if the deletion caused a section to disappear and/or a call to the -controller: didChangeObject: atIndexPath: forChangeType: newIndexPath: with a change type of NSFetchedResultsChangeDelete.

### NSManagedObjectContextDidSaveNotification

The third and final NSNotification type is fired after the NSManagedObjectContext has completed its save. This notification is observed so that the NSFetchedResults-Controller can capture any objects that are newly inserted or have been changed in another context and propagated (as discussed in Chapter 5, *Threading*, on page 77). This would typically result in a call to -controller: didChangeSection: atIndex: forChangeType: if the insertion/update caused a section to disappear or appear. It would also cause a call to -controller: didChangeObject: atIndexPath: forChangeType: newIndexPath: with any of the change types available.

Beyond listening for these notifications, the NSFetchedResultsController is just a container. The cache is most likely a serialization of the currently fetched objects (although I have not been able to figure out its exact data structure yet).

Why is this information valuable? For one, it is always helpful to understand how things work so that when they stop working, we can investigate them and resolve the issue. In addition, since the NSFetchedResultsController has such an extremely narrow focus, we don't want to use it in situations where we don't have a UITableView to populate. However, it is so useful that we really want to use some of its features outside of this narrow focus. With an understanding of how it works comes the ability to duplicate the features that are useful to us.

## 2.3 Building Our Own: ZSContextWatcher

Since the introduction of the NSFetchedResultsController, I have run into numerous situations in which I wanted to use its ability to detect data changes even when I was not using a UITableView. Frequently I would attempt to use an NSFetchedResultsController and run into one problem or another that made it more difficult than it needed to be. This led me to investigate how the NSFetched-ResultsController worked and finally resulted in the creation of the ZSContextWatcher.

The ZSContextWatcher is publicly available under the BSD license, and the latest version is always in my public GitHub repository at http://github.com/ZarraStudios/ZDS_Shared.

The goal of the ZSContextWatcher is to provide us with the ability to monitor a subset of the data that is in Core Data and to be notified when it changes. It's the same functionality that is in the NSFetchedResultsController but not as tightly coupled with the UITableView.

**ZSContextWatcher/ZSContextWatcher.h**
```
@interface ZSContextWatcher : NSObject

- (id)initWithManagedObjectContext:(NSManagedObjectContext*)context;

- (void)addEntityToWatch:(NSEntityDescription*)description
          withPredicate:(NSPredicate*)predicate;

@end
```

The API to use this class is composed of two methods.

## -initWithManagedObjectContext:

We initialize the ZSContextWatcher with an NSManagedObjectContext. This NSManagedObjectContext is used when it sets itself up as an observer on NSNotificationCenter. This avoids notifications coming from other NSManagedObjectContext instances.

**ZSContextWatcher/ZSContextWatcher.m**
```
- (id)initWithManagedObjectContext:(NSManagedObjectContext*)context;
{
  ZAssert(context, @"Context is nil!");
  if (!(self = [super init])) return nil;

  NSNotificationCenter *center = [NSNotificationCenter defaultCenter];
  [center addObserver:self
             selector:@selector(contextUpdated:)
                 name:NSManagedObjectContextDidSaveNotification
               object:context];

  return self;
}
```

## -addEntityToWatch: withPredicate:

The second method in the public API for the ZSContextWatcher allows us to define what the watcher is listening for. This is moved away from the initialization because I wanted the ability to watch more than one entity and/or more than one predicate. With this method, I can add as many entities and/or predicates as I need.

ZSContextWatcher/ZSContextWatcher.m

```
- (void)addEntityToWatch:(NSEntityDescription*)description
         withPredicate:(NSPredicate*)predicate;
{
  NSPredicate *entityPredicate = nil;
  NSPredicate *final = nil;
  NSArray *array = nil;
  entityPredicate = [NSPredicate predicateWithFormat:@"entity.name == %@",
                    [description name]];
  array = [NSArray arrayWithObjects:entityPredicate, predicate, nil];
  final = [NSCompoundPredicate andPredicateWithSubpredicates:array];

  if (![self masterPredicate]) {
    [self setMasterPredicate:finalPredicate];
    return;
  }

  array = [NSArray arrayWithObjects:[self masterPredicate], final, nil];
  finalPredicate = [NSCompoundPredicate orPredicateWithSubpredicates:array];
  [self setMasterPredicate:finalPredicate];
}
```

We do a bit of NSPredicate construction in the implementation. First, we take the passed-in NSEntityDescription and use that inside a new predicate that compares the entity name. Next, we create a compound predicate that combines the passed-in predicate with the newly created entity predicate with an AND join. Now we have a new predicate that checks to make sure the compared object is the same entity before we use the second part of the predicate against the object.

Why do we do this? If we just run the passed-in predicate against every object, we would get an error when it hits an object that doesn't have one of the properties in the predicate. By adding a prefix predicate that checks the name of the entity, we are ensuring it will run only against the correct entity.

If there is no existing predicate in our ZSContextWatcher, we set our new compound predicate as the masterPredicate and return. However, if there is already a masterPredicate set, we need to compound the existing predicate with our new one. Again, we use an NSCompoundPredicate to combine the existing masterPredicate and our new predicate. However, this time we use an OR instead of an AND in the compound predicate. Finally, we take the newly created compound predicate and set that as the masterPredicate.

### -contextUpdated:

We have constructed a predicate that we can run against a collection of NSManagedObject instances, and it will filter out any objects that we do not care

about. Now when we receive a notification from an NSManagedObjectContextDid-
SaveNotification, we can easily filter the incoming objects against our predicate.

**ZSContextWatcher/ZSContextWatcher.m**

```objc
- (void)contextUpdated:(NSNotification*)notification
{
  NSInteger totalCount = 0;
  NSSet *temp = nil;
  temp = [[notification userInfo] objectForKey:NSInsertedObjectsKey]
  NSMutableSet *inserted = [temp mutableCopy];
  if ([self masterPredicate]) {
    [inserted filterUsingPredicate:[self masterPredicate]];
  }
  totalCount += [inserted count];

  temp = [[notification userInfo] objectForKey:NSDeletedObjectsKey];
  NSMutableSet *deleted = [temp mutableCopy];
  if ([self masterPredicate]) {
    [deleted filterUsingPredicate:[self masterPredicate]];
  }
  totalCount += [deleted count];

  temp = [[notification userInfo] objectForKey:NSUpdatedObjectsKey];
  NSMutableSet *updated = [temp mutableCopy];
  if ([self masterPredicate]) {
    [updated filterUsingPredicate:[self masterPredicate]];
  }
  totalCount += [updated count];

  if (totalCount == 0) {
    return;
  }

  NSMutableDictionary *results = [NSMutableDictionary dictionary];
  if (inserted) {
    [results setObject:inserted forKey:NSInsertedObjectsKey];
  }
  if (deleted) {
    [results setObject:deleted forKey:NSDeletedObjectsKey];
  }
  if (updated) {
    [results setObject:updated forKey:NSUpdatedObjectsKey];
  }

  if ([[self delegate] respondsToSelector:[self action]]) {
    [[self delegate] performSelectorOnMainThread:[self action]
                                withObject:self
                              waitUntilDone:YES];
  }
}
```

When we receive a notification, we need to check the -userInfo and see whether there are any objects that we care about. In the -userInfo, there are up to three NSSet instances: one for updated objects, one for deleted objects, and one for inserted objects. We walk through each of these sets, grabbing a mutable copy of each one, filtering the mutable set against our masterPredicate, and keeping track of how many objects are left. If there are no objects left at the end of the filtering, we know there were none in the save that we cared about, and we can return.

If there were any objects left, we need to notify our delegate of them. Since we have already filtered the objects, we may as well pass them to our delegate so our delegate doesn't need to repeat the work. We create a new NSDictionary and add each of our NSSet instances to it using the same keys that the incoming NSNotification used. Once it is constructed, we can pass the newly created NSDictionary off to our delegate.

Now we have a class that allows us to watch any NSManagedObjectContext of our choosing and notifies us if an object that we care about has been touched in any way. We can make the predicate as broad or narrow as we want. By allowing the delegate to pass in the predicate, we've also made this class highly reusable.

## 2.4 Wrapping Up

The NSFetchedResultsController is a great time-saver when we are working with a UITableView. It can drastically reduce the amount of code we need to write and make our UITableView instances perform very well. However, it has a narrowly focused purpose, and it should be avoided when you are not working with a UITableView. Fortunately, with a little bit of effort, we can duplicate quite a bit of its functionality and create a highly flexible class that fits into a variety of situations.

# CHAPTER 3

# Versioning and Migration

Just like a battle plan, no code base ever survives contact with users. As soon as users start to use an application, they want to change it. Even if the code is just for ourselves, we, also as users, will want to change things. For example, we may need to add an attribute or a new object and then restructure things to accommodate those changes. Additions and changes can be quite involved and invariably require a change in how the data is stored. Although a data migration works even when there is no data stored, it is more useful to have some data to work with. Therefore, if you have not added any recipes yet, I recommend doing so before we proceed.

Starting with Mac OS X 10.5 Leopard and iOS 3.0, Apple has made data migration nearly trivial for users of Core Data. Taking the project outlined in Appendix 1, *Building a Foundation*, on page 209, we will add some additional features to it in succeeding versions. In version 2, we will add the ability to tag an author to a recipe as well as tag a "last used" date. That way, we know who created the delicious dish as well as the last time we made it. We certainly wouldn't want to accidentally make the same dish two days in a row!

In version 3, we will normalize the repository a bit by extracting the ingredients and forming a many-to-many relationship back to the recipes. In addition, we will add the concept of a shopping list to make it easier to ensure we pick up all the ingredients on our next trip to the store. Next, we will extract the unitOfMeasure attribute from the RecipeIngredient entity into its own entity and allow that new entity to be linked to the new ingredient entity. This step gives us one lookup list for the various units of measure and reduces the risk of human error. Lastly, we will remove the Meat and Fish entries from the Type attribute of the Recipe entity. Any recipe entries that are flagged with Meat or Fish will be updated to Entrée instead.

## 3.1 Some Maintenance Before We Migrate

Before we actually release a new version of our application that migrates the data, we need to first complete a minor "maintenance" update for our users. Normally, we would add this code to the very first version of our application, but just in case we wrote that first release before versioning was a consideration, we need to go back to our old version and add a very small amount of code to help our users.

Some users will download the new version of an application to just "try it out" and see whether it is worth the upgrade price or worth the hassle. Normally this is not an issue—until we upgrade the data underneath our users. Then things go sideways. What we *do not* want to happen is the error message shown in Figure 6, *Default model issue dialog box*, on page 38.

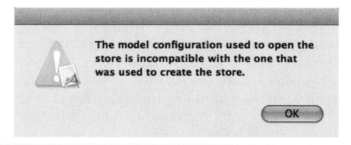

**Figure 6—Default model issue dialog box**

Note that this is the error message we would see on OS X. On iOS, our application would simply crash on launch. This is a terrible user experience and something we want to avoid. Fortunately, the way to avoid it is very easy, and we can add it to a point release of our application before we do any migration. That way, when the users open the first version of our application after "testing" the second version, they get a friendly error message; or we can take it a step further and restore/access the older version of their data.

```
Baseline/PPRecipes/PPRAppDelegateAlt2.m
dispatch_async(queue, ^{
  NSError *error = nil;
  NSPersistentStoreCoordinator *coordinator = nil;
  coordinator = [moc persistentStoreCoordinator];
  NSPersistentStore *store = nil;
  store = [coordinator addPersistentStoreWithType:NSSQLiteStoreType
                              configuration:nil
                                        URL:storeURL
                                    options:nil
                                      error:&error];
```

```
if (!store) {
  ALog(@"Error adding persistent store to coordinator %@\n%@",
      [error localizedDescription], [error userInfo]);

  NSString *msg = nil;
  msg = [NSString stringWithFormat:@"The recipes database %@%@%@\n%@\n%@",
      @"is either corrupt or was created by a newer ",
      @"version of Grokking Recipes.  Please contact ",
      @"support to assist with this error.",
      [error localizedDescription], [error userInfo]];
  UIAlertView *alertView = [[UIAlertView alloc] initWithTitle:@"Error"
                                              message:msg
                                             delegate:self
                                    cancelButtonTitle:@"Quit"
                                    otherButtonTitles:nil];
  [alertView show];
  return;
}
```

This is the new creation of the persistent store inside the -initializeCoreDataStack method. Once we have initialized our persistent store coordinator, we kick off a background process to add the NSPersistentStore to the NSPersistentStoreCoordinator. If there is an error here, we need to present it to the user and halt the application. We do this with a UIAlertView showing the error to the user, and then the delegate of the UIAlertView forces the application to quit. The resulting error message is shown in Figure 7, *Version error on iOS*, on page 40. In a production application, we would perhaps offer the user the option to reset the data as opposed to exiting. Note that we also have an ALog before the UIAlertView. When we are developing this application, we want to make *very* sure that a developer-level error fires here to ideally avoid the risk of the user ever encountering it.

## 3.2   A Simple Migration

To demonstrate a simple migration, let's add the ability to attribute recipes to authors. To begin the versioning, the first thing we need to do is create a new managed object model (MOM) based on the first one. To do that, we need to select the existing model in Xcode and then choose Design > Data Model > Add Model Version.

### Creating a Versioned Data Model

This is the first time we have added a model version, so Xcode is going to create a new bundle for us called PPRecipes.xcdatamodeld and put the original MOM inside the bundle along with a new copy of the original MOM. To make things clearer in the example project, I renamed these MOM objects to

**Figure 7—Version error on iOS**

## Your First Data Model Version

When you first set up versioning, be sure to look inside the target in Xcode and update the Compile Sources section. If you do not see the .xcdatamodeld file inside the target, remove the xcdatamodel references from it and drag the entire xcdatamodeld bundle into the target. Otherwise, your application may complain about being unable to merge entities because it will treat each version of the model as an independent model.

Once this change has been completed, it is best to clean the project (delete any previously compiled code) by choosing Product > Clean from the main menu.

v1.xcdatamodel and v2.xcdatamodel. Next, we need to select the PPRecipes.xcdatamodeld file and open the File Inspector Utility View (⌘⌥1). In the utility view, you'll see a Versioned Core Data Model section. (The Xcode templates have been bouncing back and forth on this issue over the past few versions. It is possible, depending on when you created your project, that you already have a versioned data model.) Inside of that section is a Current option, allowing us to select which model file is the current one. Make sure it references v2, as shown in Figure 8, *Setting the current model version*, on page 41.

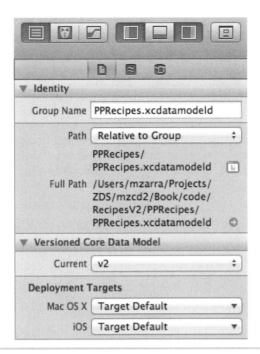

**Figure 8—Setting the current model version**

Now that we have a new version of the MOM, it's time to add the new entities and attributes. This process requires the addition of a new entity and some changes to the Recipe entity. Comparing the v1 data model and the v2 data model (Figure 9, *Versions 1 and 2 of the data model*, on page 43), you can see that we added a new Author entity along with its one-to-many relationship with the Recipe entity. Also, the Recipe entity has a new attribute called lastUsed, which is defined as a Date.

We're not quite done. If we were to run the application right now, we would trip the error that we discussed in Section 3.1, *Some Maintenance Before We Migrate*, on page 38. Clearly, something is missing.

### Turning on Automatic Data Migration

The first thing we need to do is to tell Core Data to automatically migrate data when the persistent store is not using the same model as the current version. To do this, we need to make a small change to the persistentStoreCoordinator method in our AppDelegate. Previously we were passing nil to the addPersistentStore-WithType:configuration:URL:options:error: method for the options parameter. However, we need to change that to the following:

RecipesV2/PPRecipes/PPRAppDelegate.m

```
NSMutableDictionary *options = [NSMutableDictionary dictionary];
[options setValue:[NSNumber numberWithBool:YES]
          forKey:NSMigratePersistentStoresAutomaticallyOption];
[options setValue:[NSNumber numberWithBool:YES]
          forKey:NSInferMappingModelAutomaticallyOption];

NSPersistentStore *store = nil;
store = [coordinator addPersistentStoreWithType:NSSQLiteStoreType
                            configuration:nil
                                      URL:storeURL
                                  options:options
                                    error:&error];
```

The first of these options, NSMigratePersistentStoresAutomaticallyOption, tells Core Data to attempt a migration automatically if it determines that one is needed.

The second option, NSInferMappingModelAutomaticallyOption, instructs Core Data to resolve the mapping between the persistent store and the current model. If Core Data can figure this out, it will perform the migration.

For this migration, Core Data can easily resolve the changes that need to be made and will be able to do an inferred migration for us. When the changes are more severe, we need to do a heavy, manual migration, as discussed in Section 3.4, *A Heavy/Manual Migration*, on page 44.

With those changes made, we can run our application, and Core Data automatically handles the migration for us and updates the persistent store to the new model.

## 3.3 The Difference Between Light and Heavy Migrations

There are two types of migrations for Core Data: light migration and heavy migration. When we are working with SQLite persistent stores, the difference between these two types of migration is significant enough that we should avoid doing heavy migrations if at all possible.

A light migration of a SQLite persistent store occurs within the SQLite file itself. There are no objects loaded into memory, and therefore the memory requirements of the migration are quite low. In addition, since the migration is occurring within the database file, it is very fast. While the size of the database file still affects the speed of the migration, a light migration of large database will still be remarkably faster than a heavy migration of a small database.

The speed and memory differences are so large that I recommend avoiding heavy migrations at nearly any cost.

# Version 1

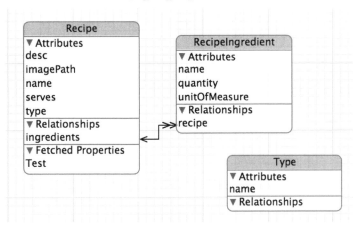

# Version 2

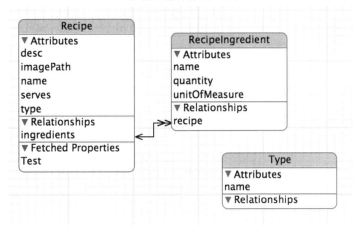

**Figure 9—Versions 1 and 2 of the data model**

A heavy migration is far more complicated than a light migration. When we perform a heavy migration, we must load each entity into memory, translate it from the old store to the new store, and then write it back out to disk. This requires two Core Data "stacks" in memory at the same time and a large amount of data processing in our application. It takes time—a lot of time. When a heavy migration is required, the application normally needs to show a wait dialog to the user so that the user knows what's going on.

In addition to the computational time, a heavy migration requires more work from the developer. When we are performing a light migration, we pass two options to Core Data and let the framework do the work. When we perform a heavy migration, we must explain the migration to Core Data. This requires us to create a mapping model, configure each entity in the mapping model, and sometimes even write code specific to a migration. As a result, there is a significant maintenance cost for the developer on top of the computational cost. All the same, it's a situation that may arise, so let's take a look at a heavy migration.

## 3.4  A Heavy/Manual Migration

A heavy migration is required when we go outside of the bounds of what a light migration can accomplish. A simple example of something that goes beyond a light migration is a *logic-based migration*. Imagine a situation in which, as part of a migration/application update, we need to change the data that is in the database. Perhaps there is a typo in the included data or a change in the logic. Changing the data during the migration is outside of the scope of a light migration. However, we can easily add it to a heavy migration.

A more complex example would be a situation that involves normalizing data. In our application, each recipe has one or more recipe ingredients. If we wanted to expand our application and extract the common parts of the recipe ingredient into new tables, we would be stepping outside the boundaries of what a light migration can accomplish.

### Creating Our First Mapping Model

In this migration, we are going to accomplish two goals. First we are going to massage the data during the migration and find every occurrence of Meat or Fish for the recipe type and replace it with Entrée. In addition, we are going to create new entities: Ingredient and UnitOfMeasure. During the migration of the RecipeIngredient entity, we are going to create or associate the appropriate Ingredient to the RecipeIngredient.

The first step is to create a mapping model for this migration. A *mapping model* is a description of how the migration is supposed to work. First we create a new file in Xcode, and select the section for Core Data. In that section, there is a template called Mapping Model, as shown in Figure 10, *Mapping Model template*, on page 45. Once we select that template, Xcode asks us to choose the data model version to use as the source. For this migration, we are going from v2 to v3, so we select v2. Then Xcode asks us to select the destination model; we'll select v3. Finally, we must name the mapping model. I named it the very descriptive FromV2toV3.

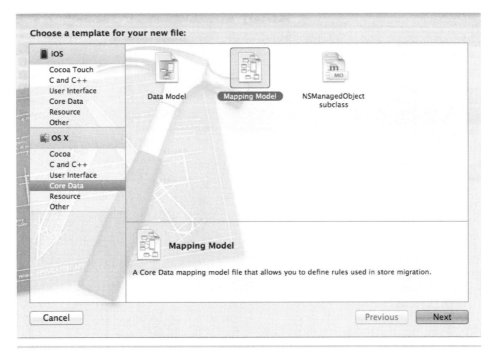

**Figure 10—Mapping Model template**

Now Xcode will do a best guess at the migration from v2 to v3 and display its results, as shown in Figure 11, *Completed mapping model*, on page 46. There is a lot of information in this view; let's go through it piece by piece. As we step through this view, keep in mind that the view represents the migration from the perspective of the destination model. Everything is described as coming *from* the source into the destination.

The *entity mappings* are on the left side of the view, just to the right of the project list. Each item in this list represents a part of the migration that will occur. They're not one-to-one with the number of entities that we have; we can actually have more or less mappings than we have entities. Specifically, as we will see when we update this mapping model, we can have more than one mapping for an entity. In addition, if an entity is no longer represented in the new model, it may not have a mapping at all.

To the right of the entity mappings are the *attribute and relationship mappings*. The attribute mappings are located at the top of the view. This section of the view describes how the attributes of an entity are mapped from the source to the destination. Since we are looking at this from the perspective of the destination, this list includes every attribute that exists in the destination entity.

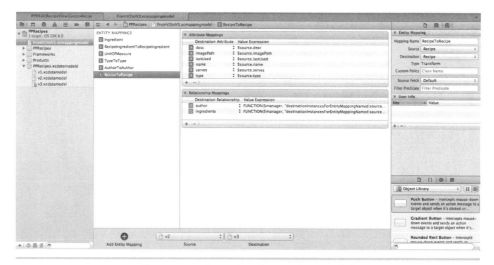

**Figure 11—Completed mapping model**

Xcode has already prepopulated the attributes and taken a guess at where the attributes come from. Reviewing what has already been populated by Xcode, we can see how the attribute mappings work. Several variables are available for these mappings:

- $manager, which references the NSMigrationManagerKey
- $source, which references the NSMigrationSourceObjectKey
- $destination, which references the NSMigrationDestinationObjectKey
- $entityMapping, which references the NSMigrationEntityMappingKey
- $propertyMapping, which references the NSMigrationPropertyMappingKey
- $entityPolicy, which references the NSMigrationEntityPolicyKey

The relationship mappings are below the entity mappings. Like the attribute mappings, these resolve the relationships for the destination entity. Normally, these mappings resolve to an instance of an entity in the destination store that existed in the source store. To accomplish this, the mapping for the object at the other end of the relationship must be higher in the list (the list is migrated in order, top to bottom). Then it is a matter of configuring the mapping properly, as shown in Figure 12, *Relationship mapping*, on page 47.

### Customizing the Heavy/Manual Migration

So far, the migration we built doesn't do very much: it migrates the entities from the old store to the new store. We need to adjust the migration to make it perform the more complicated aspects of the migration, the ones that are beyond the abilities of the light migration.

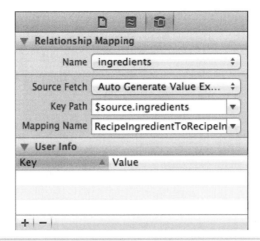

**Figure 12—Relationship mapping**

The first part of this customization is to change the Type attribute on recipes that are currently set as Fish or Meat. To do this, we need to utilize the filter feature of the migration. First, select the RecipeToRecipe mapping. Next, open the Mapping Model inspector, which is utility view 3 in Xcode (⌘⌥3). In that inspector, we see a Filter Predicate field. This filter determines which entities are migrated. Utilizing a filter, we can migrate only those recipe entities that have their type set to something other than Fish or Meat. The setting is shown here:

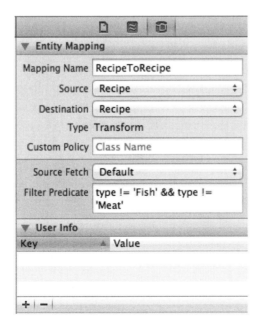

However, this leaves our meat and fish recipes unmigrated. To include them, we first duplicate the RecipeToRecipe mapping (unfortunately by hand with the current version of Xcode) and change the filter to be *inclusive* of Meat and Fish. Then, in this second mapping, we change the Value Expression setting for the Type attribute to Entrée. Taking this step will migrate all of the meat and fish recipes and change the type to Entrée.

The second part of this migration is far more complex. For each RecipeIngredient, we want to either create a new Ingredient entity or link the destination RecipeIngredient to an existing Ingredient. In addition, for each Ingredient that we create, we want to create a UnitOfMeasure entity to go with it.

To complete this very complex migration, we are going to need to resort to code. The mapping model editor is not capable of handling the complexity we need for this next bit of the migration. Fortunately, we can step in and write the code to handle the migration directly. To set this up, we start off by modifying the mapping model. The first step is to delete the mappings for Ingredient and UnitOfMeasure. There is no corresponding entity in the source model, so no mapping is needed.

Next, we need to modify the RecipeIngredientToRecipeIngredient. After selecting the RecipeIngredientToRecipeIngredient mapping, we need to look at the Mapping Model inspector and set a custom policy. The Custom Policy field tells the migration that instead of using its built-in migration policy (which will read from the mapping model), we are going to introduce custom code. This field accepts a class name that we are going to set to RecipeIngredientToIngredientAndUnitOfMeasure.

## NSEntityMigrationPolicy

Core Data will instantiate an instance of NSEntityMigrationPolicy for each mapping in the mapping model. NSEntityMigrationPolicy is designed to be subclasses so that we can override all or part of the migration. There are several methods that can be overridden in the subclass; in this example, we are overriding two methods.

```
- (BOOL)createDestinationInstancesForSourceInstance:(NSManagedObject*)source
                       entityMapping:(NSEntityMapping*)mapping
                             manager:(NSMigrationManager*)manager
                               error:(NSError**)error


- (BOOL)createRelationshipsForDestinationInstance:(NSManagedObject*)dInstance
                       entityMapping:(NSEntityMapping*)mapping
                             manager:(NSMigrationManager*)manager
                               error:(NSError**)error
```

### createDestinationInstancesForSourceInstance:

The first method, createDestinationInstancesForSourceInstance:, is called for each entity in the source store that is associated with this migration policy. For example, during the migration of the RecipeIngredient entities and the creation of the Ingredient and UnitOfMeasure entities, this method would be called for each RecipeIngredient, and it would be expected that at least an Ingredient entity would be created or associated with the incoming RecipeIngredient as a result.

The code to implement this breaks down as follows:

RecipesV3/PPRecipes/RecipeIngredientToIngredient.m
```
- (BOOL)createDestinationInstancesForSourceInstance:(NSManagedObject*)source
                            entityMapping:(NSEntityMapping*)mapping
                                manager:(NSMigrationManager*)manager
                                error:(NSError**)error
{
  NSManagedObjectContext *destMOC = [manager destinationContext];
  NSString *destEntityName = [mapping destinationEntityName];

  NSString *name = [source valueForKey:@"name"];
```

In the first part of the method, we are simply setting up references that will be needed later. Specifically, we are getting a reference to the destination NSManagedObjectContext, which we will need to create new entities, the name of the destination entity, and, most importantly, the name value from the incoming entity.

Since the incoming entity is a RecipeIngredient, the name value will be the name of the ingredient that we now want to reference.

RecipesV3/PPRecipes/RecipeIngredientToIngredient.m
```
NSMutableDictionary *userInfo = (NSMutableDictionary*)[manager userInfo];
if (!userInfo) {
  userInfo = [NSMutableDictionary dictionary];
  [manager setUserInfo:userInfo];
}
NSMutableDictionary *ingredientLookup = [userInfo valueForKey:@"ingredients"];
if (!ingredientLookup) {
  ingredientLookup = [NSMutableDictionary dictionary];
  [userInfo setValue:ingredientLookup forKey:@"ingredients"];
}

NSMutableDictionary *uofmLookup = [userInfo valueForKey:@"unitOfMeasure"];
if (!uofmLookup) {
  uofmLookup = [NSMutableDictionary dictionary];
  [userInfo setValue:uofmLookup forKey:@"unitOfMeasure"];
}
```

In this next section of code, we deal with the possibility that the Ingredient entity that we need to reference has already been created. Rather than doing a fetch against the destination context every time, we have a hash built up and stored within the NSMigrationManger. The NSMigrationManager has an NSDictionary called userInfo that is perfectly suited for this purpose. We first lazily initialize this dictionary, and then we lazily initialize another NSDictionary inside it to store references to the Ingredient entities using the name of the ingredient as the key. With this, we can make sure that each Ingredient is created only once.

For each Ingredient, we also need to create or reference a UnitOfMeasure. We also grab a reference to the UnitOfMeasure lookup or create it if it has not been created yet.

RecipesV3/PPRecipes/RecipeIngredientToIngredient.m
```
NSManagedObject *dest = [ingredientLookup valueForKey:name];
if (!dest) {
  dest = [NSEntityDescription insertNewObjectForEntityForName:destEntityName
                                inManagedObjectContext:destMOC];
  [dest setValue:name forKey:@"name"];
  [ingredientLookup setValue:dest forKey:name];

  name = [source valueForKey:@"unitOfMeasure"];
  NSManagedObject *uofm = [uofmLookup valueForKey:name];
  if (!uofm) {
    uofm = [NSEntityDescription insertNewObjectForEntityForName:@"UnitOfMeasure"
                                  inManagedObjectContext:destMOC];
    [uofm setValue:name forKey:@"name"];
    [dest setValue:uofm forKey:@"unitOfMeasure"];
    [uofmLookup setValue:uofm forKey:name];
  }
}
```

Next we attempt to locate the Ingredient in the lookup dictionary. If it is not in the dictionary, we must create it and place it in the dictionary. If we need to create the Ingredient, we must resolve the UnitOfMeasure as well. Again, if it does not exist, we create it and put a reference to it in the lookup dictionary.

RecipesV3/PPRecipes/RecipeIngredientToIngredient.m
```
  [manager associateSourceInstance:source
          withDestinationInstance:dest
                forEntityMapping:mapping];
  return YES;
}


- (BOOL)createRelationshipsForDestinationInstance:(NSManagedObject*)dInstance
                              entityMapping:(NSEntityMapping*)mapping
                                    manager:(NSMigrationManager*)manager
                                      error:(NSError**)error
```

```
{
  return YES;
}
```

**@end**

The last thing that we need to do is to tell the manager about the association. Since the manager keeps track of all associations between the two NSManagedObjectContext objects, we need to inform it of this new entity that was just created and that it is associated with the source entity that was passed in. Once that is complete, we return YES, and we are done.

**createRelationshipsForDestinationInstance:**

In a properly designed data model, this method will rarely, if ever, be needed. The intention of this method (which is called in the second pass) is to build any relationships for the new destination entity that was created in the previous method. However, if all the relationships in the model are double-sided, this method is not necessary because we already set up one side of them. If for some reason there is an entity in the model that is not double-sided, additional code would be required in this method to handle the one-sided relationship. Since we do not need that functionality in our model, we just return YES.

RecipesV3/PPRecipes/RecipeIngredientToIngredient.m
```
- (BOOL)createRelationshipsForDestinationInstance:(NSManagedObject*)dInstance
                            entityMapping:(NSEntityMapping*)mapping
                                  manager:(NSMigrationManager*)manager
                                    error:(NSError**)error
{
  return YES;
}
```

If you are thinking this is a lot of work for migration, well, you're right. Manual migrations require a great deal of effort on the part of the developer, and there isn't a lot of benefit to doing one. This, plus their poor performance, is the reason for my recommendation to avoid them at nearly any cost. However, no matter how hard we try to avoid it, sometimes heavy migration is the only answer. Fortunately, as we just examined, the option is available.

## 3.5 Fundamentals of Core Data Versioning

We've seen the nuts and bolts, but what's the magic behind all of this? How does the data migration actually work? As we already explored in the previous chapters, Core Data works with MOM (NSManagedObjectModel) objects that describe the data entities, their attributes, and their relationships. Core Data versioning works with those same MOM objects but takes the design one step further. Each entity version in each data model has a unique hash. When Core Data loads a persistent store from disk, it resolves the matching hashes in the persistent store against the MOM objects included with the application. If the matching MOM is not flagged as the "current" MOM, data migration kicks in.

## How Data Migration Works

Core Data handles data migration in a very straightforward manner. When a persistent store needs to be migrated, Core Data performs three steps.

### Copying the Entities with Attributes

In the first pass of the migration, Core Data creates new entities in the new persistent store for every entity in the old store. These entities have their attributes copied over, but not their relationships. During this phase, Core Data also keeps a reference to the old unique ID for each entity to be used in phase 2.

### Creating Relationships Between the Entities

In the second pass, Core Data builds all the relationships between the entities based on the previous relationships. This is where the reference in phase 1 is used.

### Validating the New Store

During the migration, all validation rules are turned off, and Core Data ignores the child classes defined in the MOM. Therefore, it is possible that some data validation rules may have been broken during the migration. In the final phase of the migration, Core Data goes back through the store and checks all the validation rules in order to ensure the data is in a valid state.

## Model Versions and Hashes

The word *versioning* has been used through this chapter as well as other material to describe data migration in Core Data. Unfortunately, it is an inaccurate term. Versioning implies that there is an order or precedence to the models. This is not accurate when it comes to data model versioning/migration in Core Data.

### Entity Hashes

Instead of keeping track of a version number, creation date, or some other potentially chronological identifier, Core Data generates a hash for each entity in a model. The hashes are then stored within the persistent stores created with that model for later comparison. When a persistent store is loaded, the first thing Core Data does is retrieve the metadata from that store. Inside the metadata is a list of every entity type in the store, along with the hash for that entity. Core Data then compares that list of hashes against the hashes of the "current" MOM. If they match, everything is fine, and the store is loaded. If they do not match, Core Data checks the options on the load persistent store call to see whether automatic data migration is requested. If it is not, an error message (shown in Section 3.1, *Some Maintenance Before We Migrate*, on page 38) is presented to the user.

### Changing the Hash Values

Surprisingly, not everything that changes inside a MOM causes the hash of the entities inside to change. There are actually quite a few things that we can do to a model that do not trigger data migration at all.

### Changes That Alter the Entity Hash

If any of the following are changed on an entity, the entity will report a different hash.

- Name: Changing the name of the entity
- Inheritance: Changing the parent entity
- Persistent properties: Adding or removing a property

In addition, changing the following four properties will also trigger a change to the entity hash.

- Name: The name of the property

- Optionality/read-only: Whether the property is optional or read-only

- Attribute type: The type of value stored

- Relationship: The destination, the minimum/maximum count, the delete rule, or the inverse

### Changes That *Do Not* Alter the Entity Hash

The following changes to an entity will *not* trigger a change to the entity hash:

- Class name: Changing the NSManagedObject subclass

- Transient properties: Changing properties that are not saved in the persistent store

- User info: Adding, removing, or changing the user info keys/values

- Validation predicates: Adding, removing, or changing the validation rules

- Default values: Adding, removing, or changing the default value of an attribute

In addition, the following changes to the properties of an entity will also *not* change the hash of the entity:

- User info: Adding, removing, or changing the user info key/values
- Validation predicates: Adding, removing, or changing the validation rules

The general distinction between things that do and do not affect version hashes is whether the changes impact the store schema. Details such as the class name impact only the runtime, not the structure of the persistent data.

### Mapping Models

If Core Data detects that an upgrade to the persistent store is needed, it looks for these three files in the application bundle:

- The MOM that matches the hash from the persistent store
- The current MOM
- The mapping model for those two MOM objects

Assuming that all three files are located, Core Data will then migrate the data in the persistent store from the old MOM to the new MOM. If Core Data cannot locate a mapping model, it checks to see whether inferred migration is turned on and attempts to do a lightweight migration. If inferred is not turned on or if the migration is too complex for a lightweight migration, an error will occur. Once the migration is complete, the stack (MOC, PS, and MOM) is fully initialized, and the application continues. This, of course, is the happy path, and there are several safeguards in place to allow the application developer to control failures.

Is it of vital importance that the application developer test the migration as completely as possible and that every error condition be checked during development and testing. With the delay in application releases to the App Store, it has never been more important to ensure that the migration performs correctly every time.

## 3.6   Progressive Data Migration (An Academic Exercise)

We're going to wrap up this chapter with a final section that's primarily a mental and academic exercise, one that demonstrates the flexibility available when working with Core Data migrations. Since it is possible to insert custom code at nearly every point in a migration, we can do some very interesting things. Let's take a look at an example.

What happens when our application is at version 5 of its data model and a user at version 1 decides to upgrade? Normally, we would need to provide a mapping model for every combination of source and destination object models. For the first couple of versions, this is not an issue. However, as we get further away from version 1, it becomes increasingly difficult. Fortunately, it is possible to figure out a migration path and do a *progressive migration*.

To accomplish a progressive migration, we need to handle the migration manually. The workflow is as follows:

1. If the store's model is the current model, do nothing.

2. Find a mapping model with the current store's model as its source.

3. Migrate the data to that mapping model's destination model.

4. Repeat starting at step 1.

## Creating the Migration Method

To begin this monumental task, we will be creating a new method in the AppDelegate. The method requires several pieces of information: the source path, the source type (XML, SQL, and so on), and the final model. In addition, we will pass in an error to be able to report any failures.

RecipesV3/PPRecipes/PPRAppDelegate.m

```
- (BOOL)progressivelyMigrateURL:(NSURL*)sourceStoreURL
                        ofType:(NSString*)type
                       toModel:(NSManagedObjectModel*)finalModel
                         error:(NSError**)error
{
```

It's a rather unwieldy method name, to be sure, but it contains all the information we need to figure out our migration path. Since this is going to be a recursive method, the first thing we need to do is check to see whether we are at our goal.

RecipesV3/PPRecipes/PPRAppDelegate.m

```
NSDictionary *sourceMetadata =
[NSPersistentStoreCoordinator metadataForPersistentStoreOfType:type
                                              URL:sourceStoreURL
                                            error:error];

if (!sourceMetadata) return NO;
if ([finalModel isConfiguration:nil
    compatibleWithStoreMetadata:sourceMetadata]) {
  *error = nil;
  return YES;
}
```

In this code segment, we first retrieve the metadata from the source URL. If that metadata is not nil, we ask the final model whether the metadata is compatible with it. If it is, we are happy and done. We then set the error pointer to nil and return YES. If it isn't compatible, we need to try to figure out the mapping model and potentially the interim data model to migrate to.

### Finding All the Managed Object Models

To proceed to the next step in the migration, we need to find all the managed object models in the bundle and loop through them. The goal at this point is to get all the models and figure out which one we can migrate to. Since these models will probably be in their own bundles, we have to first look for the bundles and then look inside each of them.

```
//Find the source model
NSManagedObjectModel *sourceModel = [NSManagedObjectModel
                                    mergedModelFromBundles:nil
                                    forStoreMetadata:sourceMetadata];
NSAssert(sourceModel != nil, ([NSString stringWithFormat:
                            @"Failed to find source model\n%@",
                            sourceMetadata]));
//Find all of the mom and momd files in the Resources directory
NSMutableArray *modelPaths = [NSMutableArray array];
NSArray *momdArray = [[NSBundle mainBundle] pathsForResourcesOfType:@"momd"
                                                    inDirectory:nil];
for (NSString *momdPath in momdArray) {
  NSString *resourceSubpath = [momdPath lastPathComponent];
  NSArray *array = [[NSBundle mainBundle]
                pathsForResourcesOfType:@"mom"
                inDirectory:resourceSubpath];
  [modelPaths addObjectsFromArray:array];
}
NSArray* otherModels = [[NSBundle mainBundle] pathsForResourcesOfType:@"mom"
                                                    inDirectory:nil];
[modelPaths addObjectsFromArray:otherModels];
if (!modelPaths || ![modelPaths count]) {
  //Throw an error if there are no models
  NSMutableDictionary *dict = [NSMutableDictionary dictionary];
  [dict setValue:@"No models found in bundle"
        forKey:NSLocalizedDescriptionKey];
  //Populate the error
  *error = [NSError errorWithDomain:@"Zarra" code:8001 userInfo:dict];
  return NO;
}
```

In this code block, we first grab all the resource paths from the mainBundle that are of type momd. This gives us a list of all the model bundles. We then loop through the list and look for mom resources inside each and add them to an overall array. Once that's done, we look inside the mainBundle again for any freestanding mom resources. Finally, we do a failure check to make sure we have some models to look through. If we can't find any, we populate the NSError and return NO.

## Finding the Mapping Model

Now the complicated part comes in. Since it is not currently possible to get an NSMappingModel with just the source model and then determine the destination model, we have to instead loop through every model we find, instantiate it, plug it in as a possible destination, and see whether there is a mapping model in existence. If there isn't, we continue to the next one.

```
RecipesV3/PPRecipes/PPRAppDelegate.m
NSMappingModel *mappingModel = nil;
NSManagedObjectModel *targetModel = nil;
NSString *modelPath = nil;
for (modelPath in modelPaths) {
  targetModel = [[NSManagedObjectModel alloc]
              initWithContentsOfURL:[NSURL fileURLWithPath:modelPath]];
  mappingModel = [NSMappingModel mappingModelFromBundles:nil
                                       forSourceModel:sourceModel
                                     destinationModel:targetModel];
  //If we found a mapping model then proceed
  if (mappingModel) break;
  //Release the target model and keep looking
  [targetModel release], targetModel = nil;
}
//We have tested every model, if nil here we failed
if (!mappingModel) {
  NSMutableDictionary *dict = [NSMutableDictionary dictionary];
  [dict setValue:@"No models found in bundle"
          forKey:NSLocalizedDescriptionKey];
  *error = [NSError errorWithDomain:@"Zarra"
                               code:8001
                           userInfo:dict];
  return NO;
}
```

This section is probably the most complicated piece of the progressive migration routine. In this section, we're looping through all the models that were previously discovered. For each of those models, we're instantiating the model and then asking NSMappingModel for an instance that will map between our known source model and the current model. If we find a mapping model, we break from our loop and continue. Otherwise, we release the instantiated model and continue the loop. After the loop, if the mapping model is still nil, we generate an error stating that we cannot discover the progression between the source model and the target and return NO. At this point, we should have all the components we need for one migration. The source model, target model, and mapping model are all known quantities. Now it's time to migrate!

## Performing the Migration

In this block, we are instantiating an NSMigrationManager (if we needed something special, we would build our own manager) with the source model and the destination model. We are also building up a unique path to migrate to. In this example, we are using the destination model's filename as the unique change to the source store's path. Once the destination path is built, we then tell the migration manager to perform the migration and check to see whether it was successful. If it wasn't, we simply return NO because the NSError will be populated by the NSMigrationManager. If it's successful, there are only three things left to do: move the source out of the way, replace it with the new destination store, and finally recurse.

```
RecipesV3/PPRecipes/PPRAppDelegate.m
NSMigrationManager *manager = [[NSMigrationManager alloc]
                                initWithSourceModel:sourceModel
                                destinationModel:targetModel];
NSString *modelName = [[modelPath lastPathComponent]
                        stringByDeletingPathExtension];
NSString *storeExtension = [[sourceStoreURL path] pathExtension];
NSString *storePath = [[sourceStoreURL path] stringByDeletingPathExtension];
//Build a path to write the new store
storePath = [NSString stringWithFormat:@"%@.%@.%@", storePath,
            modelName, storeExtension];
NSURL *destinationStoreURL = [NSURL fileURLWithPath:storePath];
if (![manager migrateStoreFromURL:sourceStoreURL
                            type:type
                         options:nil
                withMappingModel:mappingModel
               toDestinationURL:destinationStoreURL
                 destinationType:type
              destinationOptions:nil
                           error:error]) {
   return NO;
}
```

In this final code block, we first create a permanent location for the original store to be moved to. In this case, we will use a globally unique string generated from the NSProcessInfo class and attach the destination model's filename and the store's extension to it. Once that path is built, we move the source to it and then replace the source with the destination. At this point, we are at the same spot we were when we began except that we are now one version closer to the current model version.

Now we need to loop back to step 1 again in our workflow. Therefore, we will recursively call ourselves, returning the result of that recurse. As you can recall from the beginning of this method, if we are now at the current version, we will simply return YES, which will end the recursion.

```
RecipesV3/PPRecipes/PPRAppDelegate.m
NSString *guid = [[NSProcessInfo processInfo] globallyUniqueString];
guid = [guid stringByAppendingPathExtension:modelName];
guid = [guid stringByAppendingPathExtension:storeExtension];
NSString *appSupportPath = [storePath stringByDeletingLastPathComponent];
NSString *backupPath = [appSupportPath stringByAppendingPathComponent:guid];

NSFileManager *fileManager = [NSFileManager defaultManager];
if (![fileManager moveItemAtPath:[sourceStoreURL path]
                          toPath:backupPath
                           error:error]) {
  //Failed to copy the file
  return NO;
}
//Move the destination to the source path
if (![fileManager moveItemAtPath:storePath
                          toPath:[sourceStoreURL path]
                           error:error]) {
  //Try to back out the source move first, no point in checking it for errors
  [fileManager moveItemAtPath:backupPath
                       toPath:[sourceStoreURL path]
                        error:nil];
  return NO;
}
//We may not be at the "current" model yet, so recurse
return [self progressivelyMigrateURL:sourceStoreURL
                              ofType:type
                             toModel:finalModel
                               error:error];
```

This progressive migration can be tested by first running version 1 of our Grokking Recipes application, entering some data, and then running the third version. You will then see the data model migrate seamlessly from version 1 to version 3 with no intervention required.

## 3.7  Wrapping Up

We explored how to deal with changes and additions to our application and discussed data migration. In the next chapter, we're going to take a look at how our applications perform and ways to tune them.

# CHAPTER 4

# Performance Tuning

Brent Simmons, creator of NetNewsWire, once shared a story about a user who filed a bug report about the poor start-up performance of NetNewsWire. Upon discussion with that user, he discovered that they had more than 900,000 unread RSS feeds! The lesson I took away from that story is to expect my users to put thousands of times as much data into my applications as I would ever consider reasonable.

While we are working with Core Data, we need to consider the performance impacts of our design. We might test with a couple of dozen recipes and expect our users to load a couple hundred recipes into our application and test with those expectations. However, our users cannot read our intentions or expectations. As soon as we ship the application, some user somewhere will load 100,000 recipes into it and then file a bug report that it performs poorly.

## 4.1 Persistent Store Types

Four types of repositories are included with the Core Data API: SQLite, XML, binary, and in-memory. (XML is available only on OS X, not on iOS.) In-memory is technically not a persistent store because it is never written out to disk. Binary is effectively a serialized version of the object graph written out to disk. The XML store writes out the object graph to a human-readable text file, and SQLite stores the object graph in a relational database. When working with an iOS project, it is common to just use SQLite unless there is a very specific reason to use one of the other store formats.

### Atomic Stores

Atomic stores include XML, binary, and custom data stores. All of these stores are written to disk atomically; in other words, the entire data file is rewritten on every save. Although these store types have their advantages, they do not scale as well as the SQLite store. In addition, they are loaded fully into memory when they are accessed. This causes atomic stores to have a larger memory footprint than a SQLite store.

However, because they reside completely in memory while the application is running, atomic stores can be very fast, since the disk is hit only when the file is read into memory and when it is saved back out. SQLite, although still considered a fast store, is slower when dealing with smaller data sets because of its inherent disk access. The differences are measured in fractions of a second, so we cannot expect a dramatic speed increase by using an atomic store. But if fractions of a second matter, it may be something to consider.

## SQLite Persistent Store

In the most common cases, SQLite is the store option to use for application development. This is true on both iOS and OS X. SQLite is a software library that implements a self-contained, server-less, zero-configuration, transactional SQL database engine. SQLite is the most widely deployed SQL database engine in the world. The source code for SQLite is in the public domain.

### Better Scaling

By utilizing a relational database as the persistent store, we no longer need to load the entire data set into memory to work with it. Because the data is being stored in a relational database, our application can scale to a very large size. SQLite itself has been tested with data sets measured in terabytes and can handle just about anything that we can realistically develop. Since we are loading only the data we want at a particular moment, SQLite keeps the memory footprint of our application quite low. Likewise, SQLite makes efficient use of its disk space and therefore has a small footprint on disk as well.

### More Performance-Tuning Options

By working with a database instead of a flat file, we have access to many more performance-tuning options. For example, we can index the columns within our entities to enable faster predicates. We can also control exactly what gets loaded into memory. It is possible to get just a count of the objects, just the unique identifiers for objects, and so on. This flexibility allows us to tune the performance of our application more than any other store type. Because the SQLite store is the only format that is not fully loaded into memory, we get to control the data flow. All of the other formats require that the entire data file be loaded into memory before they can be used. The details of how to utilize these features are discussed in Section 4.3, *Fetching*, on page 67.

## 4.2 Optimizing Your Data Model

When we design our data model, we need to consider several factors. Where we put our binary data can be extremely important because its size and storage location plays a key role in the performance of our application. Likewise, relationships must be carefully balanced and used appropriately. Also, entity inheritance, a powerful feature of Core Data, must be used with a delicate hand because the underlying structure may be surprising.

Although it is easy to think of Core Data as a database API, we must remember that it is not and that structuring the data with data normalization may not yield the most efficient results. In many cases, denormalizing the data can yield greater performance gains.

### Where to Put Binary Data

One of the easiest ways to kill performance in a Core Data application is to stick large amounts of binary data into frequently accessed tables. For example, if we were to put the pictures of our recipes into the recipe table, we would start seeing performance degradation after only a couple hundred recipes had been added. Every time we accessed a Recipe entity, we would have to load its image data, even if we were not going to display the image. Since our application displays all the recipes in a list, this means every image would reside in memory immediately upon launch and remain there until the application quit. Imagine this situation with a few thousand recipes!

But where do we draw the line? What is considered a small enough piece of binary data to fit into a table, and what should not be put into the repository at all?

If you are developing an application that is targeting iOS 6.0 or greater (or Mac OS X 10.8 or greater), the answer is simple: turn on external binary storage in the model and let Core Data solve the problem for you (see Figure 13, *Turn on the external record flag*, on page 64). This feature instructs Core Data to determine how to store binary data. With this flag on, Core Data decides whether the image is small enough to store inside of the SQLite file or whether it is too big and therefore should be stored on disk separately. In either case, the decision is an implementation detail from the perspective of our application. We access the binary data just like any other attribute on the entity.

If the application is still targeting an older version of the operating system (iOS or Mac OS X), then the application is responsible for dealing with binary data in a performant way.

**Figure 13—Turn on the external record flag.**

### Small Binary Data

Anything smaller than 100 kilobytes is considered to be small binary data. Icons or small avatars are a couple examples of data of this size. When working with something this small, it is most efficient to store it directly as a property value in its corresponding table. The performance impact of binary data this size is negligible. The transformable attribute type is ideal for this use.

### Medium Binary Data

Medium binary data is anything larger than 100 kilobytes and smaller than 1 megabyte in size. Average-sized images and small audio clips are a few examples of data in this size range. Data of this size can also be stored directly in the repository. However, the data should be stored in its own table on the other end of a relationship with the primary tables. This allows the binary data to remain a fault until it is actually needed. In the previous recipe example, even though the Recipe entity would be loaded into memory for display, the image would be loaded only when it is needed by the UI.

SQLite has shown itself to be quite efficient at disk access. There are cases where loading data from the SQLite store can actually be faster than direct disk access. This is one of the reasons why medium binary data can be stored directly in the repository.

### Large Binary Data

Large binary data is anything greater than 1 megabyte in size. Large images, audio files, and video files are just some examples of data of this size. Any binary data of this size should be stored on disk as opposed to in the repository. When working with data of this size, it is best to store its path information directly in the primary entity (such as the Recipe entity) and store the binary data in a known location on disk (such as in the Application Support subdirectory for your application).

## Entity Inheritance

Entity inheritance is a very powerful feature within Core Data. It allows you to build an object-like inheritance tree in your data model. However, this feature comes at a rather large cost. For example, let's look at an example model that makes moderate use of entity inheritance, as shown here:

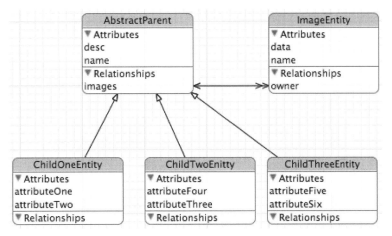

The object model itself looks quite reasonable. We are sharing name, desc, and a one-to-many relationship to the ImageEntity. However, the underlying table structure actually looks like this:

| | name | desc | attributeOne | attributeTwo | attributeThree | attributeFour | attributeFive | attributeSix |
|---|---|---|---|---|---|---|---|---|
| Entity One | | | | | | | | |
| Entity Two | | | | | | | | |
| Entity Three | | | | | | | | |

The reason for this is how Core Data handles the object model to relational table mapping. Instead of creating one table for each child object, Core Data creates one large table that includes all the properties for the parent entity as well as its children. The end result is an extremely wide and tall table in the database with a high percentage of empty values.

Although the entity inheritance feature of Core Data is extremely useful, we should be aware of what is going on underneath the object model to avoid a performance penalty. We should not treat entity inheritance as an equal to object inheritance. There is certainly some overlap, but they are not equal, and treating them as such will have a negative impact on the performance of the repository.

## Denormalizing Data to Improve Performance

Although the most powerful persistent store available for Core Data is a database, we must always be conscious of the fact that Core Data is not just a database. Core Data is an object hierarchy that can be persisted to a database format. The difference is subtle but important. Core Data is first a collection of objects that we use to display data in a user interface of some form and allow the user to access that data. Therefore, although database normalization might be the first place to look for performance improvements, we should not take it too far. There are six levels of database normalization,[1] but a Core Data repository should rarely, if ever, be taken beyond the second level. There are several cases where we can gain a greater performance benefit by denormalizing the data.

### Search-Only Properties

Searching within properties can be quite expensive. For properties that have a large amount of text or, worse, Unicode text, a single search field can cause a huge performance hit. One way to improve this situation is to create a derived attribute based on the text in an entity. For example, searching in our description property of the Recipe entity can potentially be very expensive if the user has verbose descriptions and/or uses Unicode characters in the description.

To improve the performance of searches in this field, we could create a second property on the Recipe entity that strips the Unicode characters from the description and also removes common words such as *a*, *the*, *and*, and so on. If we then perform the search on this derived property, we can drastically improve search performance.

The downside to using search-only properties is that we need to maintain them. Every time the description field is edited, we need to update the derived property as well.

### Expensive Calculations

In a normalized database, calculated values are not stored. It is considered cheaper to recalculate the value as needed than to store it in the database. However, from a user experience point of view, the opposite can frequently be true. In cases where the calculation takes a human-noticeable amount of time, it may very well be better for the user if we were to store that calculation in the entity and recalculate it only when one of its dependent values has

---

1.    See http://en.wikipedia.org/wiki/Database_normalization for details.

changed. For example, if we store the first and last names of a user in our Core Data repository, it might make sense to store the full name as well.

### Intelligent Relationships

Relationships in a Core Data model are like salt in a cooking recipe. Too much and you ruin the recipe; too little and something is missing. Fortunately, there are some simple rules we can follow when it comes to relationships in a Core Data repository.

### Follow the Object Model

Core Data is first and foremost an object model. The entities in our model should represent the data as accurately as possible. Just because a value might be duplicated across several objects (or rows from the database point of view) does not mean it should be extruded into its own table. Many times it is more efficient for us to store that string several times over in the entity itself than to traverse a relationship to get it.

Traversing a relationship is generally more expensive than accessing an attribute on the entity. Therefore, if the value being stored is simple, it's better to leave it in the entity it is associated with.

### Separate Commonly Used from Rarely Used Data

If the object design calls for a one-to-many relationship or a many-to-many relationship, we should definitely create a relationship for it. This is usually the case where the data is more than a single property or contains binary data or would be difficult to properly model inside the parent object. For example, if we have a user entity, it is more efficient to store the user's address in its own object as opposed to having several attributes in the user object for address, city, state, postal code, and so on.

A balance needs to be carefully maintained between what is stored on the other end of a relationship and what is stored in the primary entity. Crossing key paths is more expensive than accessing attributes, but creating objects that are very wide also slows down data access.

## 4.3 Fetching

*Fetching* is the term used to describe the resolving of NSManagedObject objects from the repository. When we retrieve an NSManagedObject, it is "fetched" into memory, and we can then access its properties. To help us utilize memory efficiently, fetching may not always happen all at once. Specifically, when we are using a SQLite store, it is quite possible that an object we think is in memory is actually only on disk and has yet to be read into memory. Likewise, objects that we think we are done with may actually still sit in a cache.

To demonstrate the differences in the ways that we can load data into memory from our SQLite Store, I used an older Apple demonstration application from a previous WWDC called GoFetch. (The source code for this application is available as part of this book's download.) The entire goal of this application is to generate a large amount of random data and let us control how it is fetched back into memory. Each fetch is then timed to demonstrate the speed of various options. These tests were performed with 3,417 records in the SQLite repository.

## Loading NSManagedObjectID Objects Only

The smallest amount of data that we can retrieve as part of an NSFetch-Request is just the NSManagedObjectID. The NSManagedObjectID is the unique identifier for the record and contains no content. In the test discussed earlier, it took the test machine 0.004 seconds to retrieve 3,417 records from disk.

### How to Retrieve NSManagedObjectID Objects

There is only one change required to retrieve just NSManagedObjectID objects instead of full NSManagedObject objects.

```
NSFetchRequest *fetchRequest = [[NSFetchRequest alloc] init];
[fetchRequest setEntity:[NSEntityDescription entityForName:@"Person"
 inManagedObjectContext:[self managedObjectContext]]];
[fetchRequest setResultType:NSManagedObjectIDResultType];
```

By changing the -resultType to NSManagedObjectIDResultType, our call to -executeFetchRequest:error: returns NSArray of NSManagedObjectID objects instead of NSManagedObject objects.

Why would we want only the NSManagedObjectID objects? There are several uses for this.

- *Inclusion comparison*: Since NSManagedObjectID objects guarantee uniqueness, we can use them to determine whether an object is included in a set and avoid having to retrieve the entire set for this comparison.

- *Prefetching*: Even though the properties for the associated objects are not loaded into NSManagedObject objects for us to access, they are loaded into a cache within Core Data. This means when we do access the associated NSManagedObject objects via a call to objectWithID: on NSManagedObjectContext, we will get the results much faster than if we had to make a full round-trip to the disk.

You can accomplish this by turning on property loading while keeping the -resultType as NSManagedObjectIDResultType. This is often referred to as *warming up the cache*.

## Loaded As a Fault

The next smallest amount of data we can retrieve is referred to as a *faulted* NSManagedObject. What this means is the NSFetchRequest returns an NSArray of NSManagedObject objects, but those objects contain only the NSManagedObjectID. All the properties and relationships are empty or in a faulted state. As soon as an attribute is accessed, *all of the attributes on that object are loaded in*. Likewise, as soon as a relationship is accessed, all the NSManagedObject objects on the other end of that relationship are loaded in as faults. Performing the same query as earlier in this configuration returned the 3,417 records in 0.007 seconds. Faults will be discussed in greater depth in Section 4.4, *Faulting*, on page 71.

### How to Retrieve Faulted NSManagedObject Objects

To disable the fetching of attributes as part of the NSFetchRequest, we need to disable it prior to executing the fetch.

```
NSFetchRequest *fetchRequest = [[NSFetchRequest alloc] init];
[fetchRequest setIncludesPropertyValues:NO];
[fetchRequest setEntity:[NSEntityDescription entityForName:@"Person"
 inManagedObjectContext:[self managedObjectContext]]];
```

Although this seems like a great solution, it can be a bit of a trap. Because this configuration returns empty skeletons, each object gets loaded from disk individually. This is *significantly* slower than loading all the objects needed at once. However, the time to load the objects is spread out and can be less noticeable to the user. For raw speed, it is recommended that we load all the data for the objects in one pass.

## Loading Property Values

The next step up from faulted NSManagedObject objects is to prefetch their property values. This will not retrieve the objects on the other sides of relationships. Performing this query took 0.021 seconds for the 3,417 records in the test repository.

### How to Retrieve Only Property Values

Retrieving NSManagedObject objects with attributes populated is the default for NSFetchRequest.

```
NSFetchRequest *fetchRequest = [[NSFetchRequest alloc] init];
[fetchRequest setEntity:[NSEntityDescription entityForName:@"Person"
 inManagedObjectContext:[self managedObjectContext]]];
```

This option is a very good middle ground between fetching faults and some of the following choices. In situations where only the object requested needs to be displayed right away and its relationships are not needed right away, this can be the most efficient solution.

### How to Load Property Values and NSManagedObjectID Objects

We can also combine this option with the NSManagedObjectID retrieval listed earlier to warm up the cache. The settings to accomplish this are as follows:

```
NSFetchRequest *fetchRequest = [[NSFetchRequest alloc] init];
[fetchRequest setResultType:NSManagedObjectIDResultType];
[fetchRequest setEntity:[NSEntityDescription entityForName:@"Person"
 inManagedObjectContext:[self managedObjectContext]]];
```

This can be used to excellent effect on a background thread when the entire fetch is going to take a significant amount of time. Once the NSManagedObjectID objects are retrieved, they can be safely passed to the primary thread and used to display the data to the user. Using Core Data within a multithreaded application is discussed in more detail in Chapter 5, *Threading*, on page 77.

## Loading Relationships

The next step up in the scale of loading data is to prefetch the relationships while loading the targeted entities. This does not fetch them as fully formed but as faults. This step up can have a significant impact on the performance of a Core Data application. In the test, this fetch took 1.166 seconds to retrieve 3,417 objects, each with only a *single* object on the other side of a one-to-one relationship. With a more complex data model, this becomes an even larger performance hit.

### How to Load Relationships

Fortunately, this option gives us some fine-grained control over which relationships to load. This would allow us to, for example, load only the addresses associated with a person and skip over their images, phone numbers, and so on. Accomplishing this requires passing an NSArray of NSString objects with the names of the relationships to load.

```
NSFetchRequest *fetchRequest = [[NSFetchRequest alloc] init];
NSArray *relationshipKeys = [NSArray arrayWithObject:@"addresses"];
[fetchRequest setRelationshipKeyPathsForPrefetching:relationshipKeys];
[fetchRequest setEntity:[NSEntityDescription entityForName:@"Person"
 inManagedObjectContext:[self managedObjectContext]]];
```

In this example code, we create a new NSArray that has one NSString within it that corresponds to the name of the relationship within the Person entity. We can get even more clever with this request by using a keypath in the NSArray and specifying a second level of objects to include in the fetch. For example, if our Address entities had a relationship to a postal code lookup table that contained the city and state, we could change the NSArray creation line to the following:

```
NSArray *relationshipKeys = [NSArray arrayWithObjects:@"addresses",
  @"addresses.postalCode", nil];
```

That would cause Core Data to retrieve two levels of relationships as faults. In addition, this call does check for duplication before executing the requests and thereby can be used safely when mixing keypaths. In other words, the postalCode relationship, which is probably many to many, will not be retrieved more than once.

### NSFetchRequest and Disk Access

Every time an NSFetchRequest is executed, it hits the disk. This is an important point to keep in mind when we are working with NSManaged-Object objects. If we are doing joins, adding objects to a relationship, and so on, it might seem easier and cleaner to perform an NSFetchRequest to check whether the object is already in the relationship or check for a similar function, but that action can hurt performance significantly. Even if we have all the relevant objects in memory, an NSFetchRequest is still going to hit the disk. It is far more efficient for us to use that NSPredicate against a collection that is already in memory.

We have seen in this section that with a SQLite persistent store, we have a lot of control over how our data is loaded into memory. We can tailor the load to fit our exacting needs. All of these options can be a bit overwhelming, but there is one good rule of thumb. Try to load *only* the data you need at that moment in one pass. Every fetch request can take quite a bit of time, and since the fetch requests are normally performed on the main thread, they can damage the user experience of your application.

## 4.4 Faulting

Firing faults individually is one of the most common, if not the most common, cause for the poor performance of Core Data applications. Faults are a double-edged sword that can make great improvements to the speed and performance of our applications or can drag the performance down to the depths of the unusable. The single most valuable performance improvement we can make to a Core Data application is to make sure we are fetching only the data we need when we need it. If we fetch too little, our application will feel unresponsive. If we fetch too much, our application will stall and potentially be killed by the operating system.

## Orders of Magnitude

Disk access is significantly slower than accessing memory. The times measured for each is *six orders of magnitude* different. This translates into disk access being roughly 1 million times slower than accessing data that is stored in memory, as illustrated:

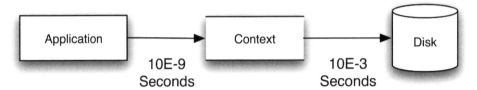

Although the actual retrieval times are closer to a few thousand times slower, the point is still clear. Avoid accessing the disk if possible. However, when we have no choice but to access the disk, we must attempt to get everything we need in one pass. Repeated small requests to the disk are significantly slower than one larger request.

## Prefetching

In Section 4.3, *Fetching*, on page 67, we reviewed the different ways we can retrieve the data from disk. To expand on that, consider each request we make from the NSManagedObjectContext and try to retrieve all the data in one request that the user is going to want to view. For example, if the user is going to be editing a user record, load that user and all its relationships at once. This will be significantly faster than grabbing the Person entity and then going back to grab three Address entities, then two Phone entities, and so on. Use the relationship prefetching option of NSFetchRequest to grab all of them at once.

If we can predict what the user is going to want to see and load it ahead of their request, the overall user experience will be vastly improved. As we are developing our applications, we need to look at each window, view, or sheet and ask, "What information will this part present?" and make sure all of that information is either already in memory or loaded at once. Having said that, we need to balance this with information overload, as discussed in Section 4.5, *Access Patterns*, on page 75.

## Warming Up the Cache

As we discussed in Section 4.3, *Fetching*, on page 67, it is possible to preload the data into the cache so that it is in memory when we need it. The easiest way to perform this step is to execute a full fetch on a background thread. For example, on launch of our recipe application, we could launch a background thread to retrieve all the Recipe entities. This would allow us to fill the cache with the Recipe entities that we know are going to be presented to the user, in turn allowing the main thread to grab those recipes from the cache instead of the disk and give the user a smoother-running application in the process. The magic behind this is based on how the NSPersistentStoreCoordinator works. Whenever any request on any thread is performed, the data is held in the NSPersistentStoreCoordinator as part of its cache. When another request is made, no matter what thread it came from, for that same data it is retrieved from the cache instead of requiring another hit to the disk.

## Saving

The numbers discussed in *Orders of Magnitude*, on page 72, also apply to writing the data back out to the disk. In fact, writing to the disk is even slower than reading from it. Therefore, it is more efficient for us to save data back out to disk in batches. Saving after every record change causes our entire application to feel sluggish to the user. Likewise, doing a huge write while the application is attempting to exit gives the appearance that our application has stopped responding and risks data loss.

As with most things when it comes to performance tuning, be aware of your saves and how much data you are saving and how frequently. Try to do saves during logical pauses in the application flow.

## Deleting

It may come as a surprise, but deleting an object can cause a performance issue. Let's review the data model from Chapter 3, *Versioning and Migration*, on page 37. Imagine that in this later version of our application we want to delete a recipe from the repository. When we delete the recipe, we have a cascade rule set up to delete all the associated RecipeIngredient entities as well. We also need to touch the Author entity, Ingredient entity, and UnitOfMeasure entity, as shown in Figure 14, *Impacts of deleting a recipe*, on page 74.

It is obvious why we need to touch the RecipeIngredient entity, but why do we need to access all the others? This is because of the relationships between the entities. For each relationship, we need to validate the relationship after the delete and confirm that there are no dangling references. If these objects

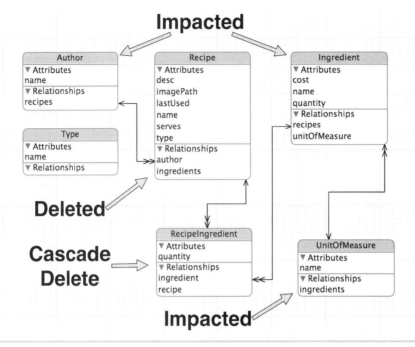

**Figure 14—Impacts of deleting a recipe**

are not currently in memory, then the NSManagedObjectContext must retrieve them from the disk to accomplish all of this.

Therefore, when we are doing deletes, especially large deletes, it can be a performance improvement to fetch all the relationships prior to the delete.

### Faulting and Disk Access

Firing a fault does not always mean that the data is going to be read from disk. Depending on how we have requested the data in the first place or what happened earlier in the NSManagedObject object's life span, it is quite possible that the data will be loaded from cache instead.

Likewise, faulting an NSManagedObject does not guarantee that it will be written back out to disk nor does it guarantee that it will be removed from the cache. If the object has no changes, then there is nothing to write to disk, and it is quite possible it will remain in the cache for an unknown period of time.

Easily one of the best ways to check to see whether the firing of a fault is in fact causing disk access is to monitor our application with Instruments. By using the Core Data template, we can use the "cache miss" instrument to check for disk hits. If we are getting far more calls to the disk than expected, we need to consider refactoring the code.

## 4.5 Access Patterns

Improving performance within Core Data is not necessarily only about the repository and order of loading the data. There are a number of things we can do within the user interface to help performance as well.

### Searching

Searching the repository can be absolute murder on performance. Whether we are searching at the request of the user or performing a search in the background, we need to be very careful to avoid impacting the performance of our application.

### Order Is Important

Just like any conditional, the order of the logic is important. Simple equality is faster than inclusions such as *in*, *contains*, and so on. When building the predicate, try to order the logic from left to right, simple to complex. This process allows Core Data to fail quickly and improve the search performance.

### Unicode and Regular Expressions

Unicode is very expensive to work with when we are searching. As suggested earlier in *Search-Only Properties*, on page 66, try to avoid searching against Unicode directly. It is cheaper to keep a derived value that strips off the Unicode than it is to do frequent searches against the Unicode text.

Likewise, regular expressions are expensive. If a situation calls for one, try to put it at the far-right end of the NSPredicate, as discussed in *Order Is Important*, on page 75.

### Limit Queries Across Relationships

Searching across objects that are joined by a relationship can be very expensive for searching. Although it is impressive to search against person.address.postalCode.city, it may not be the most efficient way to solve the problem. Consider reversing the query or breaking it down into several smaller queries to reduce the complexity of the underlying SQL. When we are working with a SQLite back end, all of our NSPredicate calls turn into SQL before hitting the database. The less complex that SQL is, the faster it will run. It may very well be faster to get an NSArray of all the Address objects within a specific city and then perform the rest of the query against that NSArray than it would be to traverse three relationships in one call.

## 4.6   Wrapping Up

A busy user interface is more than just a poor user experience; it also impacts the performance of the application. When we display a large amount of data on the screen, we must keep that information in memory, which in turn means we must load a large amount of data from disk all in one go. It is far better to break up an application user interface into consumable chunks of information than it is to try to display every last bit on the screen at once.

The careful use of tabs, sheets, and panels can improve the feel of a user interface, and that will in turn improve the performance. By splitting the user interface into smaller pieces, we have finer-grained control over what data gets loaded when, and we can reduce our disk access to manageable chunks.

Keep it simple.

# CHAPTER 5

# Threading

Multithreading is one of the great double-edged swords of programming. If it is done correctly, it can be a real boon to your application; done incorrectly, it leads to strange, unreproducible errors in the application. Multithreading has a tendency to polarize developers: they either swear that it is necessary for any application to perform properly or declare it is to be avoided at all costs. The truth, of course, is somewhere in the middle. Multithreading is a vital piece of the overall performance puzzle. While adding more threads will not make your application automatically faster, it can make your application "feel" faster to the user. That perception is what we are going to focus on in this chapter.

The problem is that Core Data is not inherently thread-safe. It still wants and expects to be run in a single thread. Therefore, when we start multithreading our applications, we must take care to work with Core Data properly to avoid threading issues. Fortunately, as of iOS 6.0 and OS X 10.8 Mountain Lion, things have improved significantly.

### Core Data and iOS 5.0

As mentioned in the introduction, we are focusing primarily on iOS 6.0. However, in this chapter in particular, many of the APIs discussed were actually introduced in iOS 5.0 (as well as OS X 10.7 Lion). Unfortunately, while the APIs were introduced at that time, they didn't work very well. In some cases, they didn't work at all. Therefore, it is my recommendation to treat iOS 5.x as if it were iOS 4.x and to avoid using *any* of the Core Data APIs that were introduced in 5.0.

## 5.1   Why Isn't Core Data Thread-Safe?

You may be surprised to learn that there are a lot of things in Cocoa and Objective-C that are not thread-safe, and Core Data is only one of the many.

For instance, whenever you make a change to a GUI widget, it is recommended you be on the main thread, because the UI is not thread-safe.

Prior to iOS 6.0 and OS X 10.8 Mountain Lion, you could get away with using Core Data incorrectly in a multithreaded environment. If you read from NSManagedObject instances only on threads other than the one that created the instance and didn't write to them, then things would work—usually. However, as of iOS 6.0 and OS X 10.8 Mountain Lion, that has changed. Core Data now monitors what thread the objects are being accessed from and will throw an exception if an improper access is detected. While this change can catch developers off-guard, it is a net win. We now have well-defined boundaries for what is correct and what is not.

Whether we are developing for the latest release of iOS or OS X or targeting an older platform, we must now follow a strict rule for thread safety with Core Data: contexts and their resulting objects must be accessed only on the thread that created them.

---

### NSOperation and NSOperationQueue

Throughout this chapter we will be using NSOperation and NSOperationQueue quite heavily. These are classes that were added to Cocoa as part of Mac OS X 10.5 Leopard specifically to make threading easier. Although we will not be going into detail on how to use these classes, it is of extreme value to fully learn these classes so that you can use them properly in your own projects.

There's a naming issue that often causes confusion while using NSOperation. The NSOperation uses a method named -main as the entry point for the work that the NSOperation is to complete while running on a background thread. The NSOperationQueue calls this method directly. However, if the NSOperation is flagged as being concurrent, then the NSOperationQueue will call -start instead. In all of the examples presented in this book, we will be using the "nonconcurrent" (which translates into "threaded") implementation of NSOperation and therefore using the -main entry point.

---

## 5.2 Creating Multiple Contexts

As of iOS 6.0 and Mac OS X Lion, there are two recommended methods for using Core Data across multiple threads. The first method, which is valid on all versions of iOS and Mac OS X that can use Core Data, involves creating a separate NSManagedObjectContext for each thread that will be interacting with Core Data.[1] The creation of the separate context on a background thread is

---

1. We will be exploring the second, updated method in Section 5.5, *Parent-Child NSManagedObjectContext Instances*, on page 92.

quite straightforward and is nearly identical to the creation of the NSManagedObjectContext on the main thread.

**Baseline/PPRecipes/PPRImportOperation.m**
```
NSManagedObjectContext *localMOC = nil;
NSPersistentStoreCoordinator *psc = nil;
localMOC = [[NSManagedObjectContext alloc] init];
psc = [[self mainContext] persistentStoreCoordinator];
[localMOC setPersistentStoreCoordinator:psc];
```

As shown in the method -main, we grab a reference to the existing NSPersistentStoreCoordinator and use that in the initialization of a new NSManagedObjectContext.

Although the NSPersistentStoreCoordinator is not thread-safe either, the NSManagedObjectContext knows how to lock it properly when in use. Therefore, we can attach as many NSManagedObjectContext instances to a single NSPersistentStoreCoordinator as we want without fear of collision.

 **Joe asks:**
## When Do I Need to Worry About Threading?

The point at which threading is appropriate is a hard one to decide upon. As a rule, I will put an operation into another thread any time that it blocks the UI thread from drawing or causes the operating system to think that the application is nonresponsive. When an application starts freezing or stuttering, it's time to optimize the application and look at threading. As your experience grows, it becomes easier to spot these trouble points ahead of time.

### Cross-thread Communication

There is one major catch when standing up multiple NSManagedObjectContext instances. Each instance is unaware of the existence and activity of the other instances. This means that when an NSManagedObject is created, edited, or deleted by one NSManagedObjectContext, the other instances aren't aware of the change.

Fortunately, Apple has given us a relatively easy way to keep all the NSManagedObjectContext instances in sync. Every time an NSManagedObjectContext completes a save operation, it broadcasts an NSNotification with the key NSManagedObjectContextDidSaveNotification. In addition, the NSNotification instance contains all the information about what is occurring in that save.

To complement the NSNotification broadcast, the NSManagedObjectContext has a method designed to consume this NSNotification and update itself based on its contents. This method, -mergeChangesFromContextDidSaveNotification:, will update the NSManagedObjectContext with the changes and also notify any observers of those changes. This means our main NSManagedObjectContext can be updated with a single call whenever the background NSManagedObjectContext instances perform a save, and our user interface will be updated automatically.

Baseline/PPRecipes/PPRImportOperation.m
```
NSNotificationCenter *center = [NSNotificationCenter defaultCenter];
[center addObserver:self
         selector:@selector(contextDidSave:)
             name:NSManagedObjectContextDidSaveNotification
           object:localMOC];
```

In this example, we listen for an NSManagedObjectContextDidSaveNotification and call -contextDidSave: whenever the notification is received. Also note that we're interested only in notifications generated from our own localMOC; this helps to avoid polluting the main NSManagedObjectContext with duplicate merges.

Baseline/PPRecipes/PPRImportOperation.m
```
- (void)contextDidSave:(NSNotification*)notification
{
  NSManagedObjectContext *moc = [self mainContext];
  void (^mergeChanges) (void) = ^ {
    [moc mergeChangesFromContextDidSaveNotification:notification];
  };
  if ([NSThread isMainThread]) {
    mergeChanges();
  } else {
    dispatch_sync(dispatch_get_main_queue(), mergeChanges);
  }
}
```

When we receive a change notification, the only thing we need to do with it is hand it off to the primary NSManagedObjectContext for consumption. However, the main NSManagedObjectContext needs to consume that notification on the main thread. To do this, we create a simple block and either call that block directly (if we are on the main thread) or pass it off to the main thread via a dispatch _sync if we are not on the main thread.

It should be noted that this call can take a human-perceivable amount of time. In fact, prior to iOS 6.0 and OS X 10.8 Mountain Lion, this was one of the greatest performance bottlenecks of Core Data that could not be avoided. Fortunately, as we discuss in Chapter 4, *Performance Tuning*, on page 61, applications targeting those platforms or newer have a solution.

## 5.3 Exporting Recipes

In our first demonstration of multithreading, we'll add the ability to export recipes from our database so that they can be shared. In this new section of the application, we will create an NSOperation, which will create its own NSManagedObjectContext and use it to copy the selected recipes into a JSON structure, which can then be used by the application in several ways (uploaded to a server, emailed to a friend, and so on).

To implement this addition to our application, we need to make a few changes to the user interface. We want to add a button to the UINavigationBar that is a generic action item. When the button is tapped, it will display an action sheet and give the user an option to mail the recipe (other options can be added later), as shown in Figure 15, *Linking the Import menu item*, on page 82.

To accomplish this, we first add the button in the storyboard and associate the button with a new method called -action:. Inside the -action: method, we construct a UIActionSheet and present it to the user.

**Baseline/PPRecipes/PPRDetailViewController.m**
```
- (IBAction)action:(id)sender;
{
  UIActionSheet *sheet = [[UIActionSheet alloc] init];
  [sheet addButtonWithTitle:@"Mail Recipe"];
  [sheet addButtonWithTitle:@"Cancel"];
  [sheet setCancelButtonIndex:([sheet numberOfButtons] - 1)];
  [sheet setDelegate:self];
  [sheet showInView:[self view]];
}
```

Once the user makes a choice with the UIActionSheet, our PPRDetailViewController will get a callback as its delegate. If the user clicked Cancel, we simply return. Otherwise, we drop into a switch statement to handle the choice the user has made. In this example, we have only one choice available.

**Baseline/PPRecipes/PPRDetailViewController.m**
```
- (void)actionSheet:(UIActionSheet*)actionSheet
didDismissWithButtonIndex:(NSInteger)buttonIndex
{
  if (buttonIndex == [actionSheet cancelButtonIndex]) return;
  switch (buttonIndex) {
    case 0: //Mail Recipe
      [self mailRecipe];
      break;
    default:
      ALog(@"Unknown index: %i", buttonIndex);
  }
}
```

Figure 15—Linking the Import menu item

When the user taps Mail Recipe, the switch statement calls our -mailRecipe method.

Baseline/PPRecipes/PPRDetailViewController.m
```
- (void)mailRecipe
{
  PPRExportOperation *operation = nil;
  operation = [[PPRExportOperation alloc] initWithRecipe:[self recipeMO]];
  [operation setCompletionBlock:^(NSData *data, NSError *error) {
    ZAssert(data || !error, @"Error: %@\n%@", [error localizedDescription],
          [error userInfo]);
    //Mail the data to a friend
  }];

  [[NSOperationQueue mainQueue] addOperation:operation];
}
```

In the -mailRecipe method, we construct a PPRExportOperation instance, passing it the recipe. We then give the PPRExportOperation a completion block. The completion block is used to handle the results of the export operation. Note that the block receives back both an NSData and an NSError. If the operation was successful, the NSData is populated. If the operation failed for any reason, the NSData is nil, and the NSError is populated. In a production application, we would want to respond to the error. For now, we have a developer-level logic check to capture the error.

## Building the PPRExportOperation

With the changes completed in the PPRDetailViewController, the next step is to build the PPRExportOperation. The goal of the operation is to accept a single recipe and turn it into a JSON structure. When the export is complete, the operation will execute a completion block and pass the resulting data back to the caller. This gives us the following header:

```
Baseline/PPRecipes/PPRExportOperation.h
#import "PPRRecipeMO.h"
typedef void (^ExportCompletionBlock)(NSData *jsonData, NSError *error);

@interface PPRExportOperation : NSOperation

@property (nonatomic, copy) ExportCompletionBlock completionBlock;

- (id)initWithRecipe:(PPRRecipeMO*)recipe;
@end
```

The initializer for our export operation needs to retain only the NSManagedObjectID of the incoming NSManagedObject. Because the initWithRecipe method is being called on the thread on which the incoming NSManagedObject was created, we can access its methods. Once we are in our own -main method, we can no longer access it. However, the NSManagedObjectID is thread-safe and can cross the boundary. So, we grab it now and hold onto it in a property. We pass in the entire NSManagedObject so that we can also grab a reference to the NSPersistentStore-Coordinator without having to explicitly request it.

```
Baseline/PPRecipes/PPRExportOperation.m
- (id)initWithRecipe:(PPRRecipeMO*)recipe;
{
  if (!(self = [super init])) return nil;

  [self setIncomingRecipeID:[recipe objectID]];
  NSManagedObjectContext *moc = [recipe managedObjectContext];
  [self setPersistentStoreCoordinator:[moc persistentStoreCoordinator]];
  return self;
}
```

Once the operation is started, we must perform a couple of start-up tasks. First, since the operation is going to be executed on a separate thread, we need to construct a new NSManagedObjectContext.

**Baseline/PPRecipes/PPRExportOperation.m**

```
- (void)main
{
  ZAssert([self completionBlock], @"No completion block set");
  NSManagedObjectContext *localMOC = nil;
  localMOC = [[NSManagedObjectContext alloc] init];

  NSPersistentStoreCoordinator *psc = nil;
  psc = [self persistentStoreCoordinator];
  [localMOC setPersistentStoreCoordinator:psc];
```

Now that we have a local NSManagedObjectContext, we need to obtain a local copy of the recipe. A call to -objectWithID: returns a local copy of the NSManagedObject. We also confirm that it did return an object for us. -objectWithID: is a method on NSManagedObjectContext that will return a context-local copy of the associated NSManagedObject. If the NSManagedObject is already loaded into the context, then it will return the object; otherwise, it will attempt to fetch it from the NSPersistentStoreCoordinator.

Once we have a local copy of the recipe, we need to turn it into a JSON structure. To do that, we must first convert the NSManagedObject into a dictionary. However, we don't want to just grab the top-level object; we also want the author, the ingredients, and so on. To get all of those, we'll have to do a bit of recursive work.

**Baseline/PPRecipes/PPRExportOperation.m**

```
- (NSDictionary*)moToDictionary:(NSManagedObject*)mo
{
  NSMutableDictionary *dict = [NSMutableDictionary dictionary];
  if (!mo) return dict;
  NSEntityDescription *entity = [mo entity];

  NSArray *attributeKeys = [[entity attributesByName] allKeys];
  NSDictionary *values = [mo dictionaryWithValuesForKeys:attributeKeys];
  [dict addEntriesFromDictionary:values];
```

The first part of the conversion involves grabbing all of the attributes (strings, numbers, dates) from the NSManagedObject and placing them into an NSMutableDictionary. By utilizing KVC, we can do this with a small amount of code. We first ask the NSEntityDescription for all of the attribute names, and then we call -dictionaryWithValuesForKeys: on the NSManagedObject. This returns a dictionary with all of the keys and values for the attributes. We then add the resulting dictionary into our NSMutableDictionary.

## Making the Copy One-Way

When performing this copy, it's easy to accidentally copy the entire Core Data repository. Because all our objects are linked via two-way relationships, if we built a recursive method to copy the objects and follow their relationships, we would end up with a complete duplicate of all the recipes.

To prevent this, we added a check into each relationship copy. Whenever it follows a relationship, it first checks to make sure that the destination entity should be copied. We do this with a key-value pair in the data model. If there's a key called ppExportRelationship and that key has a value of NO, we skip the relationship. By taking this step, we guarantee the entity tree is copied in only one direction, as shown in Figure 16, *The flow of the copy*, on page 85.

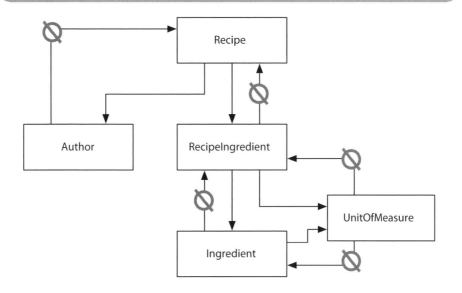

Figure 16—The flow of the copy

Baseline/PPRecipes/PPRExportOperation.m

```
NSDictionary *relationships = [entity relationshipsByName];
NSRelationshipDescription *relDesc = nil;
for (NSString *key in relationships) {
  relDesc = [relationships objectForKey:key];
  if (![[[relDesc userInfo] valueForKey:ppExportRelationship] boolValue]) {
    DLog(@"Skipping %@", [relDesc name]);
    continue;
  }
```

Next, we must deal with the relationships. Just as with the attributes, we can find out the name of each relationship from the NSEntityDescription. By looping over the resulting NSDictionary, we can process each relationship. However, to make sure we are not in an infinite recursion, we check each relationship to see whether we should be following it. If we shouldn't follow it, we simply skip to the next relationship.

Baseline/PPRecipes/PPRExportOperation.m

```
    if ([relDesc isToMany]) {
      NSMutableArray *array = [NSMutableArray array];
      for (NSManagedObject *childMO in [mo valueForKey:key]) {
        [array addObject:[self moToDictionary:childMO]];
      }
      [dict setValue:array forKey:key];
      continue;
    }
    NSManagedObject *childMO = [mo valueForKey:key];
    [dict addEntriesFromDictionary:[self moToDictionary:childMO]];
  }
  return dict;
}
```

From the perspective of the current NSManagedObject, there are two types of relationships: to-one or to-many. If it is a to-one relationship, we grab the object at the other end of the relationship and turn it into an NSDictionary for inclusion in our NSMutableDictionary.

If the relationship is a to-many, we need to iterate over the resulting set and turn each NSManagedObject into an NSDictionary and include it in a temporary array. Once we have iterated over all of the objects in the relationship, we add the entire array to our master NSMutableDictionary using the relationship name as the key.

Once all of the relationships have been processed, we return the NSMutableDictionary to the -main so that we can complete the final step.

Baseline/PPRecipes/PPRExportOperation.m

```
  NSError *error = nil;
  NSDictionary *objectStructure = [self moToDictionary:localRecipe];
  NSData *data = [NSJSONSerialization dataWithJSONObject:objectStructure
                                     options:0
                                       error:&error];

  [self completionBlock](data, error);
}
```

At the end of the -main, we use the NSJSONSerialization class to turn the NSDictionary structure into a JSON structure. Note that the PPRExportOperation does not care if the serialization is successful. It just passes the result and the potential error off to the completion block. It is up to the caller to handle any error in the processing.

## 5.4 Importing Recipes

The reverse of exporting recipes is to be able to import them. The experience we are looking for is as follows:

1. The user receives a recipe in another application (for example, in Mail).
2. The user taps the recipe, and it opens in our application.
3. Our recipe application receives the data and consumes it.

To accomplish this workflow, we need to step into our UIApplicationDelegate and do a few updates.

**Baseline/PPRecipes/PPRAppDelegate.m**
```
- (BOOL)application:(UIApplication *)application
            openURL:(NSURL *)url
  sourceApplication:(NSString *)sourceApplication
         annotation:(id)annotation
{
  if ([self managedObjectContext]) {
    [self consumeIncomingFileURL:url];
  } else {
    [self setFileToOpenURL:url];
  }
  return YES;
}
```

The first change adds the method -application: openURL: sourceApplication: annotation:. This method will be called whenever another application is requesting that we open a file. If our application has been running for a while and the Core Data stack is fully initialized, then we can process the file immediately. If the stack has not fully initialized (for instance, it freshly launched with the opening of the file), then we can store the NSURL and use it once the context has been initialized.

**Baseline/PPRecipes/PPRAppDelegate.m**
```
- (void)contextInitialized;
{
  //Finish UI initialization
  if (![self fileToOpenURL]) return;
  [self consumeIncomingFileURL:[self fileToOpenURL]];
}
```

The next change takes place in -contextInitialized. Once the context is fully initialized, we can consume the NSURL that was passed in on launch. Since we are going to be consuming the NSURL from more than one potential entry point, we abstract away the handling into a -consumeIncomingFileURL: method. Thus, the -contextInitialized just needs to check whether there is an NSURL to consume and hand it off. Since -consumeIncomingFileURL: returns a pass or fail, we can add a logic check here to help capture failures during development.

The final change is to handle the consumption of the NSURL. We have already defined the method as -consumeIncomingFileURL:.

Baseline/PPRecipes/PPRAppDelegate.m
```
- (void)consumeIncomingFileURL:(NSURL*)url;
{
  NSData *data = [NSData dataWithContentsOfURL:url];
  PPRImportOperation *op = [[PPRImportOperation alloc] initWithData:data];
  [op setMainContext:[self managedObjectContext]];
  [op setCompletionBlock:^(BOOL success, NSError *error) {
    if (success) {
      //Clear visual feedback
    } else {
      //Present an error to the user
    }
  }];
  [[NSOperationQueue mainQueue] addOperation:op];

  //Give visual feedback of the import
}
```

To consume the NSURL, we first load it into an NSData object. We can then pass the NSData instance off to a newly created PPRImportOperation. Once the operation is complete, we will display something graphically to the user and kick off the operation. The completion block for the operation checks to see whether there is an error and then reports the error or dismisses the graphical status.

## PPRImportOperation

Our PPRImportOperation has a number of similarities to the PPRExportOperation. However, there is also a bit more complexity, which we'll examine now.

Baseline/PPRecipes/PPRImportOperation.m
```
NSManagedObjectContext *localMOC = nil;
NSPersistentStoreCoordinator *psc = nil;
localMOC = [[NSManagedObjectContext alloc] init];
psc = [[self mainContext] persistentStoreCoordinator];
[localMOC setPersistentStoreCoordinator:psc];
```

As with our PPRExportOperation, we start off with the -main method. The first thing we want to do in the -main is construct a local NSManagedObjectContext.

Baseline/PPRecipes/PPRImportOperation.m

```
NSNotificationCenter *center = [NSNotificationCenter defaultCenter];
[center addObserver:self
           selector:@selector(contextDidSave:)
               name:NSManagedObjectContextDidSaveNotification
             object:localMOC];
```

Unlike its PPRExportOperation counterpart, the PPRImportOperation makes changes to the NSManagedObjectContext; we'll need to observe the changes and consume them in the primary NSManagedObjectContext.

Baseline/PPRecipes/PPRImportOperation.m

```
  NSError *error = nil;
  id recipesJSON = nil;
  recipesJSON = [NSJSONSerialization JSONObjectWithData:[self incomingData]
                                                options:0
                                                  error:&error];

  if (!recipesJSON) {
    [self completionBlock](NO, error);
    return;
  }

  NSManagedObject *recipeMO = nil;

  if ([recipesJSON isKindOfClass:[NSDictionary class]]) {
    recipeMO = [NSEntityDescription insertNewObjectForEntityForName:@"Recipe"
                                            inManagedObjectContext:localMOC];

    [self populateManagedObject:recipeMO fromDictionary:recipesJSON];
    return;
  } else {
    ZAssert([recipesJSON isKindOfClass:[NSArray class]],
            @"Unknown structure root: %@", [recipesJSON class]);
    for (id recipeDict in recipesJSON) {
      ZAssert([recipeDict isKindOfClass:[NSDictionary class]],
              @"Unknown recipe structure: %@", [recipeDict class]);
      recipeMO = [NSEntityDescription insertNewObjectForEntityForName:@"Recipe"
                                              inManagedObjectContext:localMOC];

      [self populateManagedObject:recipeMO fromDictionary:recipeDict];
    }

    ZAssert([localMOC save:&error], @"Error saving import context: %@\n%@",
            [error localizedDescription], [error userInfo]);
  }
}
```

The last portion of the -main is where the real work gets done. We start by using the NSJSONSerializer to convert the NSData into a JSON structure. If that conversion fails, we call the completion block and finish the operation.

Once we have the data in a JSON structure, we must check whether the top-level object is an NSArray or an NSDictionary. Adding this check makes the import operation more flexible and capable of handling the imported recipes. If the top-level object is an NSDictionary, we know there is a single recipe being imported and begin the import operation. If the top-level object is an NSArray, we iterate over the array and construct a recipe for each included dictionary.

For each dictionary (whether there are one or many), we construct an NSManagedObject and pass both the dictionary and the NSManagedObject into -populateManagedObject: fromDictionary:.

**Baseline/PPRecipes/PPRImportOperation.m**

```objc
- (void)populateManagedObject:(NSManagedObject*)mo
            fromDictionary:(NSDictionary*)dict
{
  NSManagedObjectContext *context = [mo managedObjectContext];
  NSEntityDescription *entity = [mo entity];
  NSArray *attKeys = [[entity attributesByName] allKeys];
  NSDictionary *atttributesDict = [dict dictionaryWithValuesForKeys:attKeys];
  [mo setValuesForKeysWithDictionary:atttributesDict];
```

In the first part of -populateManagedObject: fromDictionary:, we want to populate all the attributes of the NSManagedObject. The process is the reverse of what we accomplished in the PPRExportOperation. Here are the steps:

1. We grab an NSArray of all the attribute names for the entity.

2. We then retrieve an NSDictionary from the passed-in NSDictionary of only those attributes and their associated values.

3. We take the resulting dictionary and hand it off to the NSManagedObject via the KVC method -setValuesForKeysWithDictionary:.

**Baseline/PPRecipes/PPRImportOperation.m**

```objc
NSManagedObject* (^createChild)(NSDictionary *childDict,
                                NSEntityDescription *destEntity,
                                NSManagedObjectContext *context);
createChild = ^(NSDictionary *childDict, NSEntityDescription *destEntity,
                NSManagedObjectContext *context) {
  NSManagedObject *destMO = nil;
  destMO = [[NSManagedObject alloc] initWithEntity:destEntity
                    insertIntoManagedObjectContext:context];
  [self populateManagedObject:destMO fromDictionary:childDict];
  return destMO;
};
```

The next step is to create a block to avoid repeating ourselves later in this method. When we are dealing with the creation of the relationships, we are going to need to create one or more child objects and associate them with the NSManagedObject we are currently working on. Whether we are creating one or many child objects, the steps are virtually identical. We will use a block to perform the identical portions of the process and avoid ending up with two copies of that code.

Therefore, the purpose of the block is to construct the new NSManagedObject and recursively call -populateManagedObject: fromDictionary: for the new NSManagedObject. The block makes the rest of this method easier to follow and maintain.

**Baseline/PPRecipes/PPRImportOperation.m**

```
NSDictionary *relationshipsByName = [entity relationshipsByName];
NSManagedObject *destMO = nil;

for (NSString *key in relationshipsByName) {
  id childStructure = [dict valueForKey:key];
  if (!childStructure) continue; //Relationship not populated
  NSRelationshipDescription *relDesc = [relationshipsByName valueForKey:key];
  NSEntityDescription *destEntity = [relDesc destinationEntity];

  if (![relDesc isToMany]) { //ToOne
    destMO = createChild(childStructure, destEntity, context);
    [mo setValue:destMO forKey:key];
    continue;
  }

  NSMutableSet *childSet = [NSMutableSet set];
  for (NSDictionary *childDict in childStructure) {
    destMO = createChild(childDict, destEntity, context);
    [childSet addObject:destMO];
  }
  [self setValue:childSet forKey:key];
  }
}
```

With the attributes populated, we now need to populate the relationships. We begin by grabbing the dictionary from the NSEntityDescription that describes all of the relationships of our current NSManagedObject and iterating over them. For each relationship, we check whether there is a value set. If there is no value, then there is nothing to process. The iterator returns the key from the dictionary, which is the name of the relationship (and also the name of the accessor).

If there is a value to process, we next check whether the relationship is a to-one or a to-many. If it is a to-many, we can invoke our block and create the child NSManagedObject. We can then set the resulting NSManagedObject using KVC and the key from our relationship dictionary.

If the relationship is a to-many, we kick off an iterator to step over the collection and create one NSManagedObject for each NSDictionary inside the collection.

Once we have walked the entire JSON structure, the final step is to save the local NSManagedObjectContext. That save results in an NSManagedObjectContextDid-SaveNotification being fired and consumed in our operation. When the NSNotification fires, we consume it in our -contextDidSave: method.

Baseline/PPRecipes/PPRImportOperation.m
```
- (void)contextDidSave:(NSNotification*)notification
{
  NSManagedObjectContext *moc = [self mainContext];
  void (^mergeChanges) (void) = ^ {
    [moc mergeChangesFromContextDidSaveNotification:notification];
  };
  if ([NSThread isMainThread]) {
    mergeChanges();
  } else {
    dispatch_sync(dispatch_get_main_queue(), mergeChanges);
  }
}
```

Here again we create a block to be used within the method. Inside the block, we request that the main NSManagedObjectContext consume the notification. Why another block? The main NSManagedObjectContext should only ever be accessed from the main thread; therefore, we need to check whether we are on the main thread (most unlikely) and handle the decision appropriately. With the use of GCD, we can hand the block off to the main queue (which runs on the main thread) or run it directly. Again, we use a block to avoid repetitive code.

## 5.5 Parent-Child **NSManagedObjectContext** Instances

With the release of iOS 6.0 and Mac OS X 10.8 Mountain Lion, a number of new features have been added to Core Data. One of the more interesting changes was the introduction of parent and child contexts. Parent-child contexts allow one context to be dependent upon another. These child contexts do not have direct access to the NSPersistentStoreCoordinator but instead are dependent on their parent context. This new feature has many subtle benefits, some of which we'll demonstrate here.

### -performBlock: and -performBlockAndWait:

A lot of effort was put into the threading of Core Data with the release of iOS 6.0 and Mac OS X 10.8. To make threading a bit easier, two new methods have been introduced. Both methods accept a block and allow use of the NSManagedObjectContext, regardless of what thread we are currently running on.

## -performBlock:

The purpose of -performBlock: is to allow code to execute on the correct thread for the associated NSManagedObjectContext. By utilizing this method, we can properly and safely access an NSManagedObjectContext without necessarily being on its thread. The -performBlock: executes the block on the thread associated with the NSManagedObjectContext. Note that this method does not block the calling thread. It should also be noted that this method is not "reentrant." For example, if you call -performBlock: within a -performBlock:, the new block is added to the end of the queue, as opposed to executing immediately.

## -performBlockAndWait:

Like its counterpart -performBlock:, -performBlockAndWait: allows us to execute code against an NSManagedObjectContext regardless of the thread we are currently on. The primary difference between -performBlockAndWait: and -performBlock: is that -performBlockAndWait: is a blocking call. The calling thread waits for the block to finish execution before it continues. This also makes -performBlockAndWait: reentrant. You can nest -performBlockAndWait: calls infinitely, and they will execute in the order they are called.

## Saving the NSManagedObjectContext

With the introduction of parent and child NSManagedObjectContext instances, we need to explore how saving works. While we continue to use -save: to commit changes in an NSManagedObjectContext, the result can vary depending on the context.

To start with, if we save an NSManagedObjectContext that is associated with an NSPersistentStoreCoordinator, the changes are written to the NSPersistentStoreCoordinator, which generally means the changes are written to disk.

However, when we call -save: on a child context *that is not associated* with an NSPersistentStoreCoordinator, the changes are *not* written to the NSPersistentStoreCoordinator. Instead, those changes are "pushed up" one level to the parent of the current NSManagedObjectContext. When the changes are pushed up, they effectively dirty the parent NSManagedObjectContext, and its -hasChanges method will then return YES. It should be noted that while the changes will get pushed up to the parent context, they will not get pushed down to any existing children. It is best to treat existing children as "snapshots" of the data taken at the time that the child was created.

## Concurrency Types

There are a few requirements that must be satisfied in order to use parent and child contexts. Each NSManagedObjectContext that is associated in this way must be initialized with the new -initWithConcurrencyType: initializer. A concurrency type describes how an NSManagedObjectContext can be interacted with, because that relates to threading. Three concurrency types are available.

### NSMainQueueConcurrencyType

The first type is called NSMainQueueConcurrencyType. This concurrency type is formally declared as accessible only from the main thread. An NSManagedObject-Context that is being used by the user interface should be defined with this concurrency type. It does not matter what thread we are currently on when we initialize an NSManagedObjectContext with this concurrency type because it must always be used on the main thread.

When accessed on the main thread, it can be treated normally. All access is available. However, if it is accessed from a background/nonmain thread, it can be accessed only via the -performBlock: and -performBlockAndWait: methods.

### NSPrivateQueueConcurrencyType

The private queue concurrency type creates an NSManagedObjectContext that can be accessed *only* from its private queue. Because the queue is private, the NSManagedObjectContext can be used only via the -performBlock: and -performBlockAnd-Wait: methods.

### NSConfinementConcurrencyType

The confinement concurrency type is the "normal" concurrency type. When an NSManagedObjectContext is initialized using the -init method, this is the concurrency type that is configured. A confinement concurrency type means that the NSManagedObjectContext is confined to the thread that created it. If the NSManagedObjectContext is accessed from a thread other than the one that created it, an exception is thrown.

Let's walk through a couple of changes to our application in order to demonstrate the benefits of these new features.

## Asynchronous Saving

One of the biggest issues with threading prior to iOS 6.0 and Mac OS X 10.8 Mountain Lion had to do with *thread blocking*. No matter how cleverly we wrote our import and export operations, sooner or later we *had to* block the main thread to let the main/UI NSManagedObjectContext "catch up." With the introduction of private queue contexts, this performance issue is finally solved.

If we start our Core Data stack with a private queue NSManagedObjectContext and associate it with the NSPersistentStoreCoordinator, we can have the main/UI NSManagedObjectContext as a child of the private queue NSManagedObjectContext. Furthermore, when the main/UI NSManagedObjectContext is saved, it will not produce a disk hit and will instead be nearly instantaneous. From there, whenever we want to actually write to disk, we can kick off a save on the private queue of the private context and get asynchronous saves.See Figure 17, *Private queue for asynchronous saves*, on page 96.

Adding this ability to our application requires a relatively small change. First, we need to add a property (nonatomic, strong) to hold onto our new private NSManagedObjectContext. Next, we tweak the -initializeCoreDataStack a little bit.

**Baseline/PPRecipes/PPRAppDelegateAlt1.m**
```
NSPersistentStoreCoordinator *psc = nil;
psc = [[NSPersistentStoreCoordinator alloc] initWithManagedObjectModel:mom];
ZAssert(psc, @"Failed to initialize persistent store coordinator");

NSManagedObjectContext *private = nil;
NSUInteger type = NSPrivateQueueConcurrencyType;
private = [[NSManagedObjectContext alloc] initWithConcurrencyType:type];
[private setPersistentStoreCoordinator:psc];

type = NSMainQueueConcurrencyType;
NSManagedObjectContext *moc = nil;
moc = [[NSManagedObjectContext alloc] initWithConcurrencyType:type];
[moc setParentContext:private];
[self setPrivateContext:private];

[self setManagedObjectContext:moc];
```

Before, we had one NSManagedObjectContext configured to be on the main queue and writing to the NSPersistentStoreCoordinator. Now we have added a new NSManagedObjectContext that is of type NSPrivateQueueConcurrencyType. We set the NSPersistentStoreCoordinator to that private queue. Finally, we construct our main queue NSManagedObjectContext. Instead of handing off the NSPersistentStoreCoordinator to the main context, we give it a parent: the private queue context.

With that change, any saves on the main NSManagedObjectContext will push up the changes only to the private queue NSManagedObjectContext. No writing to the NSPersistentStoreCoordinator occurs. However, there are times when we really do want to write to disk and persist our data changes. In that case, a couple of other changes are in order.

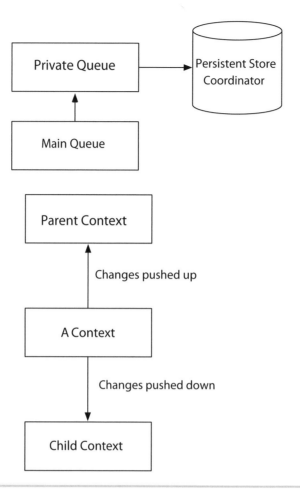

**Figure 17—Private queue for asynchronous saves**

Baseline/PPRecipes/PPRAppDelegateAlt1.m
```objc
- (void)saveContext:(BOOL)wait
{
  NSManagedObjectContext *moc = [self managedObjectContext];
  NSManagedObjectContext *private = [self privateContext];

  if (!moc) return;
  if ([moc hasChanges]) {
    [moc performBlockAndWait:^{
      NSError *error = nil;
      ZAssert([moc save:&error], @"Error saving MOC: %@\n%@",
              [error localizedDescription], [error userInfo]);
    }];
  }
```

```
  void (^savePrivate) (void) = ^{
    NSError *error = nil;
    ZAssert([private save:&error], @"Error saving private moc: %@\n%@",
            [error localizedDescription], [error userInfo]);
  };

  if ([private hasChanges]) {
    if (wait) {
      [private performBlockAndWait:savePrivate];
    } else {
      [private performBlock:savePrivate];
    }
  }
}
```

Previously in our -saveContext method, we checked to make sure we had an NSManagedObjectContext and that it had changes. We can still check to see whether we have an NSManagedObjectContext, since we create both of them at the same time. However, we now need to check both the main NSManagedObjectContext and the private NSManagedObjectContext for changes.

If the main NSManagedObjectContext has changes, we execute a -performBlockAndWait: to give the main NSManagedObjectContext all of the time that it needs to save. When the main has finished saving (or if it didn't need a save), we check the private context to see whether it also needs saving. When the private NSManagedObjectContext needs a save, we perform that save on the private context's queue. However, there are some situations in which we might want to block on the save and others where we might want it to be asynchronous. For example, when we are going into the background or terminating the application, we will want to block. If we are doing a save while the application is still running, we would want to be asynchronous. Fortunately, the -saveContext: method accepts a boolean that lets us know which method to call.

The only other alterations we need now are to change any calls from -saveContext to -saveContext: and pass in a boolean to determine whether the save blocks.

## Updating Our PPRImportOperation

Another situation in which the parent-child context design provides a huge performance gain is when we need to merge changes between contexts. There's a good example of this in our current application, in the PPRImportOperation. Without the parent-child NSManagedObjectContext design, we must block the main thread during our save of the import. If there is only one recipe coming in, there probably won't be any issue. The save will be fast enough that the user won't notice. However, if we import hundreds of recipes, the save would cause a noticeable delay.

This can be fixed.

```
Baseline/PPRecipes/PPRImportOperationAlt1.m
NSManagedObjectContext *localMOC = nil;
NSUInteger type = NSConfinementConcurrencyType;
localMOC = [[NSManagedObjectContext alloc] initWithConcurrencyType:type];
[localMOC setParentContext:[self mainContext]];
```

The first change is to initialize our local NSManagedObjectContext as a type of NSConfinementConcurrencyType. This step locks the NSManagedObjectContext to our thread. Next, we configure the NSManagedObjectContext to be a child of the main NSManagedObjectContext.

The other changes are to remove code.

First, we no longer need to listen for change notifications. As soon as we save the local NSManagedObjectContext, the changes are moved up to our parent NSManagedObjectContext.

Since we are no longer listening for change notifications, we no longer need our -contextDidSave: method. Changes now propagate automatically.

These alterations are the only changes required. Once they're in place, we will no longer block the main thread on saves. We could even increase our save frequency so the user can see the recipes coming in one at a time, if we wanted. Without a disk I/O cost or a main thread block, we have a lot more options for how to handle the user experience.

These are just two examples of how the iOS 6.0/Mac OS X 10.8 changes to Core Data can improve the performance of our applications. As developers become more familiar with these new tools, we can expect to see many more innovative ways that Core Data will be used.

## 5.6 Wrapping Up

In this chapter, we explored the often-controversial subject of multithreading. There are a number of myths about Core Data and threading, but with this foundation, deciding whether to add multithreading to your Core Data application should be a great deal clearer.

# CHAPTER 6

# Using iCloud

Starting with iOS 5.0 and Mac OS X 10.7 Lion, Apple has added the ability to sync a Core Data application to iCloud. For developers, that means we can easily add cloud sharing of our application's data without the need to build our own servers. It also means our applications can share data between devices and computers.

Unfortunately, as has been demonstrated numerous times in the past, syncing is hard, very hard. Apple did not get it working acceptably in iOS 5.0 or OS X 10.7. It was not until iOS 6.0 and OS X 10.8 that iCloud has become truly reliable. While the functionality discussed in this chapter was technically introduced in 5.0/10.7, we will be discussing it under 6.0/10.8. It is not recommended to try to implement these features prior to 6.0/10.8.

iCloud integration allows developers to sync data between any number of computers and devices; we can sync between an iPhone application, an iPad application, a Mac application, or any combination thereof. In fact, we can add the ability to sync with our very first application, and new clients added later will automatically sync once we make them available to our users.

There are two approaches to adding iCloud integration to an application on iOS. We have the option of just adding a few options to our NSPersistentStore, or we can use the new API called UIManagedDocument.

If we have an existing application, the choice is simple: adding the options to the NSPersistentStore has the smallest impact on our code base. However, in order to properly move everything into iCloud, we do need to do some additional work, as outlined in Section 6.5, *Migrating an Existing Application*, on page 113.

For a new application, it is worth looking at UIManagedDocument and deciding whether it makes sense for the particular type of application you are designing.

Once the choice between using a UIManagedDocument or a standard Core Data Stack has been made, the behavior of iCloud is the same. Therefore, we are going to start by examining UIManagedDocument and then look at wiring iCloud into a standard stack. Once we are past those differences, we will take a deeper dive into the other details of using iCloud.

## 6.1 Introducing the UIManagedDocument

In the release of iCloud, Apple introduced a new API called UIDocument. UIDocument is designed to be an abstract parent class that makes it easy to integrate applications with iCloud. One of the Core Data API changes for iOS 6.0 is UIManagedDocument, a subclass of UIDocument.

Fundamentally, the biggest advantage of using UIManagedDocument is the ability to abstract away the saving and state of your Core Data stack. With UIManaged-Document, saving is handled automatically and generally occurs asynchronously. You can request saves to occur more frequently than the autosave handles, but in general you shouldn't need to do that. In addition to managing the saving of the Core Data stack, UIManagedDocument has added features that allow you to store files outside of the persistent store that will also be pushed to iCloud.

UIManagedDocument is meant to be used in applications that have a document design. Pages, Numbers, Omnigraffle, and so on, are great examples of iOS applications that manage a form of document. Having said that, however, there is nothing stopping you from using a UIManagedDocument as your single Core Data stack enclosure. It is not specifically designed for a single stack design, but it will work. It is even appealing in some ways, since it abstracts out the creation of the stack.

iCloud/PPRecipes/PPRAppDelegate.m

```
dispatch_queue_t queue;
queue = dispatch_get_global_queue(DISPATCH_QUEUE_PRIORITY_DEFAULT, 0);

dispatch_async(queue, ^{
  NSFileManager *fileManager = [NSFileManager defaultManager];
  NSURL *storeURL = nil;
  storeURL = [[fileManager URLsForDirectory:NSDocumentDirectory
                             inDomains:NSUserDomainMask] lastObject];
  storeURL = [storeURL URLByAppendingPathComponent:@"PPRecipes"];

  NSURL *cloudURL = [fileManager URLForUbiquityContainerIdentifier:nil];
```

The first step in constructing a UIManagedDocument is to resolve the file URL where we will store the document and determine what the file URL is going to be for iCloud. The first step, where we are saving the data to, is virtually the same as when we construct a Core Data stack. We determine where the documents directory is located via a call to the NSFileManager, and then we append a path component to the end to identify our document. In this case, the document is called PPRecipes.

The second URL—the iCloud URL—is a bit different. -URLForUbiquityContainerIdentifier: is a new addition to the NSFileManager that came with iCloud. This call requests a URL in which to store information that iCloud is going to use to sync the NSPersistentStore. If iCloud is disabled on the device (iOS or OS X), this call returns nil. Once we have a URL and it is not nil, we know iCloud is available, and we need to configure it.

It is the second call that has an interesting issue; specifically, this call can take an indeterminate amount of time. If iCloud is not available or if the directory structure had previously been constructed, this call could return nearly instantaneously. However, if iCloud is enabled and the directory structure needs to be constructed, the call might take a significant amount of time—long enough that we need to worry about the watchdog killing it for taking too long to launch. Therefore, because of this method call, we need to wrap all of this construction in a dispatch queue and let it run asynchronously with the main thread.

Once we know whether iCloud is available, we can continue with our configuration.

## Configuring iCloud

To add iCloud to a Core Data stack, we need to add some additional options to the NSPersistentStore when we add the NSPersistentStore to the NSPersistentStoreCoordinator.

```
iCloud/PPRecipes/PPRAppDelegate.m
NSMutableDictionary *options = [[NSMutableDictionary alloc] init];
[options setValue:[NSNumber numberWithBool:YES]
          forKey:NSMigratePersistentStoresAutomaticallyOption];
[options setValue:[NSNumber numberWithBool:YES]
          forKey:NSInferMappingModelAutomaticallyOption];

if (cloudURL) {
  cloudURL = [cloudURL URLByAppendingPathComponent:@"PPRecipes"];

  [options setValue:[[NSBundle mainBundle] bundleIdentifier]
             forKey:NSPersistentStoreUbiquitousContentNameKey];
  [options setValue:cloudURL
             forKey:NSPersistentStoreUbiquitousContentURLKey];
}
```

The first part of this code should be familiar. We create an NSMutableDictionary and add the options both to infer a mapping model and to attempt a migration automatically. From there, if iCloud is enabled, we need to add the iCloud URL to our options dictionary. However, we do not want our document stored at the "root" of our iCloud sandbox. Rather, we want to create a directory under the root with the same name as the document we are creating locally. Therefore, we are going to append "PPRecipes" to the end of the URL. Once the URL is defined, we need to add it to our options dictionary with the key NSPersistentStoreUbiquitousContentURLKey.

In addition to the URL for the storage location, we need to tell iCloud what data it is going to sync. If we have a single application shared between iPhone and iPad, as in our current example, we can use the bundle identifier as a unique key to define what data is to be shared across the devices. However, if we are also sharing data with a desktop application, the bundle identifier may not be appropriate. The data identifier is stored in the options dictionary with the key NSPersistentStoreUbiquitousContentNameKey.

The addition of these two keys is the bare minimum required to enable iCloud for an iOS application. With that information, the operating system creates a directory for the content, downloads any content that exists in the cloud, and begins syncing the data. However, as with the URL call, the initial download (or for that matter subsequent syncing) can take an indeterminate amount of time. If there is nothing currently in the store, the creation of the directory structure will be virtually instantaneous. But if there is data to download, it could take some time, depending on the speed of the network connection and the amount of data. Therefore, the application needs to be able to handle a delay in the creation of the persistent store. There are many ways to deal with this delay, and that is an exercise left to the user experience experts.

### Building the UIManagedDocument

Once the options dictionary has been constructed, it's time to build the UIManagedDocument. The construction of the document itself is short.

iCloud/PPRecipes/PPRAppDelegate.m

```
UIManagedDocument *document = nil;
document = [[UIManagedDocument alloc] initWithFileURL:storeURL];
[document setPersistentStoreOptions:options];

NSMergePolicy *policy = [[NSMergePolicy alloc] initWithMergeType:
                         NSMergeByPropertyObjectTrumpMergePolicyType];
[[document managedObjectContext] setMergePolicy:policy];
```

```
  void (^completion)(BOOL) = ^(BOOL success) {
    if (!success) {
      ALog(@"Error saving %@\n%@", storeURL, [document debugDescription]);
      return;
    }

    dispatch_queue_t mainQueue;
    mainQueue = dispatch_get_main_queue();

    dispatch_sync(mainQueue, ^{
      [self contextInitialized];
    });
  };

  if ([[NSFileManager defaultManager] fileExistsAtPath:[storeURL path]]) {
    [document openWithCompletionHandler:completion];
    return;
  }

  [document saveToURL:storeURL
      forSaveOperation:UIDocumentSaveForCreating
    completionHandler:completion];
  [self setManagedDocument:document];
});
```

Constructing the UIManagedDocument is a case of calling +alloc and then -initWith-FileURL: and passing in the storeURL that we previously constructed. Once the UIManagedDocument is initialized, we can set the options for the NSPersistentStore via a call to -setPersistentStoreOptions:. Note that we do not have the ability to add more than one NSPersistentStore to a UIManagedDocument.

We also want to take this opportunity to set the merge policy for the UIManaged-Document. This setting is actually performed on the NSManagedObjectContext directly.

Unlike when we construct a straight Core Data stack, though, the initialization of the UIManagedDocument is not the end for us. We must now save it. We could save it later, but it is best to put all of this initialization code in the same place rather than have it spread out across our UIApplicationDelegate. To save the UIManagedDocument, we must first discover if it already exists; based on that information, we can call the appropriate method.

Whether the UIManagedDocument existed before, the process is the same: we call a method on the UIManagedDocument and pass in a completion handler. Since that completion handler is the same no matter which method we call, we construct the completion handler first and then determine which method to call.

In the completion handler, we check to see whether it completed successfully. If it was not successful, we present an error to the user and perhaps try to recover from the error. If the completion was successful, we want to notify the AppDelegate that the UIManagedDocument has been initialized and that normal program flow can resume.

With the completion block constructed, we can now ask the NSFileManager if the file already exists; if it does, we call -openWithCompletionHandler: on the UIManagedDocument. If it does not exist, we need to create it with a call to -saveToURL: forSaveOperation:UIDocumentSaveForCreating: completionHandler:. If this seems overly complicated, that's because it is. This really should be abstracted away into the framework.

### Observing Changes to the UIManagedDocument

Once our UIManagedDocument has been constructed, it can be quite useful to know its current state. Since the UIManagedDocument saves on its own accord, we won't automatically know whether it is clean or dirty. We need some kind of callback system in place to notify us. Fortunately, the UIManagedDocument does broadcast notifications when the state changes. By adding our UIApplicationDelegate as an observer to the notification UIDocumentStateChangedNotification, we are notified of those changes and can act accordingly.

**iCloud/PPRecipes/PPRAppDelegate.m**
```
- (void)contextInitialized;
{
  DLog(@"fired");
  NSNotificationCenter *center = [NSNotificationCenter defaultCenter];
  [center addObserver:self
             selector:@selector(documentStateChanged:)
                 name:UIDocumentStateChangedNotification
               object:[self managedDocument]];
```

There are several places that we could start observing this notification; placing it in the -contextInitialized is a personal preference. It is possible to start listening to it as part of the initialization of the UIManagedDocument, for example. When this notification fires, we receive the UIManagedDocument as the object of the notification. From the UIManagedDocument, we then respond accordingly.

**iCloud/PPRecipes/PPRAppDelegate.m**
```
- (void)documentStateChanged:(NSNotification*)notification
{
  switch ([[notification object] documentState]) {
    case UIDocumentStateNormal:
      DLog(@"UIDocumentStateNormal");
      break;
    case UIDocumentStateClosed:
```

```
      DLog(@"UIDocumentStateClosed %@", notification);
      break;
    case UIDocumentStateInConflict:
      DLog(@"UIDocumentStateInConflict %@", notification);
      break;
    case UIDocumentStateSavingError:
      DLog(@"UIDocumentStateSavingError %@", notification);
      break;
    case UIDocumentStateEditingDisabled:
      DLog(@"UIDocumentStateEditingDisabled %@", notification);
      break;
  }
}
```

From the state of the UIManagedDocument, we can update our user interface to reflect that state and let the user know what is going on with the underlying data.

## Manually Saving a UIManagedDocument

By default, the UIManagedDocument works to ensure that our data is saved as frequently as makes sense.

The UIDocument design knows to listen for UIApplicationWillResignActiveNotification, UIApplicationDidEnterBackgroundNotification, and UIApplicationWillTerminateNotification notifications. When it receives one of these notifications, it saves. It also saves periodically during the life of the application. On average, these periodical saves take place every five minutes.

However, we know our application better than the frameworks do. We know when something nonrecoverable or vital has just occurred, and we can decide that a save is mandatory at a specific point. Fortunately, it is possible to convey that need to UIManagedDocument.

```
iCloud/PPRecipes/PPRAppDelegate.m
NSURL *fileURL = [[self managedDocument] fileURL];
[[self managedDocument] saveToURL:fileURL
                  forSaveOperation:UIDocumentSaveForCreating
                 completionHandler:^(BOOL success) {
                   //Handle failure
                 }];
```

The call to request a save is the same we used when we were initially creating the UIManagedDocument. Further, we can request the URL for the save directly from the UIManagedDocument. The only detail left is planning how to properly respond to a failed save.

## 6.2 Direct NSManagedObjectContext to iCloud

If you have been using Core Data for a while, you will feel right at home creating a Core Data stack; otherwise, this code will look similar to the stack we discussed in Chapter 1, *Under the Hood of Core Data*, on page 1. The code to add iCloud to the Core Data stack is short, straightforward, and easy to add. This is good and bad. It's good, in that it takes a small amount of effort to add iCloud to your Core Data–based application, but it's bad because there are not very many options to configure, and it's a one-size-fits-all design. If your data model is complex or if you have elements that you do not want to sync, then lack of configurability will cause some interesting solutions. For example, if you have nonsyncable data, then you may need to split your data into more than one persistent store. Another situation that can feel limiting is if you have a very high churn rate in your data structures. iCloud prefers to have an opportunity to process the data, and a high rate of content creation or change can cause it to get backed up. In that situation, it may be necessary to "roll up" your data changes to decrease the number of entities being created or the frequency of saves. Reviewing your application's activities in Instruments (as discussed in Chapter 4, *Performance Tuning*, on page 61) will help you to determine whether you have strayed off the golden path.

### Configuring iCloud

To integrate iCloud with our Core Data stack, we insert some additional options to the NSPersistentStore when we add the NSPersistentStore to the NSPersistentStoreCoordinator.

```
iCloud/PPRecipes/PPRAppDelegate.m
NSMutableDictionary *options = [[NSMutableDictionary alloc] init];
[options setValue:[NSNumber numberWithBool:YES]
          forKey:NSMigratePersistentStoresAutomaticallyOption];
[options setValue:[NSNumber numberWithBool:YES]
          forKey:NSInferMappingModelAutomaticallyOption];
NSFileManager *fileManager = [NSFileManager defaultManager];
NSURL *cloudURL = [fileManager URLForUbiquityContainerIdentifier:nil];
if (cloudURL) {
  DLog(@"iCloud enabled: %@", cloudURL);
  cloudURL = [cloudURL URLByAppendingPathComponent:@"PPRecipes"];
  [options setValue:[[NSBundle mainBundle] bundleIdentifier]
             forKey:NSPersistentStoreUbiquitousContentNameKey];
  [options setValue:cloudURL
             forKey:NSPersistentStoreUbiquitousContentURLKey];
} else {
  DLog(@"iCloud is not enabled");
}
```

The first part of this code should be familiar. We create an NSMutableDictionary and add the options both to infer a mapping model and to attempt a migration automatically. From here, though, we are in new territory. -URLForUbiquityContainerIdentifier: is a new addition to the NSFileManager that came with iCloud. This call requests a URL used to store information that iCloud is going to use to sync the NSPersistentStore. If iCloud is disabled on this device (or Mac OS X computer), this call will return nil. Once we have the URL and have established that it is not nil, we know iCloud is available, and we can begin to configure it.

The URL we receive points to a file path; it looks something like this:

```
file://localhost/private/var/mobile/Library/
  Mobile%20Documents/K7T84T27W4~com~pragprog~PPRecipes/
```

Notice this file path is outside our application sandbox. Even so, we have some control over what goes into this directory. For example, if we use a document-based application, we could append the name of the document onto this path so that each document is kept separate. In our current example, however, we are going to create a single subdirectory for our Core Data stack. This will help us in the future if we decide to make changes or sync additional items. Once the URL is defined, we need to add it to our options dictionary with the key NSPersistentStoreUbiquitousContentURLKey.

In addition to the URL for the storage location, we must tell iCloud what data it should be syncing with. If we have a single application shared between iPhone and iPad, as in our current example, we can use the bundle identifier as a unique key to define what data is to be shared across the devices. However, if we are also sharing data with a desktop application, the bundle identifier may not be appropriate. The data identifier is stored in the options dictionary with the key NSPersistentStoreUbiquitousContentNameKey.

Once again, the addition of those two keys is the bare minimum required to enable iCloud for an iOS application. With that information, the operating system creates a directory for the content, downloads any content that exists in the cloud, and starts syncing that data for us. However, that initial download (or for that matter subsequent syncing) can take an indeterminate amount of time. If there is nothing currently in the store, the creation of the directory structure will be virtually instantaneous. However, if there is data to download, it could take some time, depending on the speed of the network connection and the amount of data. As before, we must change how we add the NSPersistentStore to the NSPersistentStoreCoordinator.

## Asynchronously Adding the NSPersistentStore

Prior to iOS 6.0 and Mac OS X Lion, we could add the NSPersistentStore to the NSPersistentStoreCoordinator directly on the main thread. While this was rarely recommended, it was extremely common. With the addition of iCloud, it's really no longer an option. The process of configuring iCloud happens when we add the NSPersistentStore to the NSPersistentStoreCoordinator, and it happens before the call returns. If iCloud needs to download data and that download takes several seconds, our application will be unresponsive while the download occurs, and our application could be potentially killed from the watchdog for taking too long to start up.

Currently, the best solution to this problem is to add the NSPersistentStore to the NSPersistentStoreCoordinator on a background thread. We can use dispatch queues and blocks to make this relatively painless.

**iCloud/PPRecipes/PPRAppDelegate.m**
```
dispatch_queue_t queue;
queue = dispatch_get_global_queue(DISPATCH_QUEUE_PRIORITY_DEFAULT, 0);
dispatch_async(queue, ^{
  NSMutableDictionary *options = [[NSMutableDictionary alloc] init];
  [options setValue:[NSNumber numberWithBool:YES]
           forKey:NSMigratePersistentStoresAutomaticallyOption];
  [options setValue:[NSNumber numberWithBool:YES]
           forKey:NSInferMappingModelAutomaticallyOption];
  NSFileManager *fileManager = [NSFileManager defaultManager];
  NSURL *cloudURL = [fileManager URLForUbiquityContainerIdentifier:nil];
  if (cloudURL) {
    DLog(@"iCloud enabled: %@", cloudURL);
    cloudURL = [cloudURL URLByAppendingPathComponent:@"PPRecipes"];
    [options setValue:[[NSBundle mainBundle] bundleIdentifier]
             forKey:NSPersistentStoreUbiquitousContentNameKey];
    [options setValue:cloudURL
             forKey:NSPersistentStoreUbiquitousContentURLKey];
  } else {
    DLog(@"iCloud is not enabled");
  }
  NSURL *storeURL = nil;
  storeURL = [[fileManager URLsForDirectory:NSDocumentDirectory
                            inDomains:NSUserDomainMask] lastObject];
  storeURL = [storeURL URLByAppendingPathComponent:@"PPRecipes-iCloud.sqlite"];
  NSError *error = nil;
  NSPersistentStoreCoordinator *coordinator = nil;
  coordinator = [[self managedObjectContext] persistentStoreCoordinator];
  NSPersistentStore *store = nil;
  store = [coordinator addPersistentStoreWithType:NSSQLiteStoreType
                              configuration:nil
                                      URL:storeURL
                                  options:options
```

```
                                        error:&error];
  if (!store) {
    ALog(@"Error adding persistent store to coordinator %@\n%@",
        [error localizedDescription], [error userInfo]);
    //Present a user facing error
  }
  dispatch_sync(dispatch_get_main_queue(), ^{
    [self contextInitialized];
  });
});
```

In this code block, we define the path for our SQLite file and gain a reference to the NSPersistentStoreCoordinator. From there, we add the NSPersistentStore to the NSPersistentStoreCoordinator. Assuming that is successful, we push another block back to the main queue and inform the application that the Core Data stack has been completed and is ready for use.

The reason we grab a fresh reference to the NSPersistentStoreCoordinator is one of safety. If we were to use the reference from the outer method, we would be incrementing the retain count of the NSPersistentStoreCoordinator and potentially causing an unnecessary reference count issue. Since we can easily obtain a fresh reference to it, there is no reason to use the reference from the outer method.

Likewise, once we have completed the construction of the NSPersistentStoreCoordinator, we want to be on the main thread (aka the UI Thread) when we call -contextInitialized so that the rest of the AppDelegate does not need to dance with threads. Keeping all of the thread jumping in one place makes it easier to maintain.

## 6.3 Consuming Changes from iCloud

Whether we are using a standard Core Data stack or a UIManagedDocument, we need to know when changes come in from iCloud. Changes will always come in asynchronously, and our NSManagedObjectContext won't know about them. It is our responsibility to notify our NSManagedObjectContext of any incoming changes. To do that, we first need to listen for the change notification via the NSNotificationCenter.

iCloud/PPRecipes/PPRAppDelegate.m
```
  NSString *name = nil;
  name = NSPersistentStoreDidImportUbiquitousContentChangesNotification;
  [center addObserver:self
            selector:@selector(mergePSCChanges:)
                name:name
              object:[[self managedObjectContext] persistentStoreCoordinator]];
}
```

Just like with the UIDocumentStateChangedNotification for the UIManagedDocument, it's a good idea to start listening for the NSPersistentStoreDidImportUbiquitousContentChanges-Notification notifications after the Core Data stack (or UIManagedDocument) has been constructed. Therefore, we put the -addObserver: selector: name: object: call in the -contextInitialized method.

When the notification fires, it can be treated exactly as if a notification from an NSManagedObjectContext is coming in from another thread, as discussed in Chapter 5, *Threading*, on page 77. Although the notification does not contain actual NSManagedObject instances, it does contain NSManagedObjectID instances, and the NSManagedObjectContext knows how to consume them as well.

iCloud/PPRecipes/PPRAppDelegate.m

```
- (void)mergePSCChanges:(NSNotification*)notification
{
  NSManagedObjectContext *moc = [self managedObjectContext];
  [moc performBlock:^{
    [moc mergeChangesFromContextDidSaveNotification:notification];
  }];
}
```

## 6.4 Under the Hood

Now that we have looked at how to integrate iCloud into our Core Data–based application, it is helpful to understand exactly how it works under the hood.

### Debug Output

Core Data has several logging levels that we can turn on to watch all of the SQL calls that are generated during an application's life cycle. There are currently three levels to this debugging log, with level 1 being the least chatty and level 3 being the most chatty. We can set this debug output by adding the runtime parameter com.apple.CoreData.SQLDebug to our application and pass along with it the level we want to be set.

In addition to the Core Data debug setting, we can also turn on an additional setting to watch all of the chatter *between* Core Data and iCloud. That additional setting is com.apple.coredata.ubiquity.logLevel. For an unknown reason, this logging code responds only to level 3, as shown in Figure 18, *Turning on iCloud debugging*, on page 111.

Looking at these logs, we can see there is a tremendous amount of activity going on behind the scenes. We can also examine the frequency with which Core Data starts a sync with iCloud and use that information when we are determining how often to generate saves from our application.

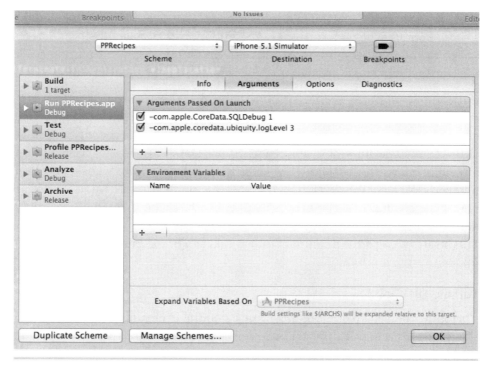

**Figure 18—Turning on iCloud debugging**

The logs can also help us watch for corruption, which appears to occur most frequently during development. Without logging's early warning system, corruption can be quite frustrating when it happens. Without the aid of logging, things just stop. No errors are generated; iCloud just stops working. With logging turned on, we can glean when something goes wrong.

Unfortunately, at this time, there is no way to determine at runtime, within our application, that corruption has occurred.

Further, once a log file has been corrupted, there is no way to clear it out. The best that we can do is to start over with a new file.

This is currently being tracked under rdar://10837238.

### Transaction Logs

iCloud functions through transaction logs. Similar to how modern version control systems work, every time a save is performed by an "iCloud-backed" persistent store, a transaction log is created that details what happened in that save. These transaction logs are kept in order and pushed up to the cloud. On other devices, the transaction logs are received and played back onto the receiving persistent store. Through this process, each persistent store is kept in sync with the other. In addition, new persistent stores can be added to the mix by simply starting with an empty store and playing back the transactions one at a time until the new store is brought up-to-date.

If the application has seen a lot of activity, there can be a large number of transaction logs. The large number of transaction logs means any new device must take a significant amount of time to "catch up" with the current state of the persistent store. For this reason, Core Data cuts a new "baseline" on a regular interval. A baseline is effectively a "roll-up" of the transaction logs to a certain point. Any logs after the baseline point will pile up as before. A new store coming into the sync starts with a baseline instead of an empty database and consumes any transaction logs generated after the baseline. This strategy keeps the amount of time it takes to bring a new persistent store up to speed to a minimum.

## Turning Off iCloud

Currently, there is an outstanding issue when the user turns off iCloud. When this event occurs, our application receives no notification. The data simply goes away. Some developers have been successful in adding a "sentinel" file to the ubiquitous container (via the URL that gets resolved when we configure iCloud) and monitoring that file. If the file goes away, then we can decide how to handle the state change. Creating a sentinel file has not been approved (or disallowed) by Apple, and this solution may not work in future versions of Core Data.

## Ordered Relationships Are Not Allowed

If we integrate iCloud into our application, we cannot use the new ordered relationships that were added as of iOS 6.0 and OS X 10.8. iCloud integration does *not* work with ordered relationships. Ideally, this deficiency will be corrected at some point.

## Data Migration

An additional limiting factor with iCloud integration is the use of lightweight migration. Heavy-weight migration (as in a migration that requires a mapping model) cannot be used if iCloud is enabled. With an iCloud-enabled NSPersistentStore, the mapping model will simply be ignored, and the migration fails. Therefore, particular care must be taken when you are doing a migration to not cross the limit of lightweight/inferred migration. If a migration requires more complexity than a lightweight migration can handle, then it is recommended that a new ubiquitous container be set up, the migration be done with iCloud turned off, and then the data be loaded into the new container. To accomplish this, you would need to follow a procedure similar to the one detailed in Section 6.5, *Migrating an Existing Application*, on page 113.

## 6.5 Migrating an Existing Application

Because Core Data keeps track of changes via transaction logs, it's impossible to just "turn on" iCloud in an existing application and expect all the data to get pushed into the cloud. A few other steps are necessary.

### Detecting a Migration

The first question when adding iCloud to an existing iOS application is whether the migration is necessary. There are two key criteria for answering this question.

- Is there any existing data to migrate?
- Has the migration already been performed?

Both of these questions can be answered easily if we do a simple filename change. For example, if our application has always used a SQLite file named PPRecipes.sqlite, then when we want to add iCloud integration to our application, we should start using a filename of PPRecipes-iCloud.sqlite. A simple "does this file exist?" check tells us whether we need to migrate our existing data.

If it is not possible or reasonable to rename the file, the fallback option is to store a flag in the NSUserDefaults to let us know whether the migration has occurred. This option is second best for a couple of reasons.

- As we will demonstrate in a moment, the file needs to be moved anyway.
- NSUserDefaults classes tend to be a bit unreliable, especially during testing.

Assuming we are going to use a file rename strategy to determine whether a migration is required, the first step is to look for the "old" filename to determine whether a migration is required. As part of this change to handle the migration, we are going to refactor the NSPersistentStoreCoordinator initialization code somewhat to make it more maintainable with these additions.

```
iCloud/PPRecipes/PPRAppDelegate.m
dispatch_queue_t queue;
queue = dispatch_get_global_queue(DISPATCH_QUEUE_PRIORITY_DEFAULT, 0);
dispatch_async(queue, ^{
  NSMutableDictionary *options = [[NSMutableDictionary alloc] init];
  [options setValue:[NSNumber numberWithBool:YES]
          forKey:NSMigratePersistentStoresAutomaticallyOption];
  [options setValue:[NSNumber numberWithBool:YES]
          forKey:NSInferMappingModelAutomaticallyOption];
```

```
NSFileManager *fileManager = [NSFileManager defaultManager];
NSURL *docURL = nil;
docURL = [[fileManager URLsForDirectory:NSDocumentDirectory
                           inDomains:NSUserDomainMask] lastObject];
NSURL *storeURL = nil;

NSError *error = nil;
NSPersistentStoreCoordinator *coordinator = nil;
coordinator = [[self managedObjectContext] persistentStoreCoordinator];
NSPersistentStore *store = nil;

NSURL *cloudURL = [fileManager URLForUbiquityContainerIdentifier:nil];
```

We start the changes at the top of the asynchronous dispatch queue. Notice that we are setting the "universal" options only for the NSPersistentStore at this point. This step allows us to reuse the dictionary no matter what path we end up taking. We are also obtaining our reference to the NSPersistentStoreCoordinator here, because that will be used through the rest of the block. Finally, we request the cloudURL from the NSFileManager so that we can start to determine how to add the NSPersistentStore to the NSPersistentStoreCoordinator.

Now we are ready to make our first decision: is iCloud available or not?

**iCloud/PPRecipes/PPRAppDelegate.m**
```
if (!cloudURL) {
  storeURL = [docURL URLByAppendingPathComponent:@"PPRecipes.sqlite"];
  store = [coordinator addPersistentStoreWithType:NSSQLiteStoreType
                                    configuration:nil
                                              URL:storeURL
                                          options:options
                                            error:&error];
  if (!store) {
    ALog(@"Error adding persistent store to coordinator %@\n%@",
        [error localizedDescription], [error userInfo]);
    //Present a user facing error
    return;
  }
  dispatch_sync(dispatch_get_main_queue(), ^{
    [self contextInitialized];
  });
}
```

Now that we've added the migration code for iCloud, it is actually the shorter path when iCloud is not enabled. Therefore, we are going to respond to that decision first. If iCloud is not available, we look for the file named PPRecipes.sqlite and add it to the persistent store. If the file does not exist, Core Data will create it. This is the traditional logic path.

Once the NSPersistentStore is added to the NSPersistentStoreCoordinator, we check to make sure it was successful and then notify our UIApplicationDelegate that the stack initialization is complete and return. It should be noted that it is possible for the user to turn iCloud back *off* and be fully robust. We should check to see whether that situation occurred. If it did, we must migrate back off of iCloud. That decision branch is left as an exercise for the reader.

iCloud/PPRecipes/PPRAppDelegate.m

```
storeURL = [docURL URLByAppendingPathComponent:@"PPRecipes-iCloud.sqlite"];
NSURL *oldURL = nil;
oldURL = [docURL URLByAppendingPathComponent:@"PPRecipes.sqlite"];
if ([fileManager fileExistsAtPath:[oldURL path]]) {
  store = [coordinator addPersistentStoreWithType:NSSQLiteStoreType
                               configuration:nil
                                         URL:oldURL
                                     options:options
                                       error:&error];

  if (!store) {
    ALog(@"Error adding OLD persistent store to coordinator %@\n%@",
        [error localizedDescription], [error userInfo]);
    //Present a user facing error
    return;
  }
}
cloudURL = [cloudURL URLByAppendingPathComponent:@"PPRecipes"];
[options setValue:[[NSBundle mainBundle] bundleIdentifier]
          forKey:NSPersistentStoreUbiquitousContentNameKey];
[options setValue:cloudURL
          forKey:NSPersistentStoreUbiquitousContentURLKey];
store = [coordinator migratePersistentStore:store
                                      toURL:storeURL
                                    options:options
                                   withType:NSSQLiteStoreType
                                      error:&error];

if (!store) {
  ALog(@"Error adding OLD persistent store to coordinator %@\n%@",
      [error localizedDescription], [error userInfo]);
  //Present a user facing error
  return;
}

ZAssert([fileManager removeItemAtURL:oldURL error:&error],
        @"Failed to remove old persistent store at %@\n%@\n%@",
        oldURL, [error localizedDescription], [error userInfo]);

dispatch_sync(dispatch_get_main_queue(), ^{
  [self contextInitialized];
});
});
```

Now we come to the more complicated decision. iCloud is enabled, but we don't know whether a migration is needed. First, we go ahead and complete the storeURL with the "new" filename, PPRecipes-iCloud.sqlite. Next, we construct the "old" file URL for PPRecipes.sqlite. If the "old" URL exists (via the NSFileManager), then we need to perform a migration.

We add the "old" file to the NSPersistentStoreCoordinator and obtain a reference to the NSPersistentStore. Once we confirm that it was loaded successfully, we can proceed with the migration.

Since we want the "new" store to be connected to iCloud, we now need to add in the options for iCloud configuration to our options dictionary. These are the options we discussed in *Configuring iCloud*, on page 106. Once the options dictionary has been updated, we can kick off the migration via a call to -migratePersistentStore: toURL: options: withType: error:. This call does several things:

- Creates a new SQLite file at the location specified by storeURL

- Copies all the data from the "old" file to the "new" file

- Registers the "new" file with iCloud per the options specified in the dictionary

- Removes the "old" store from the NSPersistentStoreCoordinator

- Adds the "new" SQLite file to the NSPersistentStoreCoordinator

It's a lot of work for one line of code, and it should be noted that this line of code can take some time. Therefore, depending on our user experience, we may want to broadcast a notification before the work begins so our user interface updates and lets the user know what's going on.

Assuming the migration was successful, we now need to delete the old SQLite file from disk so we do not accidentally repeat these steps on the next launch.

Once the migration and the deletion are complete, we are finally ready to notify the UIApplicationDelegate that the Core Data stack is ready for use.

## 6.6 Desktop iCloud Integration

So far in this chapter we have focused primarily on iOS; the reason is that the desktop implementation is actually a subset of the iOS implementation. There is no UIManagedDocument on the desktop. As a result, we must use the traditional Core Data stack and add the options to the NSPersistentStoreCoordinator ourselves. Even if we are using an NSPersistentDocument, we must still handle adding the options for the NSPersistentStoreCoordinator.

To build a new Core Data desktop application and implement iCloud data syncing, refer to Section 6.2, *Direct NSManagedObjectContext to iCloud*, on page 106 for information, because the steps are identical. Further, to migrate an existing desktop application that uses a traditional Core Data stack, refer to Section 6.5, *Migrating an Existing Application*, on page 113, because that is also identical.

If we are using an NSPersistentDocument, things get a little interesting—not a lot but enough to merit attention. The first thing we need to do is to subclass NSPersistentDocument. The reason for this is that unlike with UIManagedDocument, there is no way to pass in options to the NSPersistentStore when it is being added to the NSPersistentStoreCoordinator. That's the reason for subclassing.

**DepartmentAndEmployees/MyDocument.m**
```
- (BOOL)configurePersistentStoreCoordinatorForURL:(NSURL*)url
                                           ofType:(NSString*)fileType
                               modelConfiguration:(NSString*)configuration
                                     storeOptions:(NSDictionary*)storeOptions
                                            error:(NSError**)error
{
  NSFileManager *fileManager = [NSFileManager defaultManager];
  NSURL *cloudURL = [fileManager URLForUbiquityContainerIdentifier:nil];

  if (cloudURL) {
    NSString *pathComponent = [url lastPathComponent];
    cloudURL = [cloudURL URLByAppendingPathComponent:pathComponent];

    NSMutableDictionary *mutableOptions = [storeOptions mutableCopy];
    [mutableOptions setValue:[[NSBundle mainBundle] bundleIdentifier]
                      forKey:NSPersistentStoreUbiquitousContentNameKey];
    [mutableOptions setValue:cloudURL
                      forKey:NSPersistentStoreUbiquitousContentURLKey];

    storeOptions = mutableOptions;
  }

  return [super configurePersistentStoreCoordinatorForURL:url
                                                   ofType:fileType
                                       modelConfiguration:configuration
                                             storeOptions:storeOptions
                                                    error:error];
}
```

In this override, we first check to see whether iCloud is enabled. If it is, we build our full iCloud URL and then add the two options required to link our persistent store with iCloud. Once the options dictionary has been updated, we return control to our super's implementation.

In this example, we take the -lastPathComponent from the URL and use it as our unique sandbox within iCloud. Depending on the application's design, this may not be unique enough, so we might want to consider storing a GUID inside of the metadata of the NSPersistentStore and using that as the unique identifier within iCloud.

Once the initialization has been completed and linked to iCloud, all of the other behavior is the same between iOS and Mac OS X. We can listen for notifications about iCloud merging data into Core Data and handle those merges in the same way.

## 6.7 Data Quantities

As discussed in Section 6.4, *Under the Hood*, on page 110, Core Data uses transaction logs to keep multiple persistent stores in sync with each other. Because of that design and because of the latency of networking, there is an upper limit to the frequency in which we can create entities and save them to our Core Data application. The exact numbers are difficult to determine, but it is safe to say that if we are generating hundreds of entities per save, we may run into a performance problem.

Whenever we create an NSManagedObject and save the NSManagedObjectContext or the UIManagedDocument, a transaction log is created for that instance. The more entities we create, the larger that transaction log becomes. There is an upper threshold whereby the creation/transmission of transaction logs is unable to keep up with the frequency of entities being generated. When that threshold is hit, iCloud syncing is unable to keep up with the data generation and eventually fails. This failure usually results in a crash in your application.

Unfortunately, there is no magic number of entities to keep under. The threshold is a combination of processor speed, number of entities, size of the entities, and network speed. The slower the processor and/or network, then the fewer entities that are needed to reach the threshold. As an example, using an iPhone 4S on a performant Wi-Fi connection, it was possible to reach this threshold by generating a new entity every second with minimal size. With larger entities or a poorer network, it would be possible to reach the threshold with fewer entities.

At this time, there is no known workaround for this issue other than to decrease the amount of data that is being pushed to iCloud. The amount of data can be decreased by generating less data or by "rolling up" the data into fewer entities. Ideally, this issue will be resolved at some point in the near future.

This issue is being tracked under radr://10416604.

## 6.8 Sharing Data Between iOS and OS X

So far, we have discussed sharing data between iOS devices and linking our OS X application to iCloud. However, we have not discussed how to share data between OS X and iOS. Fortunately, there is virtually no difference between OS X and iOS iCloud integration, though there are a couple of rules that we need to follow.

### The Content Name Key Must Be the Same

The NSPersistentStoreUbiquitousContentNameKey is the unique value that iCloud uses to determine what data we are accessing. If two devices use the same value and are signed by the same developer, they will be able to access the same data. If one or more devices and one or more OS X machines use the same key, they will share the same data.

Throughout these examples, we have been using the value [[NSBundle mainBundle] bundleIdentifier]. There is nothing wrong with using that value, so long as all of our applications are using the same bundle identifier. However, if they are not, then we must use a different string to serve as this key. Apple recommends a reverse DNS notation style, and I certainly see no reason to suggest otherwise.

### The Data Model Must Be the Same

Core Data is virtually identical between iOS and OS X. We can use the same data model, even the same file, between OS X and iOS. iCloud expects and requires us to do exactly that. If the data models do not match, the transaction logs cannot be played back properly, and the synchronizing fails. The easiest way to ensure this is to share the data model (and the entity subclasses) between the OS X application and the iOS application. This step guarantees the applications are using the same model.

However, additional care must be taken when upgrading the model. If we release an update to our iOS application but not our OS X application, they can become out of sync, and iCloud integration will stop working. Once the first device with a new model touches iCloud, iCloud works only with devices that are using the updated model. Any device using the older model simply stops working with iCloud. Fortunately, as soon as the out-of-date machine updates to the latest model, iCloud starts working again.

The best way to test iCloud syncing is to have more than one application running at the same time that uses the data. We could run our existing application on an iPhone and an iPad to see the syncing work, but watching the data sync between an iOS device and an OS X machine is far more interesting. To do that, we must build an OS X client, which is what we are going to do in Chapter 7, *Adding a Desktop Foundation*, on page 121.

## 6.9 Wrapping Up

iCloud is an incredibly powerful feature of iOS/OS X and Core Data. Although it is not perfect yet, it is going to continue to improve iteratively. It is usable in its present form on iOS 6.0 and OS X 10.8. As our users get more comfortable using mobile devices, they are going to expect our applications to sync across them.

iCloud is the solution to that problem.

# CHAPTER 7

# Adding a Desktop Foundation

Until now, we've focused primarily on the iOS side of Core Data. Although nearly everything we've covered works the same on Mac OS X as it does on iOS, there are some differences. In this chapter, we're going to look a little more closely at the Mac OS X side of things.

To examine Core Data on Mac OS X, we'll follow our familiar pattern, starting off with an application on which to base our examples, another foundation. Since we've already created an application on iOS that can share its data through iCloud, it seems only fitting to develop a desktop counterpart to the application that is able to sync.

## 7.1 Our Application

Before we start building our application, here's a quick overview of how the UI will look and work (see Figure 19, *Our recipe application*, on page 122). Let's look at our breakdown.

First, in section 1, we want to allow the user to edit information about individual recipes. The user will be able to select a recipe in the list and edit its accompanying details.

In section 2, we will allow the user to enter the ingredients of the selected recipe. Each recipe will have its own list of ingredients that can be added, viewed, and edited here.

And finally, in section 3, we will allow the user to add a picture of the recipe for reference. This is a view-only element, and the addition of the image will be handled through the main menu.

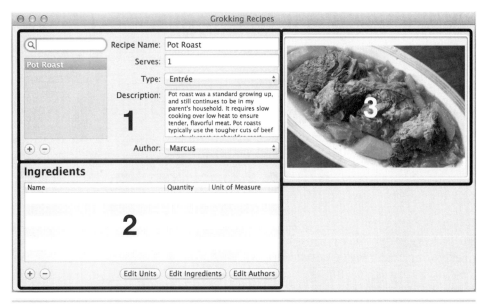

**Figure 19—Our recipe application**

## 7.2 Our Application Design

For our revised desktop application, we're going to start at the very beginning. We'll launch Xcode and proceed through the steps to create the application and bring it to a usable state. At the end of this chapter, you may be surprised that there are so few steps needed to create our Mac OS X application. This ease and efficiency are part of the allure and strength of Cocoa development. Coupled with Core Data, the efficiency is doubled. While we may be used to fairly quick development on iOS, Mac OS X is still easier and quicker to build for—at least up to the prototype stage. Once we have our prototype built and have confirmed that we can do what we want with the application, then all of the "little" things start to become obvious. This is often, lovingly, referred to as "the second 80 percent."

## 7.3 Sharing the Data Model

Since we have already developed our application for iOS, we want to leverage as much of that knowledge as possible. With Core Data, that leveraging is extensive. The xcdatamodel file structure is identical between Mac OS X and iOS. This means we can use the same data model we have been using on iOS. Further, since the data model can be shared and reused, we can share and reuse the data objects as well.

As of the writing of this book, Xcode constructs projects so that the .xcodeproj file is above all of the other files needed in the project. The purpose behind this setup is so we can more easily structure our projects to share components between iOS and Mac OS X. Therefore, we start our desktop project by creating a new project named Desktop. I suggest creating the new project in a temporary directory, perhaps on your desktop.

Once the new project is created, quit Xcode. Using Finder, move the contents of the new project in with our existing project. We could further clarify things by renaming the projects, but our main goal is to share the data model and the data objects. The final result is shown here:

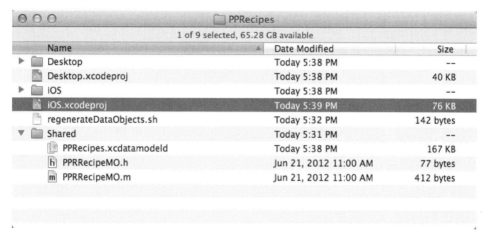

Once we have our data objects and data model in a position to be shared, drag the folder into Xcode, and add them to the desktop project. Now our data model is complete.

## 7.4   Building the Controller Layer

As you may know from experience developing Cocoa apps, Interface Builder is a large part of any project. Now that we have built our data model and have a template ready in Xcode, it's time to put together the user interface.

There are two things to note before we get into the fun of Interface Builder.

- This is not going to be Delicious Library. We will be using standard widgets for our application to help keep the non–Core Data code to a minimum.

- There are a lot of features we *could* add to this application, but we're going to hold back. Extra features, although useful, might detract from our current focus of porting the primary functionality from iOS to the desktop. Once we have that new foundation in place, we can start adding features.

## Adding Objects to the xib

The first part of the user interface we will work on is the objects in the xib file. As with most applications, we need to add the AppDelegate to the xib so it will be both instantiated on start-up and properly linked into the application itself.

### Add the AppDelegate

Depending on the whims of the templates within Xcode, the AppDelegate may already be in the xib file upon opening MainMenu.xib. If it is, great! Move on to the next section. If it's not, we need to add it. In addition, please note that depending on the version of Xcode that is running, the application delegate could have the application name prepended to it. If it does, we must substitute that name for any reference to AppDelegate in this context.

To add the AppDelegate to the xib file, follow these steps:

1.  Find the NSObject in the Library palette, and drag it to the xib's window.

2.  Click the name of the NSObject. When it is editable, change it to AppDelegate.

3.  Go to the Identity tab on the Inspector palette, and change the class of the object from NSObject to AppDelegate.

4.  Right-drag from the application to the AppDelegate object, and select Delegate.

When these steps are complete, the AppDelegate class will be instantiated when our application launches, and the application will send all delegate messages to it.

### Adding the NSArrayController Objects

We want our application to display a list of all the recipes in a single window. To accomplish this, we need to be able to reference the data so it can be displayed. So, let's add three NSArrayController objects into our xib that reference that data. Our window then references those NSArrayController objects. Once the NSArrayController objects are added and configured, the xib looks like Figure 20, *The main menu xib*, on page 125.

To add an NSArrayController for the recipe entities, follow these steps:

1.  Find the NSArrayController object in the library, and drag it to the xib file.

2.  Click the name of the NSArrayController. When it is editable, rename it to Recipes. If you have trouble getting the element into edit mode, change the

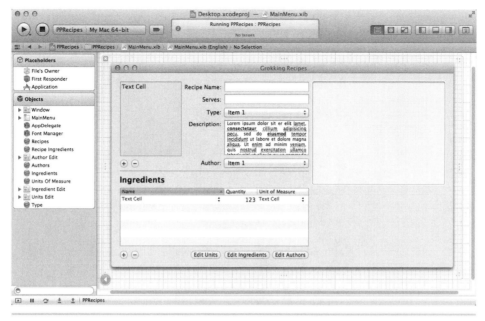

**Figure 20—The main menu xib**

name in the Identity inspector in Interface Builder, and change the Label field in the Document section.

3. On the Attributes tab of the inspector, change the mode from Class to Entity, and change the entity name to Recipe.

4. Make sure the Prepares Content flag is selected.

5. On the Bindings tab of the inspector, bind ManagedObjectContext to the AppDelegate with a model key path of managedObjectContext.

Now that we have the Recipe entity's NSArrayController built, we need to configure the other two NSArrayController instances, one for the RecipeIngredient entity and one for the Type entity. The type NSArrayController follows the same steps as our Recipe entity, but we need to set the entity name to Type so it will populate with Type objects. Other than that one difference, we follow the previous steps to complete the type's NSArrayController.

Set the identity of the last NSArrayController, the recipe ingredients' NSArrayController, to RecipeIngredient. In the Attributes inspector, choose Entity, and set the entity name to RecipeIngredient. Set the bindings as before, with one additional change: on the Bindings tab of the inspector, enable the content set in the controller content and point it at the recipe's NSArrayController with a controller key of selection and a model key path of ingredients. See Figure 21, *NSArrayController content set properties*, on page 126.

Now we are ready to build the NSWindow.

**Figure 21—NSArrayController content set properties**

## 7.5 Building the User Interface

Now that we have all the data objects referenced properly, it is time to build the user interface. Although this interface won't be winning an Apple Design Award any time soon, it does allow us to view and edit all the data objects in our model. The window we are building looks like Figure 22, *The main window*, on page 127. Let's walk through the steps to set it up. For a more detailed review of this process, take a look at Chapter 8, *OS X: Bindings, KVC, and KVO*, on page 137.

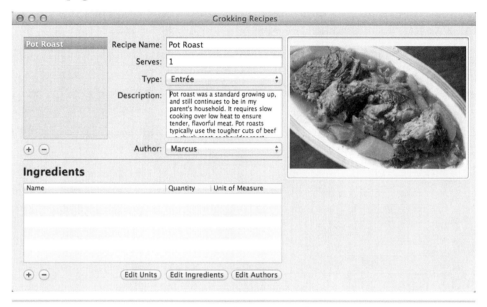

**Figure 22—The main window**

### Building the Recipe Source List

The first part of the interface we are building is in the upper-left corner, just below the search field. This view is an NSTableView configured with one column. It has no horizontal scroll bar, but it does have an automatically displaying vertical scroll bar. In addition, it has a hidden header and the highlight set to Source List. The scroll bars are configured in the inspector for the NSScrollView. The number of columns and the highlight option are configured in the NSTableView inspector. Each of the inspectors can be accessed by Control+Shift-clicking (or Shift+right-clicking) the NSTableView and selecting the appropriate view from the list. If the inspector is not on the screen, it can be displayed via the Tools > Inspector menu item.

To bind this table to our recipe's NSArrayController object, though, we need to dig down a little bit and get a hold of the NSTableColumn so we can tell that column what to display. We could click in the table view until eventually we select the NSTableColumn, but fortunately there is an easier way. As mentioned, if we Shift+right-click the table, we are presented with a pop-up listing of all of the views; we can then select the NSTableColumn (see Figure 23, *List view tree,* on page 128). With the NSTableColumn selected, we open its Bindings tab in the inspector and bind its value to the recipe's NSArrayController with a controller key of arrangedObjects and a model key path of name. Once this is set, our Recipe entities show up in this table. More importantly, when we click a recipe in this list, the recipe becomes the selection that feeds the rest of the UI.

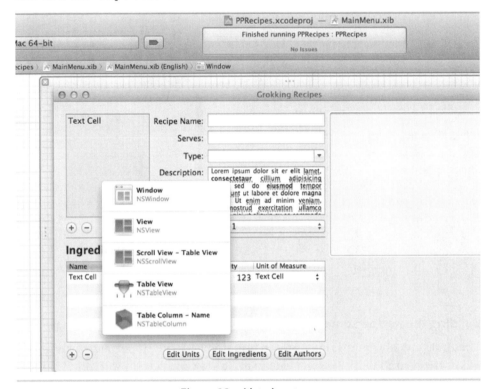

**Figure 23—List view tree**

Let's add the buttons that will control the creation and removal of Recipe entities. For this step, we drag an NSButton (it does not matter which one) from the library and place it below the Recipe table view. In the button's Attributes tab, we set its image to NSAddTemplate (a system-level image available for our use), change its style to Round Rect, and remove its title if it has one. In addition, we must select the menu item Layout > Size to Fit to get the button to the perfect size. Once these steps have been taken for the add button, select Edit > Duplicate from the main menu to create a second button, and change the second button's image to NSRemoveTemplate.

Next, we can "wire up" the buttons under the NSTableView and connect them directly to the recipe's NSArrayController. The add button will be connected to the

-add: action, and the remove button will be connected to the -remove: action on the recipe's NSArrayController. These buttons can be connected to their actions by holding down the Control key, clicking the button, and dragging from the selector sent action to the NSArrayController. With these small changes, we can now add and remove recipe entities at will.

## Adding the Recipe Details

Now that the source list in place, it's time to add the details about the recipe. These details (the name, serves, desc, and type) tie to the now-valid selection controller key on the recipe's NSArrayController. As a result, when a user clicks in the list, the relevant details of the recipe are selected.

The first two items are text fields, the third and fifth elements are pop-up boxes, and the final element is a text area, as shown in Figure 22, *The main window*, on page 127. With the exception of the pop-up boxes for the type and author, these details are configured in a very similar way. All of them have a value binding associated with the recipe's NSArrayController object through a controller key of selection and a model key path of name, serves, and desc, as appropriate. One tip with regard to the text area: be sure to turn off the Rich Text setting. When this setting is on, the field expects an NSAttributedString instead of an NSString, which can cause confusion (see Figure 24, *Remember to turn off the Rich Text setting*, on page 130). Additionally, in order to be good citizens, we should drag an NSNumberFormatter to the Serves text field and configure it to allow only whole numbers.

The pop-up boxes are a little more complex. Although each pop-up box is associated with the selected recipe, we need to populate the entire list of recipes with values. The values belong to other entities on the other side of relationships. While we want to, for example, show the selected recipe type, what we really need to display is the *name* of the recipe type being selected. Fortunately, this is a fairly common use case, and there are built-in tools to handle it. Each pop-up box is designed to be associated with an NSArrayController. And each NSArrayController references the entities we want to appear in the pop-up boxes. Furthermore, we can define each pop-up box to display a specific value from those entities.

As shown in Figure 25, *Manual data entry for the combo box*, on page 131, starting with the Type pop-up box, we need to set three sections of values.

- In the Content section, we bind to the type NSArrayController with a Controller Key setting of arrangedObjects. This step instructs the pop-up box to access the type NSArrayController for the objects it is to work with.

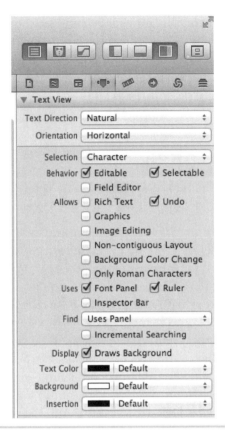

**Figure 24—Remember to turn off the Rich Text setting.**

- In the Content Values section, we bind to the type NSArrayController with a Controller Key setting of arrangedObjects. We also want to set the Model Key Path setting to name. This step instructs the pop-up to access the name property for its display value.

- In the Selected Object section, we bind to the recipe's NSArrayController and use a Controller Key setting of selection. Further, we want to set the Model Key Path setting to type. This instructs the pop-up to do several things. First, it checks the selected recipe for its type relationship and displays the value associated. Second, it updates the selected recipe when a user selects a different value in the Type pop-up list. And finally, it monitors the recipe NSArrayController and updates itself if the user selects a different recipe.

Once we have the Type pop-up box set, we need to configure the Author pop-up box. The setup here is identical to that for the Type pop-up box, except the

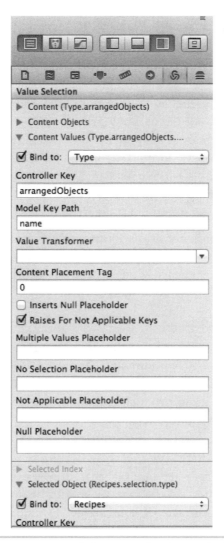

Figure 25—Manual data entry for the combo box

NSArrayController to use is the author NSArrayController, and the Selected Object Model Key Path setting will be author.

## Adding the Ingredients

Now that the recipe section of our UI is complete, it's time to add ingredients. The ingredients make up the table in the lower-left corner of our window. Fortunately, this part is almost identical to setting up the recipe source list. However, unlike the recipe source list, our NSTableView will have three columns, display its headers and its vertical scroll bar, and hide the horizontal scroll bar. We enter the column headings as Name, Quantity, and Unit of Measure.

Just as we did in the recipe source list, we bind the values for each column in the NSTableView to our recipe ingredients' NSArrayController using the controller key arrangedObjects and using the appropriate model key paths: name, quantity, and unitOfMeasure. The Quantity column (or, more specifically, the table cell in the Quantity column) should also have an NSNumberFormatter assigned to it so that the quantity is properly formatted for the value that it holds. Once those are configured, we can see the recipe ingredients for the selected recipe. Remember that we configured the recipe ingredients' NSArrayController to feed off the selected recipe, so we do not have to do anything extra at this point.

Like in the recipe source list, the add and subtract buttons are configured by binding them to the recipe ingredients' NSArrayController objects (the -add: and -remove: methods, respectively). And with that, the ingredients section is complete, and we are nearly done with our UI.

## 7.6 Adding a Splash of Code

Wondering where the code is? As it stands, our recipe application is fully functional. We can run it without any actual code on our part and start inputting recipes immediately. The combination of Cocoa and Core Data makes it possible for us to produce this application with no custom code. However, we are not stopping there.

### Displaying a Picture of the Recipe

Since our iOS counterpart is capable of taking and displaying pictures, it seems only fair that the desktop variant should be able to add and display images. Fortunately, from the UI point of view, this functionality is an easy addition. Drag an NSImageView (aka Image Well) onto our window, and connect its Value Path setting to the imagePath of the recipe's NSArrayController with a controller key of selection.

### Importing Images

Once we add the NSImageView to our user interface, we need to make our AppDelegate aware of it. In addition, we need to add a way to *set* the image path of our Recipe entities. Therefore, we must update our AppDelegate.h and add an IBOutlet for the recipe NSArrayController and an IBAction to be able to set the image path, as shown here:

Shared/Desktop/AppDelegate.h

```
#import <Cocoa/Cocoa.h>
@interface AppDelegate : NSObject
{
    IBOutlet NSWindow *window;
    IBOutlet NSImageView *imageView;
    IBOutlet NSArrayController *recipeArrayController;
    NSPersistentStoreCoordinator *persistentStoreCoordinator;
    NSManagedObjectContext *managedObjectContext;
}
- (NSPersistentStoreCoordinator *)persistentStoreCoordinator;
- (NSManagedObjectContext *)managedObjectContext;

- (IBAction)saveAction:sender;
- (IBAction)addImage:(id)sender;
@end
```

The IBAction, specifically -(IBAction)addImage:(id)sender;, is called from our main menu and displays an open file dialog box. Along with this step, we need a reference to the selected recipe in order to work with the recipe entities. To accomplish this, we add a reference to the recipe's NSArrayController that is instantiated in our nib within the AppDelegate.

Once the recipe's NSArrayController has been added to the AppDelegate header, we need to go back to Interface Builder briefly and Control+drag from the AppDelegate to the recipe's NSArrayController to complete the binding.

While we are here, let's add a menu item to the File menu that will allow the user to add an image for the recipe. We do this by making sure the MainMenu element is open in Interface Builder (it appears as a floating menu) and clicking its File menu. Next, we can either add a new NSMenuItem or use one that already exists that is not being used. Since the Save As menu item is not relevant to our application, let's go ahead and rename it Add Recipe Image. Once it is renamed, Control+drag from it to the AppDelegate, and bind the menu item to the IBAction we defined in the header, as shown in Figure 26, *Add Recipe Image menu item*, on page 134. With the bindings in place, it is time to implement the -addImage: method.

Shared/Desktop/AppDelegate.m

```
- (IBAction)addImage:(id)sender;
{
    NSManagedObject *recipe = [[recipeArrayController selectedObjects] lastObject];
    if (!recipe) return;
    NSOpenPanel *openPanel = [NSOpenPanel openPanel];
    [openPanel setCanChooseDirectories:NO];
    [openPanel setCanCreateDirectories:NO];
    [openPanel setAllowsMultipleSelection:NO];
```

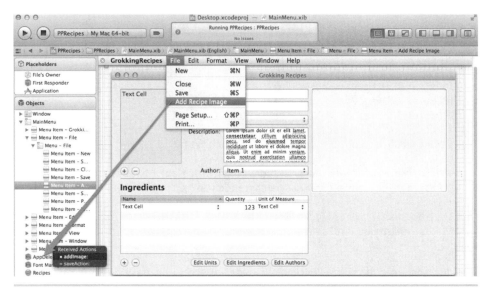

**Figure 26—Add Recipe Image menu item**

The implementation of -addImage: displays an NSOpenPanel, which attaches to the window as a sheet, making it modal to the window. Next, we tweak the NSOpenPanel a little bit so it cannot select directories or multiple files or create directories. Notice that we check to make sure a recipe has been selected before we open the panel. Otherwise, without a recipe, we would have nothing to associate the image with. A little bit of error checking can go a long way.

Since sheets work asynchronously, we need to add a completion block. The completion block will be called once the user is done interacting with the NSOpenPanel.

**Shared/Desktop/AppDelegate.m**
```
[openPanel beginSheetModalForWindow:window
                  completionHandler:^(NSInteger result) {
  if (result == NSFileHandlingPanelCancelButton) return;
  NSURL *fileURL = [[openPanel URLs] lastObject];
  NSError *error = nil;
  //Build the path we want the file to be at
  NSURL *destURL = [NSURL fileURLWithPath:[self applicationSupportFolder]];
  NSString *guid = [[NSProcessInfo processInfo] globallyUniqueString];
  destURL = [destURL URLByAppendingPathComponent:guid];
  BOOL success = [[NSFileManager defaultManager] copyItemAtURL:fileURL
                                                         toURL:destURL
                                                         error:&error];

  NSAssert2(success, @"Error copying file: %@\n%@",
           [error localizedDescription], [error userInfo]);
  [recipe setValue:[destURL path] forKey:@"imagePath"];
}];
```

Our first action in the completion block is to check whether the user canceled out of the panel. An NSInteger is passed in expressly for this reason. If the user did click Cancel, we simply return from the block, and no action is taken.

Once we know the user has selected an image file, it is time to bring it into our application. We know NSOpenPanel is configured to allow the user to select only one file, so we can grab the -lastObject from the -URLs method of the NSOpenPanel. We now know what image the user wants added. At this point, we could simply add the path to our recipe.

But what happens if the user moves the image? Or the image is intended to be temporary? To ensure the image is always available, let's copy it to a known location within our control and use *that* file path. To accomplish these steps, we grab the filename from the NSOpenPanel and construct a unique path within our Application Support directory structure. Next, we use the NSFileManager to copy the image to that location. And finally, we set the new file path into our Recipe object.

With the addition of the image menu item, we have completed the initial functionality of our desktop application. We can now share our data model across iOS and OS X. This level of code reuse allows us to maintain both applications and share functionality with a minimum of effort. As we add functionality to one, we merely need to create the UI portion for the other.

## 7.7 Wrapping Up

Coming up in the next chapter, we'll take a quick detour into the powerful features of Objective-C that allowed us to build this desktop application with virtually no code. In addition, we'll add iCloud syncing and some other features that are unique to the desktop.

# CHAPTER 8

# OS X: Bindings, KVC, and KVO

Cocoa Bindings provides a lot of the magic behind Core Data. It consists of a number of APIs and concepts that together allow us to develop our applications using the Model View Controller paradigm, without requiring a tight coupling of the three aspects.

Cocoa Bindings allows us to design views, controllers, and models that all expect data in a specific format, without requiring that we bind them to specific classes. This means we can use views in multiple places and swap out controllers and even models without the need for extensive recoding, if any.

In this chapter, we look at some of the key components of Cocoa Bindings and then delve into the specifics of how Core Data works with those bindings. The two primary APIs we discuss are Key Value Coding and Key Value Observing. These APIs are part of the foundation that allows Interface Builder to function. Between the two of them, they give us a tremendous amount of flexibility in our design. In addition, Core Data uses these APIs heavily in order to allow us to focus on the business logic of our applications, as opposed to the data layer. With the combination of Cocoa Bindings and Core Data, the amount of code that we need to write, and therefore debug and maintain, is drastically reduced.

While this chapter is primarily focused on OS X, there are some fundamental portions that affect both OS X and iOS. Specifically, KVC and KVO are available on both platforms. While the Cocoa Bindings discussed in depth in this chapter applies only on OS X, it is highly recommended that iOS developers become familiar with these technologies as well.

## 8.1 Key Value Coding

Key Value Coding (KVC) is one of the cornerstones of Cocoa Bindings. KVC allows us to access the attributes of an object without calling the accessors of that object directly. Key Value Coding is implemented through an informal protocol on NSObject itself and is used mainly through the getter/setter pair -valueForKey: and -setValue:forKey:.

## -valueForKey:

The method -valueForKey: is a generic accessor that retrieves an attribute on an object. For example, if we had an object called Recipe and it had an attribute called name, normally we would access that attribute via the following:

```
Recipe *myRecipe = ...
NSString *recipeName = [myRecipe name];
```

However, this requires specific knowledge about the Recipe object to exist in the calling method and generally requires that we import the header file of the Recipe object. However, with Key Value Coding, we can obtain this same attribute without any preexisting knowledge about the Recipe object.

```
id myRecipe = ...
NSString *recipeName = [myRecipe valueForKey:@"name"];
```

By itself, this is not all that useful. However, there are huge benefits that are not obvious on the surface. Here's an example of how you might better take advantage of this ability:

```
- (NSString*)description
{
  NSMutableString *string = [NSMutableString stringWithFormat:@"[%@] {",
    [self class]];
  NSEntityDescription *desc = [self entity];
  for (NSString *name in [desc attributeKeys]) {
    [string appendFormat:@"\n\t%@ = '%@'", name, [self valueForKey:name]];
  }
  [string appendString:@"\n}"];
  return string;
}
```

In this example, we utilize the NSEntityDescription class (discussed in greater detail in Chapter 1, *Under the Hood of Core Data*, on page 1) to retrieve the names all of the attributes of an NSManagedObject subclass and generate an NSString for display in the logs. With this method, we can reuse it in every NSManagedObject subclass that we create, rather than having to create a custom -description method for each subclass.

There are a couple of things to note in this example. First, the target object is not required to have accessor methods for the attribute being queried. If our target object has only an ivar or property for a name, it will still be resolved and retrieved properly. (*ivar* stands for instance variable, which is different from a static or local variable.) In addition, if the target object has neither an accessor nor an ivar, the target object will still have a chance to respond to the request before an error occurs via the -valueForUndefinedKey: method. Lastly, all the properties of an NSManagedObject are queryable via the KVC protocol. What this means is if we have an NSManagedObject defined in our model, we can retrieve an instance of that object and access its properties without having to implement a *single line of code* in the target object!

## -setValue:forKey:

Dynamically accessing properties on an object is a useful skill, but it's only half of what KVC does. The other half is the ability to dynamically set attributes on an object in much the same manner that we can retrieve them. Normally, we would change the name attribute on an Recipe object by calling the setter method.

```
Recipe *myRecipe = ...
[myRecipe setName:@"Yummy Cookies"];
```

As in the earlier getter accessor, preexisting knowledge of the Recipe object is required in order to use that accessor without compiler warnings. However, with KVC, we can access it in a more dynamic manner.

```
id myRecipe = ...
[myRecipe setValue:@"Yummy Cookies" forKey:@"name"];
```

This call attempts to use the setter -setName: if it is available; if it is not, the call will look for and use the attribute directly if it is available, and failing that, it will call -setValue:forUndefinedKey: on the target object. The combination of the dynamic getter coupled with the dynamic setter allows us to manipulate objects without having to write accessors and without having to know (or care!) if they exist. This is used to great effect in one of the Core Data recipes to create a preferences singleton object that reads its values from a properties table. See Chapter 10, *Dynamic Parameters*, on page 179.

## @property

In addition, as of OS X 10.5 Leopard, we have the keyword @property, which allows us to synthesize accessors to attributes on an object. This feature plays very nicely with KVC, and the two can be used together to produce extremely dynamic and flexible code. By utilizing the @property keyword, we can instruct the compiler to generate getter and setter accessors that are KVO-compliant. In a 32-bit application, we can define the @property that has the same object type and name as a defined ivar. This will tell the compiler that getter and setter accessors exist or will exist for that ivar. In a 64-bit application, the ivar itself is not required because the property definition handles that for us, as well. For example, if we had an object with the following header:

```
@interface MyObject : NSObject
{
    NSString *myString; //Only required for a 32-bit application
}

@property (retain) NSString *myString;
@end
```

Xcode would interpret it the same as the following header:

```
@interface MyObject : NSObject
{
  NSString *myString;
}

- (NSString*)myString;
- (void)setMyString:(NSString*)string;
@end
```

In combination with the @property keyword, we have the @synthesize and @dynamic keywords for use in our implementation files. @synthesize will generate the actual accessors that the @property alludes to in the header. Therefore, in our example MyObject.m file, we can declare the following:

```
#import "MyObject.h"
@implementation MyObject
@synthesize myString;
@end
```

and have the same effective code as this:

```
#import "MyObject.h"
@implementation MyObject

- (NSString*)myString;
{
  return myString;
}

- (void)setMyString:(NSString*)string;
{
  @synchronized(self) {
    if ([string isEqualToString:myString]) return;
    [myString release];
    myString = [string retain];
  }
}
@end
```

The compiler adds the retain in the setter because we specified it in the property. If we had set it to assign instead, no retain would have occurred. Likewise, the locking of the ivar is a default option that we could have turned off by adding the nonatomic option to the property definition.

When dealing with multiple properties on an object, this can be a great time-saver. There have also been indications that the accessors generated by the compiler are faster than the "normal" accessors that developers write. In addition to generating accessors, the @synthesize keyword is smart about what it implements. If we need to implement our own setter for a property, it will not overwrite that setter.

Alongside the @synthesize property, we have the @dynamic property. Unlike @synthesize, which generates the accessors for us, @dynamic tells the compiler that while the accessors for the property are not there at compile time, they will be at runtime, and it instructs the compiler not to produce a warning for them. @synthesize and @dynamic are sibling keywords. For each property, we can use one or the other but not both. However, neither is required in a situation where we are implementing the accessors ourselves. If the accessor methods will be implemented at runtime, we would use the @dynamic property instead of the @synthesize property so that the compiler does not produce a warning. This is particularly useful for Core Data subclasses, discussed in Chapter 1, *Under the Hood of Core Data*, on page 1.

It should be noted that it is possible to have one @property definition that does not match the name of the ivar. For example, it is fairly common to have ivars that start with an underscore, but the accessors do not include the underscore. The @property can handle this as well as part of the @synthesize and @dynamic calls.

```
@interface MyObject : NSObject
{
  NSString *_myString; //Only required for 32-bit
}

@property (retain) NSString *myString;
@end
@implementation MyObject
@synthesize myString = _myString;
@end
```

Note that as of iOS 6.0 and Mac OS X 10.8, the ivar is different from the property name by default. Unless you override the default, the ivar name will have an underscore prefix.

## 8.2 Key Value Observing

Key Value Observing (KVO) is the sister API to KVC. KVO allows us to request notifications when an attribute has changed. By observing attributes on an object, we can react when those attributes are changed. KVO is also implemented via an informal protocol on the NSObject, and we register and remove observers using -addObserver:for-KeyPath:options:context: and -removeObserver:forKeyPath:. These are the two primary methods, although there are other methods involved in the protocol, just as with KVC.

If we wanted to observe the name value on a recipe, we would add ourselves (or another object) as an observer for that value, like so:

```
static NSString *kPragProgObserver = @"PragProgObserver"
id myRecipe = ...
[myRecipe addObserver:self
        forKeyPath:@"name"
            options:(NSKeyValueObservingOptionNew|NSKeyValueObservingOptionOld)
            context:kPragProgObserver];
```

This snippet of code adds self as an observer to the myRecipe object and requests that when the name value changes to notify self of that change and include both the old value and the new value in that notification. We pass along a context so we can ensure we are acting on observations meant only for us and that they are not accidentally intercepted.

We do this because it is possible that our code is not the only code in our application observing a value, and this method may be called with the intention of being received by our superclass. To ensure that the notification we receive is in fact intended for us, we check the context that is passed in. After this code has been called, any time the name property is changed on *that instance of Recipe*, the -observeValueForKeyPath:ofObject:change:context: is called upon self. We can then handle the change notification as appropriate.

```
- (void)observeValueForKeyPath:(NSString*)keyPath
                      ofObject:(id)object
                        change:(NSDictionary*)change
                       context:(void*)context
{
  if (context != kPragProgObserver) {
    [super observeValueForKeyPath:keyPath
                      ofObject:object
                        change:change
                       context:context];
    return;
  }
```

```
    NSLog(@"Attribute %@ changed from %@ to %@", keyPath,
       [change valueForKey:NSKeyValueChangeOldKey],
       [change valueForKey:NSKeyValueChangeNewKey]);
}
```

When the variable is changed, we see output similar to the following:

```
Attribute name changed from untitled to Beef Chili
```

When we are done observing a value, we can stop receiving messages by passing -removeObserver:forKeyPath: to the observed object.

```
id myRecipe = ...
[myRecipe removeObserver:self
            forKeyPath:@"name"];
```

KVO allows views to automatically refresh themselves from the model when the data has changed. When a view is initialized, it uses KVO to connect all its components to the underlying objects and uses the notifications to refresh itself.

## 8.3 Cocoa Bindings and Core Data

The combination of KVO/KVC (collectively referred to as Cocoa Bindings) and Core Data reduces the amount of code that we are required to write by a considerable amount. In the previous chapter, we wrote almost no code to create and display our recipe objects. Nearly all the work that we did was in Interface Builder. In this section, we discuss each of the interface objects that we used and how they work with Core Data.

How does this apply to our application? Let's review the user interface that we built in Chapter 7, *Adding a Desktop Foundation*, on page 121 and how we used KVO and KVC.

### NSTableView

Our recipe application makes heavy use of the NSTableView. In the main window of our application, we have two table views: one to list all of the recipes and another to list the ingredients for those recipes. Whenever an application needs to display a list of items or a grid of data, the NSTableView is the element to use.

In an NSTableView, like in the NSOutlineView, we do not actually bind the table itself to the NSArrayController. Instead, we select each column individually and bind it to a property of the objects in the NSArrayController (see Figure 27, *Select each NSTableColumn individually*, on page 144). As we did in Chapter 7, *Adding a Desktop Foundation*, on page 121, we bind the column to the arrangedObjects controller key and the model key path to the value we want displayed in that column, as shown in Figure 28, *Bind the table column to the Core Data property*, on page 144.

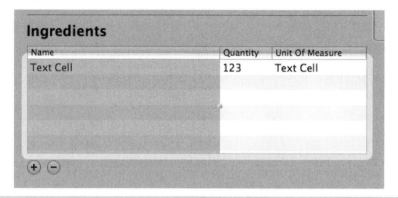

Figure 27—Select each **NSTableColumn** individually.

Figure 28—Bind the table column to the Core Data property.

NSTableView, like NSOutlineView (as discussed in *NSOutlineView*, on page 148), plays very nicely with Core Data. This is especially true when the NSTableView is backed by an NSArrayController that is feeding the data. It is possible to use NSTableView with a custom data source, if that is appropriate for the problem at hand. However, when bound with an NSArrayController, the NSTableView can be manipulated with other objects, such as the NSSearchView (discussed in a moment), to produce interfaces that integrate smoothly and provide a great user experience.

With this configuration, the NSTableView displays the data from the NSArrayController automatically and, thanks to KVO, stays in sync with the data stored in the persistence layer.

## NSArrayController

NSArrayController is an extremely useful object when working with Core Data because it is aware of the Core Data layer and knows how to talk to it without any additional code on our part. When we configure it within Interface Builder, all that we really need to give it is the NSManagedObjectContext and a data object type. The rest of the work—retrieving the objects, updating those objects, and creating new ones—is all handled for us.

NSArrayController also understands relationships between objects when it is working with Core Data. In our recipe application, we have one NSArrayController configured to manage RecipeIngredient objects. Based on our data model, these are child objects that are bound to a specific recipe. Because NSArrayController understands these relationships, we can configure it to pull and display only those RecipeIngredient objects that are connected to a Recipe object that is selected in another NSArrayController. This again is made possible by KVC and KVO. When we configure the RecipeIngredient's NSArrayController to provide only those ingredients that are related to the specific recipe, what it is doing behind the scenes is accessing the Recipe object and requesting its ingredients property via KVC. In the RecipeIngredient's NSArrayController, we bind the NSManagedObjectContext so that new ingredients can be added. In addition to properly being able to create (and remove) objects from the persistence layer, the NSArrayController will also manage the relationship between the newly created or removed RecipeIngredient and the parent Recipe object.

All of this works because Core Data is the entire persistence layer and is accessed in a consistent way no matter what object is being dealt with. Because Core Data uses KVO and KVC, our controller objects do not need to know very much about the objects, other than the name of the objects and where they are stored. The rest is all resolved at runtime based on the settings that we provide in Interface Builder. In our recipe application, we have one NSArrayController that is bound to the Recipe entity in Core Data. Because we also bound that NSArrayController to our NSManagedObjectContext, it is able to retrieve those Recipe entities automatically and make them available to the rest of the user interface. When our interface is loaded, those NSArrayController objects go out to that NSManagedObjectContext and ask for the entities that currently exist. Once they are loaded into the NSArrayController objects, any view element associated with them will be notified, via KVO, that the data is available for display. All of this happens behind the scenes; we're not required to write code for any of it.

## NSFormatter

Users expect fields in the interface to accept their input and format it appropriately. This is where NSFormatter objects come into play. When dealing with any type of number, it is best to add an NSNumberFormatter to the text field or table column and define its display. Likewise, when working with dates, use an NSDateFormatter on the field or column to ensure the data is formatted and validated correctly before it is stored in the Core Data repository. When working with Core Data, it is sometimes necessary to manipulate the display of the data so the user's input can be validated and also so it can be displayed in a usable form. For instance, we're not creating a very good user experience if we display currency as 3.99 rather than $3.99 or display a date in raw seconds.

In our application, we used an NSNumberFormatter to display the quantity in the Ingredients column of our second NSTableView. If we were to add a shopping list to our application, we would also use NSNumberFormatter objects to display currency and NSDateFormatter objects to show date and time information.

To add an NSFormatter to a field (either a column or a text field), select it in the Library palette and drag it onto the interface element. Once it is in place, we can configure its details in the Attributes inspector, as shown in Figure 29, *NSNumberFormatter Attributes inspector*, on page 147. The Attributes inspector allows us to configure exactly how the data is presented to the user.

In addition to properly displaying number and date data, the NSFormatter classes accept input from the user and send that input back to the model in the correct format. For example, by applying NSNumberFormatter to the Quantity column of the ingredients table, we are guaranteed to receive an NSNumber back from the user interface.

**Figure 29—NSNumberFormatter Attributes inspector**

Once an NSFormatter has been applied to an object, it can be a little tricky to reference it again to make changes. To change or remove an NSFormatter once it has been applied, select the number formatter in the element list on the left side of the Interface Builder view. Selecting the line item references the NSFormatter again so that it can be manipulated. See Figure 30, *Accessing an existing NSFormatter on an element*, on page 148.

## 8.4 Other Interface Elements That Use KVO, KVC, and Core Data

Although the previous sections show how to access the Core Data repository in our recipe application with KVO and KVC, let's quickly review the other elements that, if we wanted or needed to, could be utilized to display the data in our application as well.

### NSObjectController

NSObjectController shares a lot of similarities with the NSArrayController discussed earlier. However, unlike the NSArrayController, the NSObjectController is designed to represent *one* instance rather than an array of instances. A common usage of the NSObjectController is to represent the selected object of an NSArrayController, thereby making it clearer as to what data is being displayed in the interface elements that are bound to the NSObjectController, as opposed to an NSArrayController. Another common usage is to have an entire interface, such as a detail sheet or child window, be bound to the values within an NSObjectController and then have the File's Owner reference and populate that NSObjectController. In this design, the File's Owner (usually a subclass of NSWindowController) simply has to populate the NSObjectController with a call to -setContent:, and the entire UI is

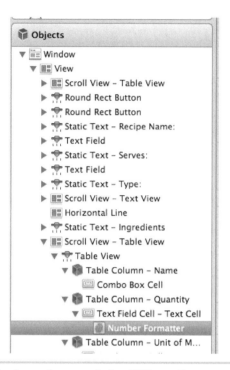

**Figure 30—Accessing an existing NSFormatter on an element**

automatically populated. This again makes the maintenance of the code very easy and also improves readability.

## NSOutlineView

If we wanted to change the look of our application, we could display a single NSOutlineView instead of the two table views we are currently using. With an NSOutlineView, we could display a list of recipes with a hierarchy of ingredients listed under them, as depicted in Figure 31, *Outline view of recipes*, on page 149.

NSOutlineView shares a lot in common with the NSTableView object. In fact, it is a subclass of NSTableView. The major difference is that the NSOutlineView displays data in both a column format as well as a hierarchal format. This changes how the data needs to be represented and accessed. Instead of a flat array of objects, the NSOutlineView expects the data to be in a tree structure. Fortunately, there is a controller designed just for that use: NSTreeController. Some care must be taken when working with Core Data and an NSOutlineView. In general, the NSOutlineView and the NSTreeController expect the data to be in a fairly organized state. NSTreeController expects each parent (or branch) to have children accessible via the same methods. This is a bit counterintuitive to having descriptive

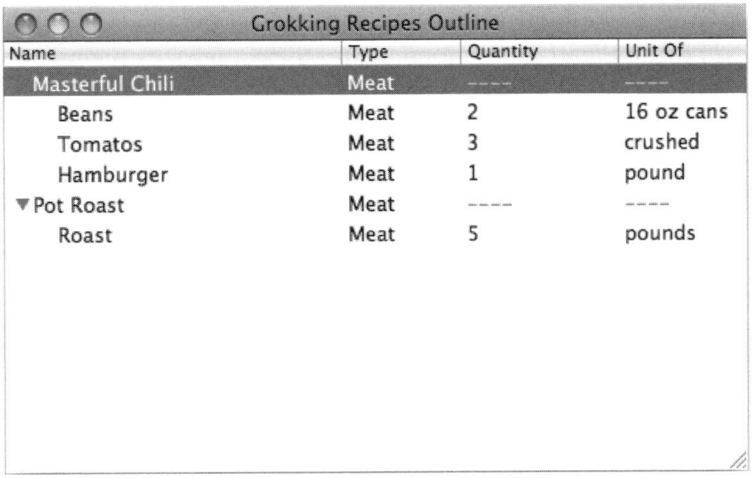

**Figure 31—Outline view of recipes**

names for relationships between objects, and I normally implement accessors instead of making my relationships generic. For instance, if we had a recipe that has children named RecipeIngredients, I would add another accessor to that relationship called children, purely for the NSOutlineView to use. We discuss custom NSManagedObject classes in Chapter 1, *Under the Hood of Core Data*, on page 1.

Unlike its parent object, NSTableView, the NSOutlineView does not work as cleanly as we might expect. We can combine it with the NSTreeController, but we get a lot more functionality and control by implementing the data source protocol for the NSOutlineView instead of using the NSTreeController object.

## NSTreeController

As discussed in *NSOutlineView*, on page 148, NSTreeController objects are primarily used by the NSOutlineView interface element. Although they can store any data that lends itself to a tree structure, they are best suited as a controller for NSOutlineView objects. Unfortunately, there is still quite a bit of work to be done with the NSTreeController, and the results we get from working with it can be unexpected and unclear. Therefore, I recommend skipping it at this time and implementing the data source protocol instead when working with tree data.

## NSSearchField

The NSSearchField interface element is an extremely useful tool and can provide an extra bit of polish to an interface. Its primary purpose is to filter the objects in an NSArrayController. That may not seem like much, until we remember that, thanks to KVO, any tables or interface elements associated with that NSArray-Controller will get updated automatically and instantly. This means if we put a search field into our application and link it to our NSArrayController of Recipe objects, our source list of recipes will automatically be filtered based on the user input into that NSSearchField. Even better, we don't have to write any code! All we need to do to implement it is configure the bindings for the NSSearchField.

To accomplish this, we first add an NSSearchField to our application. In Figure 32, *Adding an NSSearchField to our application*, on page 150, we have decreased the vertical size of the recipe source list and inserted an NSSearchField above it. Next, we configure its bindings.

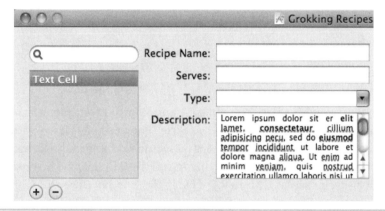

**Figure 32—Adding an NSSearchField to our application**

As shown in Figure 33, *NSSearchField bindings*, on page 151, the NSSearchField interface element works with an NSPredicate. We write the predicate in the Predicate Format field, substituting $value for whatever the user inputs into the search field and using the controller key and value transformer to bind it to our data. In this example, we want to filter on the name of recipes; therefore, we bind the NSSearchField to our recipe's NSArrayController using the controller key of filterPredicate and a predicate of name contains[c] $value.

Once we add one predicate, another appears on the Bindings tab for the NSSearchField. This is so we can use a search field for more than one type of search. Each search will be shown in the drop-down on the NSSearchField, and the Display Name binding will be shown to the user. This allows us to create one NSSearchField that can search for recipe names, ingredients, descriptions, or anything else we may need.

Once the binding is complete, we are done adding a basic search field. Running the application shows that text entered into the search field impacts the list

Figure 33—NSSearchField bindings

of recipes, as shown in Figure 34, *Search filter running against the recipe list*, on page 151.

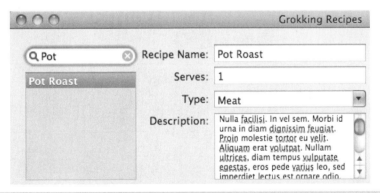

Figure 34—Search filter running against the recipe list

## 8.5 Wrapping Up

Now that we have an understanding of Cocoa Bindings, KVO, and KVC, what else can we add to our desktop application that is specific to the desktop? In Chapter 9, *Spotlight, Quick Look, and Core Data*, on page 153, we will look at additions to our application that will be used *outside* of our application.

# Spotlight, Quick Look, and Core Data

Developing for Mac OS X is about functionality meeting quality. When our applications have one without the other, we leave our users wanting more. They may not be able to define it, but "something" will be missing. Spotlight and Quick Look integration are two of those things that users don't look for when trying a new application but are pleasantly surprised by when they stumble upon them. Surprisingly, not a lot of developers handle this integration. Perhaps it is because Spotlight does not get along with Core Data very well. Perhaps the feature is too abstracted away. But one thing is for certain —integrating with Spotlight is the right move going forward. Spotlight is here to stay, and users will be using it more often and in more creative ways.

Unfortunately, for technical reasons, Spotlight and Core Data are at odds with each other. Spotlight works on the metadata of individual files, and Core Data stores everything in a single file. Because Spotlight is designed to work with the metadata of a file to discover things about the file, it will not work very well with a single file design such as Core Data. When Tiger was first released, there were a number of applications (such as Entourage) that, because of their single file design, did not play nicely with Spotlight. In fact, Apple rearchitected Mail for that reason.

The incompatibility between Spotlight and Core Data was corrected in Snow Leopard but was never backported to Leopard; the correction was for Snow Leopard only and is not backward-compatible with Mac OS X 10.5 Leopard. How? It's in a manner that is very similar to the solution described in this chapter. Going forward, Core Data and Spotlight play nicely together assuming that your application is targeted for Mac OS X 10.6 or newer.

In this chapter, we will integrate Spotlight into our recipes application. Once we are done, our users will be able to search for *Pot Roast* and find it in our application. In addition, when they select that search result, our application will not only open but open to Pot Roast. While we are solving the Spotlight issue, we are also going to take a look at Quick Look. Although on the surface these two technologies appear to be completely different, they are handled in a very similar fashion by Mac OS X and the Finder. And although it is not 100 percent appropriate for our sample application (since we have only a single data file and that data file is hidden away in the Library/Application Support directory), it is very useful to understand how Quick Look works for document-based Core Data applications because it makes them easier to find in Finder, Spotlight, Time Machine, Mail, and many other applications. Lastly, Quick Look and Spotlight integrate rather well together. If our users activate Quick Look on a Spotlight result, we want them to see information about the recipe, not a picture of a generic file.

### Should I Just Use Separate Files?

Throughout this book, the application we are designing uses a single Core Data file. This is done for the sake of clarity and focus on Core Data. Depending on the application that is being designed, it is highly likely that it will be document-based, and therefore it would be appropriate to have one Core Data repository per document. In that situation, Spotlight and Quick Look can be a lot easier to integrate.

However, for applications that are not document-based, it is preferable to use a single Core Data repository, as opposed to individual files. Although individual files make Spotlight easier to work with, they would be the tail wagging the dog. The main focus of object persistence (in other words, data files) is to quickly and easily access the data in a logical and reproducible manner. Core Data solves all those problems quite neatly—with the unfortunate minor wrinkle of not being fully compatible with Spotlight.

## 9.1 Integrating with Spotlight

The issue, as mentioned, is one of multiple files. Ideally, for our recipe application, we want one Spotlight "record" for each recipe in our Core Data repository. For Spotlight to work properly, we would need one file on the disk for each recipe, along with its associated metadata. Therefore, to make Spotlight happy, we will do exactly that. However, since all our data is being stored in a Core Data repository, there is no reason to store any data in these files. These additional files exist purely for Spotlight (and Quick Look) to utilize. Since Spotlight does not need any data in the files to work (it just needs metadata), we will create very simple files and link them back to our Core Data repository.

The other gotcha with Spotlight is that the importer needs to be as fast as possible. What might be acceptable for processing one file or ten files is not going to fly when Spotlight has to chug through thousands of files. Since the same importer that we are writing for use inside our application could potentially be used in a server situation, it needs to be as fast as we can make it. So, we're going to cheat a bit. Instead of looking up the metadata in our Core Data repository upon request from Spotlight, we'll instead store the metadata in the files we are creating for Spotlight. That way, our importer has to touch the metadata files only and does not need to initialize the entire Core Data "stack" (that is, NSManagedObjectContext, NSPersistentStoreCoordinator, and NSManagedObjectModel).

## Creating the Metadata Files

We first need to produce and update the metadata files on the fly. To keep them as simple as possible, we just use plist files, as opposed to a binary representation or some other format. Since NSDictionary understands plist files, it reduces the amount of overhead needed for loading and saving the files.

To begin, let's create our first NSManagedObject subclass. This subclass handles producing the NSDictionary that will contain all the metadata. Since we are creating a subclass, we might as well implement some of the properties we will be using to reduce the code complexity and make it easier to maintain.

Therefore, our header file looks as follows:

```
Spotlight/PPRecipe.h
#import <Cocoa/Cocoa.h>

extern NSString *kPPImagePath;
extern NSString *kPPObjectID;
extern NSString *kPPServes;

@interface PPRecipe : NSManagedObject {

}

@property (assign) NSString *desc;
@property (assign) NSString *name;
@property (assign) NSString *type;
@property (assign) NSManagedObject *author;
@property (assign) NSDate *lastUsed;

- (NSDictionary*)metadata;
- (NSString*)metadataFilename;

@end
```

We need to make sure we change the Class setting in the latest data model so Core Data uses our subclass rather than the default NSManagedObject. See Figure 35, *Changing the entity's class*, on page 156.

**Figure 35—Changing the entity's class**

### Implementing the Metadata Method

The goal of this metadata file is to contain just enough information to populate Spotlight and Quick Look but not so much information that the files become large and cumbersome. We must pretend there will be thousands of these files (even if in reality that would be impractical), and we do not want to impact the users' performance or their hard drive capacity. For our metadata files, we really need only the following information:

- The name of the recipe
- The number of people it serves
- The image for the recipe
- The last time it was served
- The description of how to prepare it

Most of that list is very light—just text. However, the image is probably too large to cram into the plist file, especially since we cannot be sure how large that file will be. In addition, it would complicate the file format by including binary data. Therefore, we will put in the path of the image instead of the actual image. Since the image is stored on disk, we just access that copy.

In addition to this list, we need to add one more item that is not user-facing. We want a way to link back to the recipe record in our Core Data repository so if the user tries to open the metadata file, instead our application will open and select the correct record. To do this, we use the NSManagedObjectID of the recipe and store its URIRepresentation (which is actually an NSURL) as a string in the metadata.

```
Spotlight/PPRecipe.m
- (NSDictionary*)metadata;
{
  NSMutableDictionary *metadataDict = [NSMutableDictionary dictionary];

  [metadataDict setValue:[self name]
              forKey:(id)kMDItemTitle];
  [metadataDict setValue:[self desc]
              forKey:(id)kMDItemTextContent];
  [metadataDict setValue:[[self author] valueForKey:@"name"]
              forKey:(id)kMDItemAuthors];
  [metadataDict setValue:[self valueForKey:@"imagePath"]
              forKey:kPPImagePath];
  [metadataDict setValue:[self lastUsed] forKey:(id)kMDItemLastUsedDate];
  [metadataDict setValue:[self valueForKey:@"serves"] forKey:kPPServes];
  [metadataDict setValue:[NSString stringWithFormat:@"Recipe: %@", [self name]]
              forKey:(id)kMDItemDisplayName];
  [metadataDict setValue:[[[self objectID] URIRepresentation] absoluteString]
              forKey:kPPObjectID];
  return metadataDict;
}
```

### Implementing the metadataName Method

Because we want users to be able to view the actual metadata files in the Finder, the filenames should represent the recipe rather than an abstract name. We use the name attribute of the recipe itself as the filename.

```
Spotlight/PPRecipe.m
- (NSString*)metadataFilename;
{
  return [[self name] stringByAppendingPathExtension:@"grokkingrecipe"];
}
```

### Generating and Updating the Metadata Files

Now that we have an implementation for generating the metadata per recipe, we need to add the ability to populate these files and keep them up-to-date. Ideally, we want to refresh the metadata files every time that the NSManagedObjectContext is saved. To do this, we add a new -save: method to our AppDelegate and route all of our saves through it.

Spotlight/AppDelegate.m

```
- (BOOL)save:(NSError**)error;
{
  NSManagedObjectContext *moc = [self managedObjectContext];
  if (!moc) return YES;

  if (![moc hasChanges]) return YES;

  //Grab a reference to all of the objects we will need to work with
  NSSet *deleted = [moc deletedObjects];
  NSMutableSet *deletedPaths = [NSMutableSet set];
  for (NSManagedObject *object in deleted) {
    if (![object isKindOfClass:[PPRecipe class]]) continue;
    [deletedPaths addObject:[object valueForKey:@"metadataFilename"]];
  }

  NSMutableSet *updated = [NSMutableSet setWithSet:[moc insertedObjects]];
  [updated unionSet:[moc updatedObjects]];

  //Save the context
  if (![moc save:error]) {
    return NO;
  }
  return [self updateMetadataForObjects:updated
                      andDeletedObjects:deletedPaths
                                  error:error];
}
```

In this new -save: method, we are doing a couple of things before calling save on the NSManagedObjectContext. Since the NSManagedObjectContext knows what objects have been deleted, updated, or inserted, we want to grab a reference to that information before the -save: occurs. Once the -save: is complete, that information is no longer available. Therefore, we grab a reference to the NSSet of deleted objects, updated objects, and inserted objects. Because the deleted objects will be, well, deleted once the -save: is performed, we want to extract the information we care about beforehand. So, we loop over the deleted objects looking for Recipe instances. When we find one, we extract its metadataFilename and store it in a new NSMutableSet. In addition, since we will be doing the same thing to the inserted and the updated objects, we merge them into one set. Once we have that information, we go ahead and save the context. If the save fails, we just abort and let the calling code handle the error. When the save is successful, it is time to update the metadata.

Spotlight/AppDelegate.m

```
if ((!updatedObjects || ![updatedObjects count]) &&
    (!deletedObjects || ![deletedObjects count])) return YES;

NSString *path = [self metadataFolder:error];
```

```
if (!path) return NO;

BOOL directory = NO;

NSFileManager *fileManager = [NSFileManager defaultManager];
if (![fileManager fileExistsAtPath:path isDirectory:&directory]) {
  if (![fileManager createDirectoryAtPath:path
              withIntermediateDirectories:YES
                               attributes:nil
                                    error:error]) {
    return NO;
  }
  directory = YES;
}
if (!directory) {
  NSMutableDictionary *errorDict = [NSMutableDictionary dictionary];
  NSString *msg = NSLocalizedString(@"File in place of metadata directory",
    @"metadata directory is a file error description");
  [errorDict setValue:msg forKey:NSLocalizedDescriptionKey];
  *error = [NSError errorWithDomain:@"pragprog" code:1001 userInfo:errorDict];
  return NO;
}
```

Because we want to be in the habit of assuming nothing, let's first check that
there is something to update or delete. Once we are past that check, we next
need to confirm that the cache directory is in place, and either our metadata
directory is in place or we can create it. If any of this fails, we update the
NSError object and return.

```
Spotlight/AppDelegate.m
NSString *filePath = nil;
if (deletedObjects && [deletedObjects count]) {
  for (NSString *filename in deletedObjects) {
    filePath = [path stringByAppendingPathComponent:filename];
    if (![fileManager fileExistsAtPath:filePath]) continue;
    if (![fileManager removeItemAtPath:filePath error:error]) return NO;
  }
}
```

The next part of updating the metadata is to remove any files that are no
longer appropriate. Therefore, if the passed-in deletedObjects set contains any
objects, we need to loop over it. Since we know that the name of the metadata
file is stored in the deletedObjects variable, we append it to the metadata directory path and check for the existence of the file. If it exists, we delete it. (It
may be possible that a recipe got created and deleted without ever being saved
to disk. It's unlikely, but why take chances?) If we run into an issue deleting
the file, we abort the update and let the calling method handle the error.

**Spotlight/AppDelegate.m**
```
if (![updatedObjects] || ![updatedObjects count]) return YES;

NSNumber *_YES = [NSNumber numberWithBool:YES];
NSDictionary *attributesDictionary = [NSDictionary
                                dictionaryWithObject:_YES
                                forKey:NSFileExtensionHidden];
for (id object in updatedObjects) {
  if (![object isKindOfClass:[PPRecipe class]]) continue;
  PPRecipe *recipe = object;
  NSDictionary *metadata = [recipe metadata];
  filePath = [recipe metadataFilename];
  filePath = [path stringByAppendingPathComponent:filePath];
  [metadata writeToFile:filePath atomically:YES];
  [fileManager changeFileAttributes:attributesDictionary atPath:filePath];
}

return YES;
```

The last part of updating the metadata files is to process existing or new recipes. As with the deleted objects earlier, we first check to see whether there are any objects to update, and if there aren't, we are done. If there are new or updated objects, we again loop through the NSSet looking for PPRecipe entities. For each recipe we find, we request its metadata NSDictionary object from the metadata method we created earlier. Using that NSDictionary along with the metadataFilename method, we write the NSDictionary to disk. For one last bit of polish, we update the attributes on the newly created (or updated) file and tell it to hide its file extension. This gives us the cleanest appearance when viewed inside the Finder.

Now that the -save: method has been written, we need to route all the -save: calls that exist to call this method instead of calling -save: directly on the NSManagedObjectContext. Currently, this requires modifying both the -(NSApplication-TerminateReply)applicationShouldTerminate: method and the -(IBAction)saveAction: method. In each case, we just need to change the following:

```
[[self managedObjectContext] save:&error];
```

to a message to the -save: method on the AppDelegate.

```
[self save:&error];
```

There is one last situation we need to handle. If we have existing users and are adding the Spotlight integration after v1.0, we need some way to bring our users up to speed. To do this, we add a check to the -(void)applicationDidFinishLaunching: method. If the metadata directory does not exist, we must do a full push of all the metadata in the persistent store.

```
Spotlight/AppDelegate.m
NSError *error = nil;
NSString *path = [self metadataFolder:&error];
if (!path) {
  NSLog(@"%@:%s Error resolving cache path: %@", [self class], _cmd, error);
  return;
}
if ([[NSFileManager defaultManager] fileExistsAtPath:path]) return;

NSManagedObjectContext *moc = [self managedObjectContext];
NSFetchRequest *request = [[[NSFetchRequest alloc] init] autorelease];
[request setEntity:[NSEntityDescription entityForName:@"Recipe"
                              inManagedObjectContext:moc]];

NSSet *recipes = [NSSet setWithArray:[moc executeFetchRequest:request
                                              error:&error]];
if (error) {
  NSLog(@"%@:%s Error: %@", [self class], _cmd, error);
  return;
}
[self updateMetadataForObjects:recipes andDeletedObjects:nil error:&error];
if (error) {
  NSLog(@"%@:%s Error: %@", [self class], _cmd, error);
  return;
}
```

Here we are looking for the metadata cache directory, and if it does not exist, we fetch every recipe entity in the persistent store and pass the NSSet to our metadata-building method. This also protects us from users who like to periodically delete their cache directory. This method calls the -metadataFolder method to determine where the metadata should be stored.

```
Spotlight/AppDelegate.m
- (NSString*)metadataFolder:(NSError**)error
{
  NSString *path = [NSSearchPathForDirectoriesInDomains(NSCachesDirectory,
                                              NSUserDomainMask, YES)
                    lastObject];
  if (!path) {
    NSMutableDictionary *errorDict = [NSMutableDictionary dictionary];
    [errorDict setValue:NSLocalizedString(@"Failed to locate caches directory",
                                  @"caches directory error description")
              forKey:NSLocalizedDescriptionKey];
    *error = [NSError errorWithDomain:@"pragprog" code:1000 userInfo:errorDict];
    return nil;
  }
  path = [path stringByAppendingPathComponent:@"Metadata"];
  path = [path stringByAppendingPathComponent:@"GrokkingRecipes"];
  return path;
}
```

In the -metadataFolder, we first request a list of the cache directories from the NSSearchPathForDirectoriesInDomain method and append the path components Metadata and GrokkingRecipes to it. We do not check to see whether the path exists at this point but instead let our caller decide how to handle that.

## Creating the Spotlight Importer

Now that we have some metadata to work with, it's time to build the Spotlight importer. To start this part of the application, we need to first address UTIs.

### Uniform Type Identifiers (UTIs)

Both Spotlight and Quick Look use UTIs rather than filename extensions to connect files on disk with (Spotlight) importers and (Quick Look) generators. A UTI is a unique string that identifies the type of data stored in a given file. It is recommended that UTIs identify the company and application that created the data file, and like bundle identifiers, a reverse domain name is ideal for this purpose. (It should be noted that bundle identifiers are in fact UTIs themselves.) Since our application uses com.pragprog.grokkingrecipes as its unique bundle identifier, we will use the same UTI as the value of the LSItemContentTypes to identify the files.

```
Spotlight/Info.plist
<key>CFBundleDocumentTypes</key>
<array>
        <dict>
                <key>CFBundleTypeExtensions</key>
                <array>
                        <string>grokkingrecipe</string>
                </array>
                <key>CFBundleTypeIconFile</key>
                <string>book.icns</string>
                <key>CFBundleTypeName</key>
                <string>Grokking Recipe</string>
                <key>CFBundleTypeRole</key>
                <string>Editor</string>
                <key>LSItemContentTypes</key>
                <array>
                        <string>com.pragprog.grokkingrecipe</string>
                </array>
                <key>NSPersistentStoreTypeKey</key>
                <string>XML</string>
        </dict>
</array>
```

The UTExportedTypeDeclarations section is probably very familiar. Xcode generates it to describe any file that is handled by the application being built. The one difference is that, instead of defining a file extension (like .txt), we are defining a UTI that is being handled by our application. Since this UTI is unknown by the system, we need to describe it, again in our Info.plist file.

Spotlight/Info.plist

```
<key>UTExportedTypeDeclarations</key>
<array>
        <dict>
                <key>UTTypeConformsTo</key>
                <array>
                        <string>public.data</string>
                        <string>public.content</string>
                </array>
                <key>UTTypeDescription</key>
                <string>Grokking Recipe</string>
                <key>UTTypeIdentifier</key>
                <string>com.pragprog.grokkingrecipe</string>
                <key>UTTypeTagSpecification</key>
                <dict>
                        <key>public.filename-extension</key>
                        <string>grokkingrecipe</string>
                </dict>
        </dict>
</array>
```

This key describes exporting our UTI and tells Mac OS X how to link it to different file extensions. In addition, this section describes the data to Mac OS X, telling the OS a descriptive name for the data type and where in the UTI tree it fits.[1]

## Xcode Subproject

Our Spotlight importer is actually its own application. Xcode handles this with a separate project for the importer. (It is actually possible to include the plug-in as part of the main application project, but I have found that to be more hassle than it is worth.) Since we want to include the importer as part of our primary application and we do not want to have to remember to rebuild the subproject every time we build our main project, we will set it up as a dependent or subproject within our primary project. To do this, we start with creating a project in Xcode and selecting the Spotlight importer, as shown in Figure 36, *Select the Spotlight template*, on page 164.

We want to save this project in a directory inside our primary recipe project, and we don't want to be too clever. We'll give the subproject an obvious name like SpotlightPlugin and include it with the Spotlight example project. To make

---

1. For more information on UTIs, I suggest reviewing http://developer.apple.com/library/ios/#documentation/general/conceptual/DevPedia-CocoaCore/UniformTypeIdentifier.html.

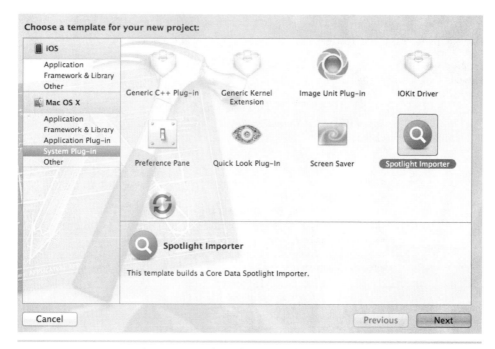

**Figure 36—Select the Spotlight template.**

Xcode build this plug-in every time we build the main project, we need to link the two together. This is accomplished with the following steps:

1. Drag the subproject into the main project. See Figure 37, *Drag the subproject into the main project*, on page 165.
2. Open the target in the main project, and select the General tab.
3. Add the subproject as a dependency.
4. Add a new copy phase to the main project's target, and set its destination to wrapper and path to Contents/Library/Spotlight.
5. Drag the Spotlight plug-in into the new build phase. See Figure 38, *Drag the plug-in into its build phase*, on page 165.

Now, whenever we clean or build the main project, the subproject is cleaned/built. Taking this step also allows the subproject to be built with the same settings as the primary project.

### Linking the Spotlight Importer to the UTI

With our Spotlight importer subproject in place, it is time to link the importer to the UTI for our metadata files. To do this, we need to update the Info.plist of our Spotlight subproject to let the operating system know which UTIs this importer handles.

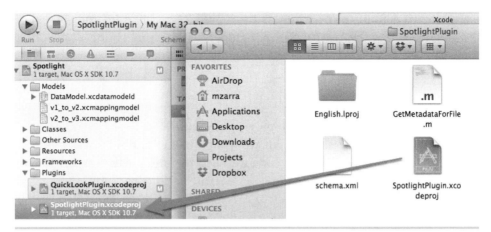

**Figure 37—Drag the subproject into the main project.**

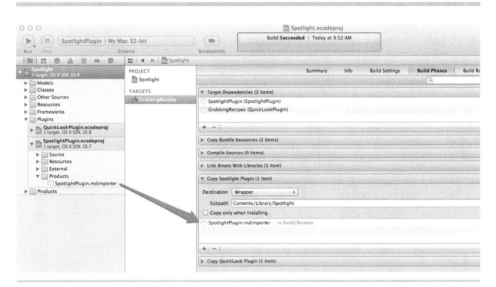

**Figure 38—Drag the plug-in into its build phase.**

```
<array>
  <dict>
    <key>CFBundleTypeRole</key>
    <string>MDImporter</string>
    <key>LSItemContentTypes</key>
    <array>
      <string>com.pragprog.grokkingrecipe</string>
    </array>
  </dict>
</array>
```

Here, we are defining our plug-in as having an MDImporter role, and the list of UTIs contains just the one for our metadata file. With this change, Mac OS X knows to use this importer to retrieve the information for our metadata files.

### Building the Spotlight Importer

Now that everything is connected, it is time to build the importer. Fortunately, this is the easiest and shortest part of the entire process. The Spotlight template created the main.m file that we will be using, and it contains all the boilerplate code for us. The only code we need to write for the importer is in the GetMetadataForFile.m file. The template generates a GetMetadataForFile.c file, and that file will not accept any Objective-C code. Since I prefer Objective-C over straight C, the first thing I did was rename the .c file to an .m file. This tells Xcode to compile it as Objective-C rather than C. Since we will be using Foundation APIs, we need to include Foundation.framework as well.

**Spotlight/SpotlightPlugin/GetMetadataForFile.m**

```
#include <CoreFoundation/CoreFoundation.h>
#include <CoreServices/CoreServices.h>

#import <Foundation/Foundation.h>

Boolean GetMetadataForFile(void* thisInterface,
                           CFMutableDictionaryRef attributes,
                           CFStringRef contentTypeUTI,
                           CFStringRef pathToFile)
{
  NSAutoreleasePool *pool = [[NSAutoreleasePool alloc] init];
  NSDictionary *metadata;
  metadata = [NSDictionary dictionaryWithContentsOfFile:(NSString*)pathToFile];
  for (NSString *key in [metadata allKeys]) {
    [(id)attributes setObject:[metadata objectForKey:key] forKey:key];
  }
  [pool release], pool = nil;
  return TRUE;
}
```

The actual code for the importer is almost laughably simple. We are just loading the metadata file back into an NSDictionary, looping over the keys using the allKeys method, and adding each associated value to the passed-in CFMutableDictionaryRef. Once we are done with the NSDictionary, we return TRUE and are done. Since we are running inside a C function, we need to wrap the entire procedure in an NSAutoreleasePool so that we are not leaking any memory.

### Testing the Spotlight Importer

There are a couple of ways to test the importer to make sure everything is working properly. The first thing we need to do is generate the metadata files, which we accomplish by running our application. Once the metadata files are created, we can test the importer.

We can get a lot of information about our importer directly on the command line. Mac OS X includes a command-line tool called mdimport. A quick review of the man page reveals there are three switches for this command that are of immediate use. First, we need to tell Spotlight to load our importer.

```
mdimport -r ${path to our project}/build/Debug/GrokkingRecipes.app/
   Contents/Library/Spotlight/SpotlightPlugin.mdimporter
```

Once Spotlight is aware of our importer, we can start querying it, again from the command line using the mdimport command.

```
cd ~/Library/Caches/Metadata/GrokkingRecipes
mdimport -d2 Test.grokkingrecipe
```

We can change the debug level from 1 to 4 to display different quantities of information about the metadata file. Level 2 tells us that the importer is working and gives us a basic summary of the data contained inside the file.

The other way to test the importer is to just search for one of our recipes! Click the spotlight magnifying glass in the upper-right corner, and enter the name of one of the recipes, as in Figure 39, *The Pot Roast recipe in Spotlight*, on page 167. But what happens when we try to open this file?

Figure 39—The Pot Roast recipe in Spotlight

## Accepting Metadata Files

Since we linked our metadata files to the primary application, Mac OS X attempts to open our application and pass the file to us. However, we have no way of handling that yet.

```
Spotlight/AppDelegate.m
- (BOOL)application:(NSApplication*)theApplication
           openFile:(NSString*)filename
{
  NSDictionary *metadata = [NSDictionary dictionaryWithContentsOfFile:filename];
  NSString *objectIDString = [metadata valueForKey:(id)kPPObjectID];
  NSURL *objectURI = [NSURL URLWithString:objectIDString];
  NSPersistentStoreCoordinator *coordinator;
  coordinator = [[self managedObjectContext] persistentStoreCoordinator];

  NSManagedObjectID *objectID;
  objectID = [coordinator managedObjectIDForURIRepresentation:objectURI];

  NSManagedObject *recipe = [[self managedObjectContext] objectWithID:objectID];
  if (!recipe) return NO;

  dispatch_async(dispatch_get_main_queue(), ^{
    NSArray *array = [NSArray arrayWithObject:recipe];
    [[self recipeArrayController] setSelectedObjects:array];
  });

  return YES;
}
```

In our application delegate, we need to add the method -(BOOL)application:openFile: that will be called when the operating system attempts to open one of our metadata files. In that method, we load the metadata file into an NSDictionary and retrieve the URIRepresentation of the NSManagedObjectID. With the NSManagedObjectID in hand, we can load the represented Recipe entity and display it to the user. Since we want to return from this method as quickly as possible (the operating system is waiting on an answer), we display the recipe *after* we return from this method.

To do that, we wrap the call to display the recipe in a dispatch_async, which updates the recipeArrayController with the selected recipe and allows the UI to update. By doing a dispatch_async and putting the execution block onto the main queue, we are effectively telling the OS to please run the block right after the current runloop completes.

With that code in place, we can select a recipe from Spotlight, and our application opens with the correct recipe selected. The first part of our OS integration is now in place.

## 9.2  Integrating with Quick Look

There are two different ways to implement Quick Look. The application can generate images as part of the data bundle, or a generator can be written that generates the images on the fly. Storing images with the data is viable only if the data is stored in a bundle similar to the way that Pages or Numbers does. When the data is stored in a flat file, like our metadata files, a generator is the only way to integrate with Quick Look. Fortunately, writing a Quick Look generator is only slightly more complicated than a Spotlight importer.

### Adding the Subproject

Just like the Spotlight importer, the Quick Look generator is created within its own subproject.

Like the Spotlight importer subproject we added earlier, we need to perform the following steps:

1. Create a subproject under our recipes project. Again, I gave mine the very clever title of QuickLookPlugin.

2. Drag the project into the main project, and flag it as a dependency.

3. Add a new copy phase to the main project's target, and set its destination to wrapper and path to Contents/Library/QuickLook.

4. Drag the Quick Look plug-in into the new build phase.

If any of these steps are confusing, please see *Xcode Subproject*, on page 163. Once the Quick Look subproject has been added, the main project's tree should look similar to Figure 40, *The Xcode project tree with all plug-ins added*, on page 170.

Once the subproject has been set up properly, we will go ahead and rename the two .c files to .m files so that we can use Objective-C inside them. We need to also add Foundation.framework to the subproject so that we can utilize the Foundation APIs.

Unlike Spotlight, Quick Look has two components. There is a thumbnail generation and a preview generation. The thumbnail is used by the Finder both in place of a standard file icon and in Cover Flow. The preview is used when Quick Look is invoked in Finder, Mail, and so on. Therefore, the Quick Look template creates two .c (now .m) files, one for each. Let's tackle the thumbnail file first.

### Generating the Quick Look Thumbnail

The file GenerateThumbnailForURL.m has one function inside it that is called by the Quick Look manager (part of the operating system). This function expects we will be populating the QLThumbnailRequestRef and returning the OSStatus of noErr.

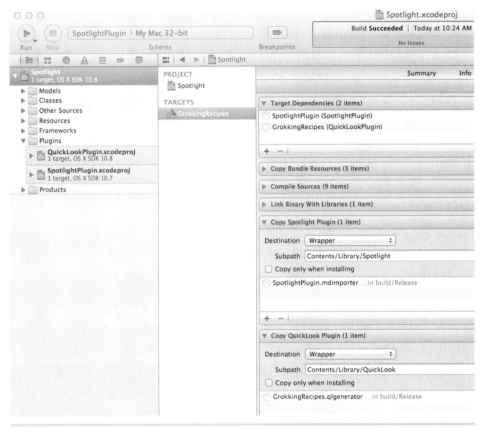

**Figure 40—The Xcode project tree with all plug-ins added**

Based on the documentation for Quick Look, even if we suffer a complete failure inside our plug-in, we should always return noErr.

As you can probably guess, our thumbnail generation code is going to be very simple. Since we already have an image included with each recipe, we are simply going to pass that image back whenever it is requested.

**Spotlight/QuickLookPlugin/GenerateThumbnailForURL.m**
```
OSStatus GenerateThumbnailForURL(void *thisInterface,
                                 QLThumbnailRequestRef thumbnail,
                                 CFURLRef url,
                                 CFStringRef contentTypeUTI,
                                 CFDictionaryRef options,
                                 CGSize maxSize)
{
  NSAutoreleasePool *pool = [[NSAutoreleasePool alloc] init];
  @try {
    NSDictionary *metadata;
```

```
    metadata = [NSDictionary dictionaryWithContentsOfURL:(NSURL*)url];
    NSString *pathToImage = [metadata valueForKey:@"kPPImagePath"];
    if (!pathToImage) {
      //No image available
      return noErr;
    }
    NSData *imageData = [NSData dataWithContentsOfFile:pathToImage];
    if (!imageData) {
      //Unable to load the data for some reason.
      return noErr;
    }
    QLThumbnailRequestSetImageWithData(thumbnail, (CFDataRef)imageData, NULL);
  } @finally {
    [pool release], pool = nil;
  }
  return noErr;
}
```

In this method, we are again retrieving the metadata file and loading it into an NSDictionary. From that dictionary, we are retrieving the path to the image for the recipe and loading the image into an NSData object. From there, we call the QLThumbnailRequestSetImageWithData(QLThumbnailRequestRef, CFDataRect, CFDictionaryRef) method, which populates the QLThumbnailRequestRef. After that is done, we pop the NSAutoreleasePool and return noErr. From there, Quick Look uses the image we have provided whenever it needs a thumbnail for the file.

### Generating the Quick Look Preview

The Quick Look preview is understandably more complex than generating a thumbnail image. If we do absolutely nothing for this part of Quick Look, we would still get a rather satisfying preview, as shown in the figure below. But why stop there when we can do so much more?

Like the thumbnail generator in *Generating the Quick Look Thumbnail*, on page 169, the preview generator is contained within one function call, and we are expected to populate the QLPreviewRequestRef and return noErr. Also, like the thumbnail generator, we will always return noErr no matter what happens within our function call.

Unlike the thumbnail generator, we are not going to be working with just the image for the recipe. Instead, we will generate a full HTML page that contains a large amount of information about the recipe and use that as our preview. Although it would be possible to generate the entire HTML page in code, I am rather lazy and would rather avoid that. Instead, let's take advantage of some XPath queries to locate the correct nodes inside a template HTML file, change the values to be appropriate for our current recipe, and use that to generate the QLPreviewRequestRef.

**Spotlight/QuickLookPlugin/GeneratePreviewForURL.m**
```
NSString *bundleID = @"com.pragprog.quicklook.grokkingrecipe";

OSStatus GeneratePreviewForURL(void *thisInterface,
                               QLPreviewRequestRef preview,
                               CFURLRef url,
                               CFStringRef contentTypeUTI,
                               CFDictionaryRef options)
{
  NSAutoreleasePool *pool = [[NSAutoreleasePool alloc] init];
  @try {
    NSDictionary *metadata;
    metadata = [NSDictionary dictionaryWithContentsOfURL:(NSURL*)url];
    if (!metadata) return noErr;
    NSLog(@"metadata: %@", metadata);

    NSString *imagePath = [metadata valueForKey:@"kPPImagePath"];
    NSData *imageData = [[NSData alloc] initWithContentsOfFile:imagePath];
    if (!imageData) return noErr;
```

To start with, we load the metadata dictionary as we have previously. We are also going to load the image data into an NSData object again. Assuming there are no issues with either the metadata or the image loading, the next step is to set up the options for the HTML page.

**Spotlight/QuickLookPlugin/GeneratePreviewForURL.m**
```
NSMutableDictionary *imageDict = [NSMutableDictionary dictionary];
[imageDict setValue:imageData
             forKey:(id)kQLPreviewPropertyAttachmentDataKey];

if (QLPreviewRequestIsCancelled(preview)) return noErr;

NSMutableDictionary *attachments = [NSMutableDictionary dictionary];
```

```
[attachments setValue:imageDict forKey:@"preview-image"];

NSMutableDictionary *properties = [NSMutableDictionary dictionary];
[properties setValue:attachments
            forKey:(id)kQLPreviewPropertyAttachmentsKey];
[properties setValue:@"text/html"
            forKey:(id)kQLPreviewPropertyMIMETypeKey];
[properties setValue:@"UTF-8"
            forKey:(id)kQLPreviewPropertyTextEncodingNameKey];
[properties setValue:@"Recipe"
            forKey:(id)kQLPreviewPropertyDisplayNameKey];
```

For Quick Look to be able to use the HTML page that we are handing to it, it requires that we describe the document and include any attachments it has. This helps improve the performance of the HTML rendering, since it does not have to fetch any of the attachments. Therefore, in this section, we are setting up the properties for the HTML page, including specifying its encoding, the MIME type, and the attachments. We also give it a display name that will be used outside the HTML page.

**Spotlight/QuickLookPlugin/GeneratePreviewForURL.m**
```
NSBundle *bundle = [NSBundle bundleWithIdentifier:bundleID];
NSString *templatePath = [bundle pathForResource:@"preview" ofType:@"html"];
NSURL *templateURL = [NSURL fileURLWithPath:templatePath];

NSError *error = nil;
NSXMLDocument *template;
template = [[[NSXMLDocument alloc] initWithContentsOfURL:(NSURL*)templateURL
                                          options:NSXMLDocumentTidyHTML
                                            error:&error] autorelease];
if (!template) {
  NSLog(@"Failed to build template: %@", error);
  return noErr;
}
```

Once all the preliminaries are complete, we need to retrieve the HTML template from our bundle. Since this code is not actually being called from our bundle, we cannot just perform [NSBundle mainBundle] and get a reference to our NSBundle. (If we tried, we would actually get a reference to /usr/bin/qlmanage!) Instead, we have to request it by its UTI. With a reference to the bundle, we can then retrieve the path to preview.html, which we will be using as our template. Once we have loaded the HTML file into an NSXMLDocument, it is time to substitute the placeholders in that file with real data.

**Spotlight/QuickLookPlugin/GeneratePreviewForURL.m**
```
//Updating the Title
error = nil;
NSXMLElement *element = [[template nodesForXPath:
```

```objc
                                    @"/html/body/div/*[@id='title']"
                                          error:&error] lastObject];
if (!element) {
  NSLog(@"Failed to find element: %@", error);
  return noErr;
}
[element setStringValue:[metadata valueForKey:(id)kMDItemDisplayName]];

//Updating the description
error = nil;
element = [[template nodesForXPath:@"/html/body/div/*[@id='description']"
                            error:&error] lastObject];
if (!element) {
  NSLog(@"Failed to find element: %@", error);
  return noErr;
}
[element setStringValue:[metadata valueForKey:(id)kMDItemTextContent]];

//Updating the serves value
error = nil;
element = [[template nodesForXPath:@"/html/body/div/*[@id='serves']"
                            error:&error] lastObject];
if (!element) {
  NSLog(@"Failed to find element: %@", error);
  return noErr;
}
NSNumber *serves = [metadata valueForKey:@"kPPServes"];
[element setStringValue:[NSString stringWithFormat:@"Serves: %i",
                        [serves integerValue]]];

//Updating the last served value
error = nil;
element = [[template nodesForXPath:@"/html/body/div/*[@id='last_served']"
                            error:&error] lastObject];
if (!element) {
  NSLog(@"Failed to find element: %@", error);
  return noErr;
}
NSDate *lastServedDate = [metadata valueForKey:(id)kMDItemLastUsedDate];
if (lastServedDate) {
  NSDateFormatter *dateFormatter;
  dateFormatter = [[[NSDateFormatter alloc] init]  autorelease];
  [dateFormatter setDateStyle:NSDateFormatterMediumStyle];
  [dateFormatter setTimeStyle:NSDateFormatterNoStyle];
  [element setStringValue:[NSString stringWithFormat:@"Last Served: %@",
                          [dateFormatter stringFromDate:lastServedDate]]];
} else {
  [element setStringValue:@"Last Served: Never"];
}
```

Since we know the shape of the HTML document, we can build simple XPath queries to retrieve each part of the document and replace its value component with data from our metadata in NSDictionary.

```
Spotlight/QuickLookPlugin/GeneratePreviewForURL.m
    QLPreviewRequestSetDataRepresentation(preview,
                                         (CFDataRef)[template XMLData],
                                         kUTTypeHTML,
                                         (CFDictionaryRef)properties);
  } @finally {
    [pool release], pool = nil;
  }
  return noErr;
}
```

Once all the data has been put into the HTML document, it is time to render it and set the QLPreviewRequestRef. As this section of code shows, we are passing in the reference along with the HTML file as data and the property NSDictionary. When this is complete, we pop the NSAutoreleasePool and return noErr. Quick Look now generates our preview and presents it to the user.

### Testing the Quick Look Plug-In

At the time of this writing, testing the Quick Look plug-in is a little more challenging than testing its Spotlight counterpart. Although there is a command-line option to test it, getting the system to recognize the plug-in is a bit trickier. The issue is that the system tends to ignore what generator we want it to use and will use the generator defined for the system.

In writing this chapter, I used the following workflow to test the Quick Look plug-in:

1. Clean and build the main recipe application.

2. On the command line, execute qlmanage -r to reset the Quick Look generators.

3. Run the recipe application, which causes our Quick Look generator to get registered.

4. From the command line (can also be done in Xcode), I ran qlmanage -p ${path to metadata test file}, which generated the preview. Using the -t switch instead would produce the thumbnail.

5. Rinse and repeat.

## 9.3 Putting It All Together

With a Spotlight importer and a Quick Look generator, it is possible to do some very interesting things in Mac OS X. For example, we can build a smart folder that finds all our recipes. We can then put that smart folder in the sidebar of Finder and easily access all our recipes directly from the Finder. Further, we can turn on Cover Flow for this smart folder and smoothly browse through the pictures of our recipes, as shown here:

With the included metadata, this opens up quite a few ideas. For example, along with each recipe, we are storing the time it was last served in the metadata. We can use this information to further refine our smart folder to display only those recipes that we have not served in the last thirty days. It is possible to get quite creative with metadata now that the operating system is aware of it.

## 9.4 Wrapping Up

With UTIs, it is possible to integrate even further with the operating system, Spotlight, and Quick Look. It is possible to publish a full description of the UTI—effectively injecting it into the tree and thus having the data type appear in Spotlight rules and more. However, this is beyond the scope of this book.

### Decreasing the Size of the Metadata Files

Depending on the application, it is possible to reduce the metadata files dramatically. Since the importer (and the generator) can stand up the entire Core

Data stack, it is possible to just have the `NSManaged-ObjectID` (or even a unique identifier within the `Recipe` object) stored in the metadata file and have the importers and generators retrieve all the metadata information from the Core Data stack instead. (This is probably very similar to how Core Data does it internally.) This would also simplify the updating of the metadata, since the only action required at that point would be to delete metadata files for records that no longer exist. However, care must be taken with this approach because performance may suffer greatly.

### Improving the Quick Look Thumbnail Generator

You may have noticed that we ignored the Max Size setting of the Quick Look thumbnail generator. That was done for the sake of clarity, and in a production system we should be sizing down the image to accommodate that setting. By doing so, we would be good citizens as well as be helping the performance of Quick Look whenever our files are involved.

### Document-Based Applications

When writing an application that uses a document model as opposed to a single repository, integrating Spotlight and Quick Look is even easier. Instead of having separate metadata files, we can simply store the relevant information in the metadata of the actual documents. This allows the importers to read the metadata without having to initialize the entire Core Data stack and still allows for very quick access to the relevant information.

# CHAPTER 10

# Dynamic Parameters

If you have a document-style application, you will need to work with document-specific parameters or settings. For example, in a word processor, some settings are specific to one document, and some settings apply to the entire application. We have access to a great implementation for storing application-level parameters: NSUserDefaults. However, there is no reusable storage system for document-level parameters provided by the APIs. In this chapter, we'll build that reusable storage system within Core Data.

System-level and user-level preferences are extremely useful and easy to access on OS X. One call to standardDefaults on NSUserDefaults from anywhere in the application instantly gives you access to the defaults for the currently logged in user. However, sometimes we don't want to store preferences at the user level but would prefer to store them at the file level.

When working with a Core Data application, the natural first solution may seem to be to create a table for these parameters and access them from within the Core Data API. The problem with this solution occurs when we are accessing those parameters. No longer is it a single call to standardDefaults on NSUserDefaults; now it looks more like this:

**CDPreferences/MyDocument.m**
```objc
- (void)clunkyParameterAccess
{
  NSManagedObjectContext *moc = [self managedObjectContext];
  NSFetchRequest *request = [[NSFetchRequest alloc] init];
  [request setEntity:[NSEntityDescription entityForName:@"parameter"
                                 inManagedObjectContext:moc]];
  [request setPredicate:[NSPredicate predicateWithFormat:@"name == %@",
                       @"default1"]];
  NSError *error = nil;
  NSManagedObject *param = [[moc executeFetchRequest:request
                                               error:&error] lastObject];
```

```
if (error) {
  DLog(@"Error fetching param: %@\n%@", [error localizedDescription],
      [error userInfo]);
  return;
}

NSLog(@"Parameter value %@", [param valueForKey:@"value"]);
}
```

Worse is when we need to *set* a parameter.

CDPreferences/MyDocument.m
```
- (void)clunkyParameterWrite
{
  NSManagedObjectContext *moc = [self managedObjectContext];
  NSFetchRequest *request = [[NSFetchRequest alloc] init];
  [request setEntity:[NSEntityDescription entityForName:@"parameter"
                                 inManagedObjectContext:moc]];

  [request setPredicate:[NSPredicate predicateWithFormat:@"name == %@",
                      @"default1"]];

  NSError *error = nil;
  NSManagedObject *param = [[moc executeFetchRequest:request
                                               error:&error] lastObject];
  if (error) {
    DLog(@"Error fetching param: %@\n%@", [error localizedDescription],
        [error userInfo]);
    return;
  }
  if (!param) {
    param = [NSEntityDescription insertNewObjectForEntityForName:@"Parameter"
                                      inManagedObjectContext:moc];
    [param setValue:@"default1" forKey:@"name"];
  }
  [param setValue:@"SomeValue" forKey:@"value"];
}
```

The most obvious answer to this problem is to abstract away most of the code somewhere so we can hit it with only one line of code. Wouldn't it be nice if we could access our document-level parameters with code like this:

CDPreferences/MyDocument.m
```
if ([[[self preferences] valueForKey:@"default1"] boolValue]) {
  //Do something clever
}
```

and be able to set them with something like this:

CDPreferences/MyDocument.m
```
[[self preferences] setValue:@"New Value" forKey:@"newKey"];
```

In this example, that is exactly what we are going to do. As we discussed briefly in Chapter 8, *OS X: Bindings, KVC, and KVO*, on page 137, every object responds to the -valueForUndefinedKey: and -setValue:forUndefinedKey: methods. We can use (or abuse) these methods and make them do all of the heavy lifting for us.

## 10.1 Building the Xcode Example Project

To start this project, we'll use the Core Data Document-based Application template from within Xcode. In a document-based application, each document object has its own Core Data stack, as opposed to a single Core Data stack for the entire application.

Once we have created the project, named CDPreferences, we need to create the data model. For this example, we are going to focus only on the parameters and build the parameters table shown in Figure 41, *Parameter table model*, on page 181. Each parameter has two properties: a name that is a nonoptional string and a value that is an optional string. By making the value optional, we can have parameters that are nullable.

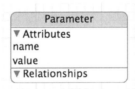

Figure 41—Parameter table model

With no additional code changes, our application will correctly start up and display an empty document. Since each document has its own persistent store, the persistent store becomes the document that is being saved to disk. The next step is to build the object that will manage the parameters.

## 10.2 The DocumentPreferences Object

To build a system that imitates the NSUserDefaults, we need to have a single object that manages the parameters table for us. By doing so, we can treat the entire parameters table as if it were a single object with a dynamic number of accessors. However, we do not want to have to write an accessor every time that we add a parameter; ideally, we want to just call -valueForKey: and -setValue:forKey: and not worry about the persistence of these values. Lastly, we want to be able to set up some default values.

An important point about the defaults is that they are not persisted to disk. If they get persisted, then later versions that change the default would require additional code to check for persisted defaults and reset them. If, however, we do not persist them, users of newer versions of the application automatically get the newer defaults for free and, more importantly, do not get their preferences destroyed if they have changed the value from its default.

The DocumentPreferences object accomplishes all of these goals.

CDPreferences/DocumentPreferences.h

```
@interface DocumentPreferences : NSObject
{
  NSDictionary *_defaults;
  NSPersistentDocument *_associatedDocument;
}
@property (assign) NSPersistentDocument *associatedDocument;
@property (assign) NSDictionary *defaults;
- (id)initWithDocument:(NSPersistentDocument*)associatedDocument;
- (NSArray*)allParameterNames;
- (NSDictionary*)allParameters;
@end
```

Our DocumentPreferences object expects to receive a reference to its NSPersistentDocument upon initialization. From the passed-in reference, our DocumentPreferences will be able to access the underlying NSManagedObjectContext. We could also just incorporate this design directly into a subclass of NSPersistentDocument; however, that can cause the document object to become quite large and difficult to maintain. Therefore, even though there is a one-to-one relationship between NSPersistentDocument objects and DocumentPreferences objects, we keep them separate to reduce code complexity.

The one thing that's missing from this header file is any way to access the parameters themselves. There are no methods for this access because we are going to take advantage of KVC. Whenever another piece of code requests a parameter from our DocumentPreferences object, the -valueForUndefinedKey: method is called, and that is where we handle access to the parameters table.

### -valueForUndefinedKey:

CDPreferences/DocumentPreferences.m

```
- (id)valueForUndefinedKey:(NSString*)key
{
  id parameter = [self findParameter:key];
  if (!parameter && [[self defaults] objectForKey:key]) {
    return [[self defaults] objectForKey:key];
  }
  return [parameter valueForKey:@"value"];
}
```

In this method, we receive the name of the value that the caller is attempting to retrieve. We use this name to retrieve the NSManagedObject via the -findParameter: method and return the NSManagedObject object's value property. If there is no parameter with the passed-in name, we check the defaults NSDictionary to see whether there is a default for it. If there is no default set, we let the -valueForKey: method return nil to the caller.

### -findParameter:

```
CDPreferences/DocumentPreferences.m
- (NSManagedObject*)findParameter:(NSString*)name;
{
  NSManagedObjectContext *moc;
  NSManagedObject *param;
  NSError *error = nil;
  moc = [[self associatedDocument] managedObjectContext];
  NSFetchRequest *request = [[NSFetchRequest alloc] init];
  [request setEntity:[NSEntityDescription entityForName:@"Parameter"
                                inManagedObjectContext:moc]];
  [request setPredicate:[NSPredicate predicateWithFormat:@"name == %@", name]];

  param = [[moc executeFetchRequest:request error:&error] lastObject];
  if (error) {
    DLog(@"Error fetching parameter: %@\n%@", [error localizedDescription],
        [error userInfo]);
    return nil;
  }
  [request release], request = nil;
  return param;
}
```

In the -findParameter: method, we construct an NSFetchRequest against the parameters table using a compare on the name property to filter it down to a single result. Assuming there is no error on the fetch, we return the NSManagedObject. In this method, we are using the -lastObject method on the resulting array as a convenience. -lastObject automatically checks for an empty array and returns nil if the array is empty. This reduces the code complexity and gives us the result we want in a single call. If there is an error accessing the Core Data stack, we report the error and return nil. Note that we do not create a parameter if there is not one in this method. We intentionally separate this out so that we are not creating potentially empty parameters. This allows us to request a parameter and check whether it is nil without the concern of parameters being generated unnecessarily.

## -setValue:forUndefinedKey:

CDPreferences/DocumentPreferences.m

```
- (void)setValue:(id)value forUndefinedKey:(NSString*)key
{
  [self willChangeValueForKey:key];
  NSManagedObject *parameter = [self findParameter:key];
  if (!parameter) {
    if ([[self defaults] valueForKey:key] &&
        [value isEqualTo:[[self defaults] valueForKey:key]]) {
      [self didChangeValueForKey:key];
      return;
    }
    parameter = [self createParameter:key];
  } else {
    if ([[self defaults] valueForKey:key] &&
        [value isEqualTo:[[self defaults] valueForKey:key]]) {
      [self willChangeValueForKey:key];
      [[[self associatedDocument] managedObjectContext] deleteObject:parameter];
      [self didChangeValueForKey:key];
      return;
    }
  }
  if ([value isKindOfClass:[NSNumber class]]) {
    [parameter setValue:[value stringValue] forKey:@"value"];
  } else if ([value isKindOfClass:[NSDate class]]) {
    [parameter setValue:[value description] forKey:@"value"];
  } else {
    [parameter setValue:value forKey:@"value"];
  }
  [self didChangeValueForKey:key];
}
```

In addition to being able to access a parameter, we also need to set parameters. This is done in the counterpart method of -valueForUndefinedKey: called -setValue:forUndefinedKey:. In this method, we first notify the system we are going to be changing the value associated with the passed-in key. This is part of KVO and is required so that notifications work correctly. After starting the KVO notification, we attempt to retrieve the NSManagedObject from the parameters table. If there is no NSManagedObject for the passed-in key, we check the defaults NSDictionary to see whether there is a default. If there is a default set and the passed-in value matches the default, we complete the KVO notification and return. If the default value does not match the passed-in value, we create a new NSManagedObject for the passed-in key.

If there is an NSManagedObject and a default set for the key, we compare the default value to the passed-in value. If they match, we *delete* the NSManagedObject, which effectively resets the parameter to the default. Once we pass the checks against the default and/or create the NSManagedObject, we test the value to see whether it is an NSNumber or NSDate. If it is, we pass in its -stringValue or -description as the value for the NSManagedObject. Otherwise, we pass in the value directly to the NSManagedObject. Once the value is set, we call -didChangeValueForKey: to complete the KVO notification.

### -createParameter:

CDPreferences/DocumentPreferences.m
```
- (NSManagedObject*)createParameter:(NSString*)name
{
  NSManagedObject *param;
  NSManagedObjectContext *moc;
  moc = [[self associatedDocument] managedObjectContext];
  param = [NSEntityDescription insertNewObjectForEntityForName:@"Parameter"
                                     inManagedObjectContext:moc];
  [param setValue:name forKey:@"name"];
  return param;
}
```

The -createParameter: method creates a new NSManagedObject and sets the name property with the passed-in value. It does not set the value property, leaving that up to the caller. This allows us to set a nil parameter if we really need one.

### -allParameters

CDPreferences/DocumentPreferences.m
```
- (NSDictionary*)allParameters;
{
  NSManagedObjectContext *moc;
  NSError *error = nil;
  moc = [[self associatedDocument] managedObjectContext];
  NSFetchRequest *request = [[NSFetchRequest alloc] init];
  [request setEntity:[NSEntityDescription entityForName:@"Parameter"
                                  inManagedObjectContext:moc]];
  NSArray *params = [moc executeFetchRequest:request error:&error];
  if (error) {
    DLog(@"Error fetching parameter: %@\n%@", [error localizedDescription],
        [error userInfo]);
    return nil;
  }
  NSMutableDictionary *dict = [[self defaults] mutableCopy];
  for (NSManagedObject *param in params) {
    NSString *name = [param valueForKey:@"name"];
    NSString *value = [param valueForKey:@"value"];
    [dict setValue: value forKey:name];
  }
  return dict;
}
```

In addition to the primary function of this class, we have a couple of convenience methods that have proven useful. The first one, -allParameters, returns an NSDictionary of all the parameters, including the defaults. In this method, we create an NSFetchRequest for the Parameter entity without an NSPredicate. We take the resulting NSArray from the fetch and loop over it. Within that loop, we add each NSManagedObject to an NSMutableDictionary derived from the default NSDictionary. This ensures we have both the default values and the Parameter entries included in the final NSDictionary.

### -allParameterNames

CDPreferences/DocumentPreferences.m

```
- (NSArray*)allParameterNames;
{
  NSManagedObjectContext *moc;
  NSError *error = nil;
  moc = [[self associatedDocument] managedObjectContext];
  NSFetchRequest *request = [[NSFetchRequest alloc] init];
  [request setEntity:[NSEntityDescription entityForName:@"Parameter"
                              inManagedObjectContext:moc]];
  NSArray *params = [moc executeFetchRequest:request error:&error];
  if (error) {
    DLog(@"Error fetching parameter: %@\n%@", [error localizedDescription],
        [error userInfo]);
    return nil;
  }

  NSMutableArray *keys = [[[self defaults] allKeys] mutableCopy];
  for (NSManagedObject *param in params) {
    NSString *name = [param valueForKey:@"name"];
    [keys addObject:name];
  }
  return keys;
}
```

Like -allParameters, -allParameterNames is a convenience method that returns an NSArray of the keys currently set or defaulted. Just like the -allParameters method, it retrieves all the parameter NSManagedObject objects and loops over them. Within that loop, it adds the name property to an NSMutableArray derived from the defaults NSDictionary.

## 10.3 Wrapping Up

With this design, we can access our parameters within each document without having to worry about the underlying structure. We also don't need to stop coding just to hop over and add a parameter to the object. We can work with DocumentPreferences in the same manner that we work with NSUserDefaults.

This same design can be used in a nondocument application by changing the DocumentPreferences object by directly adding the methods -valueForUndefinedKey: and -setValue:forUndefinedKey: to the NSApplicationDelegate along with the NSManagedObjectContext.

Whether we are working in a document model or not, we can now access persistent store–specific parameters with a single call similar to the following:

```
NSString *value = [[self preferences] valueForKey:@"exampleKey1"];
```

We can also set them with a call similar to the following:

```
[[self preferences] setValue:@"someValue" forKey:@"someKey"];
```

In both of these examples, we are calling -valueForKey: and -setValue:forKey: directly on the DocumentPreferences object and not worrying about whether the value exists. If it does not exist, we will receive a nil. If it has been set as a default, we get the default back, and if we have overridden the default or previously set the property, it is returned.

Lastly, like the NSUserDefaults, the default values are not persisted to disk. Therefore, we need to set them every time we initialize the DocumentPreferences.

**CDPreferences/MyDocument.m**
```
NSMutableDictionary *defaults = [NSMutableDictionary dictionary];
[defaults setValue:[NSNumber numberWithBool:YES] forKey:@"default1"];
[defaults setValue:@"DefaultValue2" forKey:@"default2"];
[defaults setValue:@"DefaultValue3" forKey:@"default3"];
[[self preferences] setDefaults:defaults];
```

However, we do not need to worry about changing the defaults at a later date. If we change the defaults in a subsequent version, they will automatically be updated if the user has not overridden them.

Now that we have addressed making our code cleaner and more integrated on the inside, we need to look at making our application cleaner and more integrated with the overall operating system. As you will see in Chapter 9, *Spotlight, Quick Look, and Core Data*, on page 153, with a small amount of work we can make our application a true first-class Mac OS X citizen.

# CHAPTER 11

# Distributed Core Data

Imagine if all the users in a family had our recipe application and wanted to be able to see everyone else's recipes. You can probably come up with many such scenarios for sharing data across a local area network. If your application sits on a user's desktop and laptop, there is a fair chance the user wants to keep that data in sync. Of course, this can be done with iCloud for a single user, but imagine a small office environment or family of computers. Not every user has the same iCloud account, and you may not want to share the entire data set to every user. Being able to set up a local area sharing can solve the need to share partial or complete data in a local environment.

Core Data is generally considered to be a single-user/single-application persistent store. However, as we explored in Chapter 6, *Using iCloud*, on page 99, Core Data can be used beyond the single-user/single-application design with iCloud along more than one application and/or device to access the same data. In this chapter, we are going to explore using Core Data with distributed objects. Distributed objects enable a Cocoa application to call an object in a different Cocoa application (or a different thread in the same application). The applications can even be running on different computers on a network.

To take this idea one step further, we are going to add Bonjour into the design. Bonjour, also known as *zero-configuration networking*, enables automatic discovery of computers, devices, and services on IP networks. With this combination, we can provide access to a Core Data repository to any client on the network "automatically"—without user interaction.

Before we go into the details, let's examine the cons for this design.

- *Scalability*: This design does not scale well at all. When we are working with a couple of clients on a network, the design performs just fine. But when we start scaling it to half a dozen or more clients, it starts to slow down very quickly. There are optimizations that we can do, but if you have more than a couple of clients, it's better to use a full database solution instead of Core Data.

- *Threading*: Although all the calls to the server are performed on the main thread, calls within objects passed by reference are not by their very nature. Therefore, if we pass an NSManagedObject by reference to a client and that client makes a change to the NSManagedObject, we are in a worst-case situation with regard to threading.

## 11.1 Building the Server

In a normal client-server application, the server would be a background or GUI-less application. In this demonstration, we are going to start with a normal single persistent store Cocoa application instead. There is no benefit to having a UI for a server in a production environment, but for testing, it is useful to see the activity on the server. Therefore, we start with creating a Core Data Cocoa application called DistributedCDServer. The user interface for the server is a single window with a table view displaying the list of items in the Core Data persistent store, as shown here:

The data model for this example is composed of two entities. The top-level entity is named Test and has two properties: name and children. The second entity is called Child and also has two properties: name and parent. The two objects share a many-to-one relationship between the properties children and parent. The resulting model looks like this:

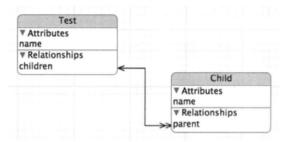

## Distributed Objects Protocol

When I am working with distributed objects, I prefer to contain the contract between the client and the server within a protocol. For this application, we are going to have a few methods that the clients can use to query the server, but we are not going to have any server to client queries.

The resulting protocol is as follows:

```
DistributedCDServer/PPDistributedProtocol.h
#define kDomainName @"local."
#define kServiceName @"_pragProgExample._tcp"

@protocol PPDistributedProtocol

- (oneway void)ping;

- (byref NSManagedObject*)createObject;
- (byref NSManagedObject*)createChildForObject:(byref NSManagedObject*)parent;
- (oneway void)deleteObject:(byref NSManagedObject*)object;
- (byref NSArray*)allObjects;
- (byref NSArray*)objectsOfName:(bycopy NSString*)name
                  withPredicate:(bycopy NSPredicate*)predicate;

@end
```

When we are working with distributed objects, we need to define how nonscalar attributes are handled. (These are discussed in depth in Apple's documentation.) In our protocol, we are passing most of the objects byref, which means an NSDistantObject is created on the receiver as a proxy to the object residing on the server. This is different from bycopy, which makes a copy of the object on the receiving end. One of the interesting differences between these is that KVO works across a distributed object when it is passed byref. This will be demonstrated as we build the application.

## Broadcasting the Service

Distributed objects work by using good old Unix sockets. Fortunately, these are wrapped with NSSocketPort for us, so we do not need to use the raw C functions and all the complexity that entails. To use sockets, we need to know the address and port of the socket to talk to. This can be entered by the user, which is a suboptimal experience, or we can discover it using Bonjour. To use Bonjour, we must set up a broadcast on the server for the client to discover.

**DistributedCDServer/AppDelegate.m**
```objc
- (void)startBroadcasting
{
  receiveSocket = [[NSSocketPort alloc] init];
  int receivePort = [self portFromSocket:receiveSocket];
  myConnection = [[NSConnection alloc] initWithReceivePort:receiveSocket
                                                  sendPort:nil];
  [myConnection setRootObject:self];
  myService = [[NSNetService alloc] initWithDomain:kDomainName
                                              type:kServiceName
                                              name:kServerName
                                              port:receivePort];

  [myService setDelegate:self];
  [myService publish];
}
```

In the -startBroadcasting method, we first initialize a new NSSocketPort. When we use the default -init method, the NSSocketPort chooses a random open port for us to use. However, we need to broadcast this port information as part of the Bonjour service. Therefore, we need to extract the port information from the NSSocketPort object. In a production environment, we probably want to define a port to use instead of selecting one at random.

**DistributedCDServer/AppDelegate.m**
```objc
- (int)portFromSocket:(NSSocketPort*)socket
{
  struct sockaddr *address = (struct sockaddr*)[[receiveSocket address] bytes];
  uint16_t port;
  if (address->sa_family == AF_INET) {
    port = ntohs(((struct sockaddr_in*)address)->sin_port);
  } else if (address->sa_family == AF_INET6) {
    port = ntohs(((struct sockaddr_in6*)address)->sin6_port);
  } else {
    @throw [NSException exceptionWithName:@"Socket Error"
                                  reason:@"Unknown network type"
                                userInfo:nil];
  }
  return port;
}
```

This bit of C code determines whether the address received from the NSSocketPort is IPv4 or IPv6 and, based on that decision, extracts the port information from the address and returns it to the caller.

With the port number in hand, we next construct an NSConnection and assign the AppDelegate as the root object. The root object is what will be "proxied" to any clients, and any methods they call on that proxy object will be transferred to the root object on the receiver. In a more complex example, it would make sense to have a separate object used as the proxy instead of the AppDelegate. With the NSConnection created, we can initialize the NSNetService. The NSNetService handles the broadcasting using Bonjour. Bonjour requires four pieces of information: the domain, type, name, and port. We discovered the port previously, and we defined the domain and type within the PPDistributedProtocol. The last value is the name of server and should be unique per machine. With this information, we can instantiate the NSNetService, set its delegate, and publish it. Once we call -publish, other machines can see the service.

## Starting the Server

The -startBroadcasting method is invoked from -applicationDidFinishLaunching:

**DistributedCDServer/AppDelegate.m**
```
- (void)applicationDidFinishLaunching:(NSNotification*)notification
{
  [self startBroadcasting];

  saveTimer = [NSTimer scheduledTimerWithTimeInterval:(5.0 * 60.0)
                                               target:self
                                             selector:@selector(saveAction:)
                                             userInfo:nil
                                              repeats:YES];
}
```

In addition to broadcasting the service on start-up, we schedule an autosave of the NSManagedObjectContext. In this example, we automatically save every five minutes.

**DistributedCDServer/AppDelegate.m**
```
- (IBAction)saveAction:(id)sender
{
  NSError *error = nil;
  NSManagedObjectContext *context = [self managedObjectContext];
  if (![context hasChanges]) return;
  if (![context save:&error]) {
    [self logError:error];
  }
}
```

The -saveAction: is similar to a save in any Core Data application. There are a couple of changes that we made just for protection. Before we attempt a save call, we first check to see whether there are any changes to save. In addition, instead of handing off the error (if there is one) to the NSApplication to present via the UI, we instead log the error to the console via a call to -logError:. By logging the error, we can see all the issues in a more programmer-friendly setup.

**DistributedCDServer/AppDelegate.m**
```
- (void)logError:(NSError*)error
{
  id sub = [[error userInfo] valueForKey:@"NSUnderlyingException"];
  if (!sub) {
    sub = [[error userInfo] valueForKey:NSUnderlyingErrorKey];
  }
  if (!sub) {
    NSLog(@"%@:%s Error Received: %@", [self class], __PRETTY_FUNCTION__,
        [error localizedDescription]);
    return;
  }

  if ([sub isKindOfClass:[NSArray class]] ||
      [sub isKindOfClass:[NSSet class]]) {
    for (NSError *subError in sub) {
      NSLog(@"%@:%s SubError: %@", [self class], __PRETTY_FUNCTION__,
          [subError localizedDescription]);
    }
  } else {
    NSLog(@"%@:%s exception %@", [self class], __PRETTY_FUNCTION__,
        [sub description]);
  }
}
```

The -logError: attempts to extract the NSUnderlyingException from the userInfo of the passed-in NSError. If something goes wrong within Core Data that is not part of the normal failure path, it is possible to get information about the failure via the stored NSUnderlyingException. If there is no NSUnderlyingException, we look for a value stored under the key NSUnderlyingErrorKey. If we get something back from that key, we check to see whether it is a collection, which would indicate multiple validation errors and print the -localizedDescription to the console. If we cannot locate either an NSUnderlyingException or an NSUnderlyingErrorKey, we dump the -localizedDescription for the NSError that is passed in.

Once the Bonjour service has started and the save thread has begun, the server waits for requests from clients. In a distributed object application, the server does not get notified when a client connects; it simply starts getting calls to the exposed methods.

## Receiving Requests from Clients

Working with distributed objects is deceptively easy. Other than the minor alterations to the method signatures, there are no changes to the methods and how they are handled. However, whenever we write a method that is going to be accessed via distributed objects, we need to remember it is not being called locally; therefore, we need to keep a few things in mind.

- The server configuration we have built in this example has one incoming socket: it can process only one request at a time. If a request takes too long (demonstrated in a moment), all the other clients wait in line, including calls from the same client.

- Although we can pass objects by reference to the client, if those objects get passed back to the server by reference, it can cause confusion. This is especially true when dealing with NSManagedObject objects. Therefore, whenever we receive an NSManagedObject from the client, we resolve a local reference and perform any actions on the local reference instead of trying to use the client reference a second time on the server.

### -ping Implementation

The first method I always implement when building a distributed object application is -ping. I use this method to test the connectivity between the client and the server. Since this method does nothing other than print out a console message, I am guaranteed that no other programming errors will be introduced while I test the connectivity.

**DistributedCDServer/AppDelegate.m**
```
- (oneway void)ping
{
  NSLog(@"%@:%s received", [self class], __PRETTY_FUNCTION__);
}
```

### -allObjects Implementation

This is one of those methods that is at risk of taking too long.

**DistributedCDServer/AppDelegate.m**
```
- (byref NSArray*)allObjects
{
  NSManagedObjectContext *context = [self managedObjectContext];
  NSFetchRequest *request = [[NSFetchRequest alloc] init];
  NSEntityDescription *entity = [NSEntityDescription entityForName:@"Test"
                                      inManagedObjectContext:context];
  [request setEntity:entity];
```

```
NSError *error = nil;
NSArray *objects = [context executeFetchRequest:request error:&error];
[request release], request = nil;

if (error) {
  NSLog(@"%@:%s error: %@", [self class], __PRETTY_FUNCTION__, error);
  return nil;
}
return objects;
}
```

In this method, we retrieve a reference to the NSManagedObjectContext and build an NSFetchRequest to retrieve all the Test entities from the persistent store. If there are any errors, we log them and return nil. Otherwise, we return the resulting NSArray.

This method, although useful for demonstrating distributed objects and Core Data, is a very poor performer. When we're working with tens of thousands of entities in the persistent store, they take a long time to pass over the network. This hampers the performance of not just the client making the request but every client waiting in line to make a request on the server. If our requirements involve data of this size, we should consider other options. One option that has met great success is to keep a local copy of the entire repository on each machine and, when the machines sync, merely pass deltas back and forth instead of a true client-server environment.

### -createObject Implementation

**DistributedCDServer/AppDelegate.m**
```
- (byref NSManagedObject*)createObject;
{
  NSManagedObjectContext *context = [self managedObjectContext];
  NSManagedObject *object = nil;
  object = [NSEntityDescription insertNewObjectForEntityForName:@"Test"
                                        inManagedObjectContext:context];
  return object;
}
```

The -createObject method demonstrates a more performant distributed object method. In this method, we again retrieve a reference to the NSManagedObject-Context and use that reference to create a new Test object. We create and delete all objects on the server as opposed to pulling the NSManagedObjectContext to the client and trying to delete it remotely. This helps prevent any threading issues while working with the NSManagedObjectContext.

> ⍀// **Joe asks:**
> ℥ᵋ **Can We Pass the NSManagedObjectContext by Reference?**
>
> Although this is feasible, it's not recommended. When we pass objects by reference, a proxy object is created on the receiver that sends all messages back to the server to be performed. This is fine for objects with low complexity, but when we're dealing with highly complex objects, such as the NSManagedObjectContext, performance suffers. During experimentation, I received some very unusual errors deep within the Core Data API when the NSManagedObjectContext was passed by reference. It's probably best to avoid this approach.

### -deleteObject Implementation

DistributedCDServer/AppDelegate.m

```
- (oneway void)deleteObject:(byref NSManagedObject*)object;
{
  NSManagedObjectContext *context = [self managedObjectContext];
  NSManagedObject *local = [context objectWithID:[object objectID]];
  if ([local isDeleted]) {
    return;
  }
  if (![local isInserted]) {
    [self saveAction:self];
  }
  [context deleteObject:local];
}
```

The -deleteObject is similar to the -createObject discussed earlier. However, in this method, we need to retrieve a local reference to a passed-in NSManagedObject. If we attempt to delete the referenced NSManagedObject directly, the NSManagedObjectContext implodes deep within the API. No doubt this is caused by the double proxy of looping to the remote and then back again to the server. To solve this issue, we retrieve the NSManagedObjectID from the referenced NSManagedObject and use it to retrieve a local reference to the NSManagedObject via the -objectWithID: of the NSManagedObjectContext. Once we have a local reference to the NSManagedObject, we check to see whether it is freshly inserted or already deleted. If it is freshly inserted, we need to persist it before we can delete it. Therefore, we save the NSManagedObjectContext and then delete the NSManagedObject. If the NSManagedObject has already been deleted, we return to the caller.

## -createChildForObject: Implementation

DistributedCDServer/AppDelegate.m

```
- (byref NSManagedObject*)createChildForObject:(byref NSManagedObject*)parent;
{
  NSManagedObjectContext *context = [self managedObjectContext];
  NSManagedObject *localParent = [context objectWithID:[parent objectID]];
  NSManagedObject *object = nil;
  object = [NSEntityDescription insertNewObjectForEntityForName:@"Child"
                                        inManagedObjectContext:context];
  [object setValue:localParent forKey:@"parent"];
  return object;
}
```

The -createChildForObject: implementation is similar to the -createObject implementation discussed earlier. There is one important difference, though. Since we defined the Child entity to have a nonoptional parent property, we set it immediately while we are still on the main thread of the server. This again is a protection against the uncontrollably multithreaded nature of distributed objects. We could just create the Child entity and return it to the caller, but there is a fair chance that a save will occur before the relationship is updated on the client, and an error would result.

In addition to setting the parent property on the Child object, we also grab a local reference to the passed-in NSManagedObject. Although I did not receive any errors while testing this method by using the remote proxy, there is no reason to risk it.

## -objectsOfName:withPredicate: Implementation

DistributedCDServer/AppDelegate.m

```
- (byref NSArray*)objectsOfName:(bycopy NSString*)name
                  withPredicate:(bycopy NSPredicate*)predicate;
{
  NSManagedObjectContext *context = [self managedObjectContext];
  NSError *error = nil;
  NSFetchRequest *request = [[NSFetchRequest alloc] init];
  [request setEntity:[NSEntityDescription entityForName:name
                                 inManagedObjectContext:context]];
  [request setPredicate:predicate];
  NSArray *results = [context executeFetchRequest:request error:&error];
  [request release], request = nil;
  if (error) {
    NSLog(@"%@:%s Error on fetch %@", [self class], __PRETTY_FUNCTION__, error);
    return nil;
  }
  return results;
}
```

In this previous example method, we deal with a more complicated situation. During the development of this method, I started by passing an NSFetchRequest between the server and clients. This resulted in some terminal errors within the Core Data stack, which led me to this solution instead. Based on these experiments, it is clear to me that passing around the NSManagedObjectContext itself results in some risky situations and should be avoided. However, NSPredicate objects can be passed around without any issue. Therefore, in this method, we accept the name of the entity and the NSPredicate to use in the NSFetchRequest. From this, we build the NSFetchRequest and execute it against the local NSManagedObjectContext. If there is an error, we print it to the console and return nil. Otherwise, we return the resulting array.

## 11.2 Building the Client

The client side of this application is both more complicated and easier than the server side. Configuring Bonjour and setting up the distributed objects is a bit more complicated than it is on the server. However, once the distributed object is configured, the rest of the setup is significantly easier.

In this example, we are going to build a client designed to stress test the server, as opposed to being truly functional in a user perspective. Our client is going to connect to the first server it finds, and once the connection is complete, it will run NSTimer objects to fire against each of the methods on the server in quick succession. With this type of client, we can stress test the server with multiple clients and look for race conditions and threading/locking issues.

### Configuring the Xcode Project

Unlike the server, the client is going to start with a Cocoa non–Core Data application. Because the server is maintaining the Core Data repository, the client does not need to be configured as a Core Data application. However, like the server, our user interface is a single window with a single table displaying the results of one of the method calls to the server. See Figure 42, *The distributed client user interface*, on page 200.

Once the DistributedCDClient project has been created, we need to copy the PPDistributedProtocol.h file from the server into the project. Normally I would just reference the file directly from the server project so that both are using the same file, but the example has a copy in each project to prevent any errors in the referencing. Next we need create a new class called AppDelegate and add it to the project. Once the AppDelegate has been added to the project, we will need to configure the user interface.

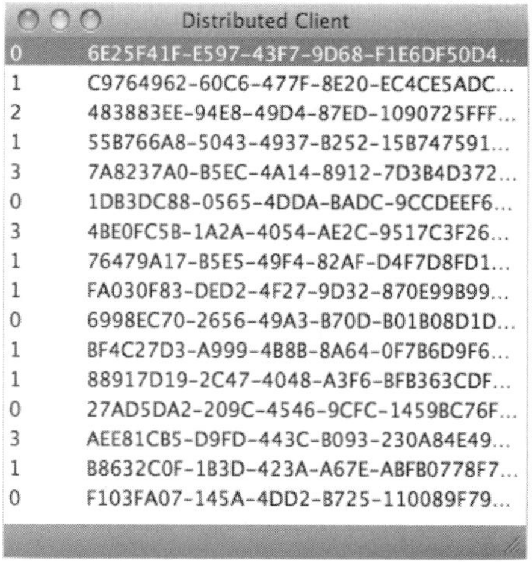

| | Distributed Client |
|---|---|
| 0 | 6E25F41F-E597-43F7-9D68-F1E6DF50D4... |
| 1 | C9764962-60C6-477F-8E20-EC4CE5ADC... |
| 2 | 483883EE-94E8-49D4-87ED-1090725FFF... |
| 1 | 55B766A8-5043-4937-B252-15B747591... |
| 3 | 7A8237A0-B5EC-4A14-8912-7D3B4D372... |
| 0 | 1DB3DC88-0565-4DDA-BADC-9CCDEEF6... |
| 3 | 4BE0FC5B-1A2A-4054-AE2C-9517C3F26... |
| 1 | 76479A17-B5E5-49F4-82AF-D4F7D8FD1... |
| 1 | FA030F83-DED2-4F27-9D32-870E99B99... |
| 0 | 6998EC70-2656-49A3-B70D-B01B08D1D... |
| 1 | BF4C27D3-A999-4B8B-8A64-0F7B6D9F6... |
| 1 | 88917D19-2C47-4048-A3F6-BFB363CDF... |
| 0 | 27AD5DA2-209C-4546-9CFC-1459BC76F... |
| 3 | AEE81CB5-D9FD-443C-B093-230A84E49... |
| 1 | B8632C0F-1B3D-423A-A67E-ABFB0778F7... |
| 0 | F103FA07-145A-4DD2-B725-110089F79... |

**Figure 42—The distributed client user interface**

Opening the MainMenu.xib file in Interface Builder, we add a new NSObject to the xib and set its class to AppDelegate. We then need to bind the NSApplication delegate outlet to the AppDelegate. Next we add an NSArrayController to the xib and bind its content array to the AppDelegate with a model key of filteredObjects. Lastly, we add an NSTableView to the window, expanding it to take up the entire window and assigning the first column to the NSArrayController with a controller key of arrangedObjects and the model key path set to childCount. The second column's value should also be set to the NSArrayController with a controller key of arrangedObjects and the model key path set to name. Once that is complete, we can close Interface Builder and open the AppDelegate.

### -applicationDidFinishLaunching: Implementation

Like most application delegate objects, our custom code will start in the -applicationDidFinishLaunching:. The first thing our client needs to do is find a server to connect to. To accomplish this task, we initialize an NSNetServiceBrowser and set our AppDelegate as its delegate. We then configure it to search for our server using the #define settings in the protocol that we imported. The browser will run in the background and start searching for servers on the local network. If it finds a server, it calls -netServiceBrowser:didFindService:moreComing:.

DistributedCDClient/AppDelegate.m
```
- (void)applicationDidFinishLaunching:(NSNotification*)notification
{
  NSNetServiceBrowser *myBrowser = [[NSNetServiceBrowser alloc] init];
  [myBrowser setDelegate:self];
  [myBrowser searchForServicesOfType:kServiceName inDomain:kDomainName];
}
```

### -netServiceBrowser:didFindService: Implementation

Every time the NSNetServiceBrowser finds a service, it calls this method. If it finds more than one server in a single sweep of the network, it calls this method once per service, and the moreComing: will be set to YES.

DistributedCDClient/AppDelegate.m
```
- (void)netServiceBrowser:(NSNetServiceBrowser*)browser
           didFindService:(NSNetService*)service
              moreComing:(BOOL)more
{
  [service retain];
  [service setDelegate:self];
  [service resolveWithTimeout:5.0];
  [service startMonitoring];
  [browser stop];
  [browser release], browser = nil;
}
```

In our implementation, we want to connect to a server as soon as we find one. We are not worried about multiple servers on the network, so the first that comes in will do. Once we receive notice that a service matching our search criteria is available, we start monitoring it. This causes the NSNetService-Browser to attempt to resolve the service. Once the service is resolved, the service's delegate receives notification. Therefore, we set the AppDelegate as the delegate to the service. Since we care about only a single service, we shut down the browser and release it.

### -netServiceDidResolveAddress: Implementation

Once the service has been resolved, the NSNetService calls -netService-DidResolveAd-dress: on its delegate. When this method is called, we can retrieve the address and port information about the service, which lets us connect to it and begin using distributed objects.

DistributedCDClient/AppDelegate.m
```
- (void)netServiceDidResolveAddress:(NSNetService*)service
{
  NSConnection *clientConnection = nil;
  NSSocketPort *socket = nil;
  NSData *address = [[service addresses] lastObject];
  u_char family = ((struct sockaddr*)[address bytes])->sa_family;
  socket = [[NSSocketPort alloc] initRemoteWithProtocolFamily:family
                                                 socketType:SOCK_STREAM
                                                   protocol:IPPROTO_TCP
                                                    address:address];
  clientConnection = [NSConnection connectionWithReceivePort:nil
                                                    sendPort:socket];
  server = [clientConnection rootProxy];
```

```
    [socket release], socket = nil;
    [service stop];
    [service release];
    [self startTestTimers];
}
```

Once the NSNetService has been resolved, we can retrieve its addresses and connect to it. With access to the address from the NSNetService, we can initialize an NSSocketPort to connect to the server hosting the service. With the NSSocketPort initialized, we can then initialize an NSConnection and finally get a reference to the -rootProxy of the NSConnection, which is actually an NSDistantObject proxy for the AppDelegate of the server.

Once we have the server referenced properly, we can shut down the Bonjour NSNetService and start our tests.

## 11.3 Testing the Networking Code

Whenever I build an application that needs to communicate to a server or another device, I always start off with simple tests to confirm that the connection is working. I generally leave these tests in place until the code goes to production. This both provides me with a simple way to test the connectivity and gives me a base to fall back upon if some of the higher-level functions start to fail. For this application, let's start by setting up a group of timers that will fire off our test methods.

### -startTestTimers Implementation

To simulate a large amount of client-server traffic, this application runs several timers at a fairly high pace. This will help us catch any race conditions or other issues with the distributed nature of this application.

DistributedCDClient/AppDelegate.m
```
- (void)startTestTimers
{
  SEL selector = @selector(testPing);
  pingTimer = [NSTimer scheduledTimerWithTimeInterval:0.5
                                               target:self
                                             selector:selector
                                             userInfo:nil
                                              repeats:YES];
  selector = @selector(testObjectInsertion);
  insertTimer = [NSTimer scheduledTimerWithTimeInterval:0.5
                                                 target:self
                                               selector:selector
                                               userInfo:nil
                                                repeats:YES];
  selector = @selector(testObjectDeletion);
```

```
deleteTimer = [NSTimer scheduledTimerWithTimeInterval:1.0
                                               target:self
                                             selector:selector
                                             userInfo:nil
                                              repeats:YES];
selector = @selector(testChildInsertion);
childInsertTimer = [NSTimer scheduledTimerWithTimeInterval:1.0
                                                    target:self
                                                  selector:selector
                                                  userInfo:nil
                                                   repeats:YES];
selector = @selector(testChildDeletion);
childDeleteTimer = [NSTimer scheduledTimerWithTimeInterval:1.0
                                                    target:self
                                                  selector:selector
                                                  userInfo:nil
                                                   repeats:YES];
selector = @selector(testObjectFetch);
fetchTimer = [NSTimer scheduledTimerWithTimeInterval:15.0
                                              target:self
                                            selector:selector
                                            userInfo:nil
                                             repeats:YES];
}
```

The -startTestTimers fires up a number of timers that continuously call our test methods. We retain a reference to each of these timers so we can later shut them down gracefully.

## -disconnect Implementation

Whenever we shut down the client application, we want to shut down the timers, and we want to close the connection to the server. The -disconnect walks through each of the NSTimer references and invalidates them. Once all the timers are shut down, it retrieves the NSConnection from the server proxy and invalidates it.

**DistributedCDClient/AppDelegate.m**
```
- (void)disconnect
{
  [pingTimer invalidate], pingTimer = nil;
  [fetchTimer invalidate], fetchTimer = nil;
  [insertTimer invalidate], insertTimer = nil;
  [deleteTimer invalidate], deleteTimer = nil;
  [childDeleteTimer invalidate], childDeleteTimer = nil;
  [childInsertTimer invalidate], childInsertTimer = nil;
  NSConnection *connection = [(NSDistantObject*)server connectionForProxy];
  [connection invalidate];
  server = nil;
}
```

## -testPing Implementation

The first of our test methods is also the simplest. We call the -ping method on the server, and nothing else. We do not expect a return from the server at all. This method causes a log statement to be generated on the server, allowing us to watch the server and see that connections are in fact coming in. It also keeps the testing simple. With this method, we can confirm that the Bonjour service and the distributed objects are working properly without having to wonder whether some other logic in some other part of our application is the real source of a failure. If the ping is not getting through, we know either the Bonjour service or the distributed objects are failing.

DistributedCDClient/AppDelegate.m
```
- (void)testPing
{
  [server ping];
}
```

## -testObjectFetch Implementation

The -testObjectFetch is the first complicated method that we are testing across the distributed objects link. In this test, we construct an NSPredicate that we pass to the server to be executed against the NSManagedObjectContext. As I mentioned, passing the NSManagedObjectContext itself across distributed objects produced some terminal exceptions within the Core Data stack itself, so we are avoiding this by performing as much of the Core Data work as possible on the server. Here we are passing in the name of the entity we want to search against and the NSPredicate. The server returns an NSArray of the entities that fit the NSPredicate. One interesting thing to note in this method is that we are not using the new for loop to access the returned NSArray. Since the NSArray is actually an NSDistant proxy for the NSArray on the server, the newer fast enumeration does not handle it properly. Therefore, we need to use the older NSEnumerator instead.

DistributedCDClient/AppDelegate.m
```
- (void)testObjectFetch
{
  NSString *test = [GUID substringToIndex:3];
  NSPredicate *predicate = nil;
  predicate = [NSPredicate predicateWithFormat:@"name contains[c] %@", test];
  NSArray *results = [server objectsOfName:@"Test" withPredicate:predicate];
  NSEnumerator *enumerator = [results objectEnumerator];
  NSManagedObject *object;
  while (object = [enumerator nextObject]) {
    [object setValue:GUID forKey:@"name"];
  }
  [self setFilteredObjects:results];
}
```

To show and test KVO across the distributed objects, we loop over the NSManagedObject objects within the NSArray and update their name to a globally unique string that we retrieve from NSProcessInfo, using a #define to make it a little easier to read. The #define is as follows:

```
#define GUID [[NSProcessInfo processInfo] globallyUniqueString]
```

## -testObjectInsertion Implementation

Testing object creation is only a single call to the server. However, to test that we can start using the object immediately, we also set its name using a globally unique string received from the NSProcessInfo. In addition, we added a random into this method so that approximately 50 percent of the time it would not do an insertion. This step adds a bit of randomness to the data testing and helps keep the number of Test entities on the server low.

```
DistributedCDClient/AppDelegate.m
- (void)testObjectInsertion
{
  if ((rand() % 2) == NO) return;
  NSManagedObject *object = [server createObject];
  [object setValue:GUID forKey:@"name"];
}
```

## -testObjectDeletion Implementation

-testObjectDeletion is a fair bit more complicated than -testObjectInsertion because we need to have a reference to an object first before we can delete it. Therefore, this method starts off by calling -allObjects on the server to get an NSArray of Test entities. From that NSArray, we randomly select an entity to delete and call -deleteObject: on the server.

```
DistributedCDClient/AppDelegate.m
- (void)testObjectDeletion
{
  NSArray *objects = [server allObjects];

  if (![objects count]) return;

  int index = (rand() % [objects count]);
  NSManagedObject *toBeDeleted = [objects objectAtIndex:index];

  [server deleteObject:toBeDeleted];
}
```

## -testChildInsertion Implementation

Two methods are available to us for testing relationships: child creation and child deletion. In the first, -testChildInsertion, we start off by getting an NSArray of all the Test entities. From there, we call -createChildForObject: on the server, randomly using one of the Test entities from the retrieved NSArray. We let the server handle the actual creation of the relationship between these objects to ensure there are no issues with the distributed objects themselves. During testing, Core Data got confused when the relationship was created on the client as opposed to the server. Therefore, to avoid any risks in this area, we pass the parent back to the server to let the server both create the child and set the relationship between the two objects.

**DistributedCDClient/AppDelegate.m**
```
- (void)testChildInsertion
{
  NSArray *objects = [server allObjects];
  id object = [objects objectAtIndex:(rand() % [objects count])];
  id child = [server createChildForObject:object];
  [child setValue:GUID forKey:@"name"];
}
```

### -testChildDeletion Implementation

The last test method is the deletion of a child object. In this test, we again retrieve all the Test entities from the server and randomly select one. We then check to see whether the Test entity has a child, and if it does, we grab one of them and call -deleteObject: on the server with that child as the parameter.

**DistributedCDClient/AppDelegate.m**
```
- (void)testChildDeletion
{
  NSArray *objects = [server allObjects];

  int index = (rand() % [objects count]);
  id object = [objects objectAtIndex:index];

  NSSet *children = [object valueForKey:@"children"];

  if (![children count]) return;
  id child = [children anyObject];
  [server deleteObject:child];
}
```

## 11.4 Wrapping Up

Whenever we start working with multiple computers on a network or interapplication communication, the code starts to get extremely complex. However, at least with this design, we can keep the Core Data/persistence separated from the distributed objects/networking as much as possible. By doing so, we avoid the need for a large number of locks and synchronization that would otherwise be required.

As we discussed at the beginning of this chapter, it is not a very scalable design, but in situations where a formal stand-alone database is overkill, this design actually works quite well. There is no user configuration, and there is no need to set up an external application; we just start one application on one machine and another application on another and let them talk. The biggest gotcha is with the `NSManagedObjectContext`. As long as we don't try to share it across distributed objects, we can use Core Data fairly transparently.

The design built here can also be used in a peer environment, as opposed to the client-server design. Multiple peers could use Bonjour to discover each other and use distributed objects to sync their data stores so that each device has a complete and up-to-date copy of the data set. In a situation like that, users could have our application on each of their machines, and whenever they are near each other (that is, on the same local network), they would automatically update each other. Talk about a pleasant user experience!

# Building a Foundation

On our journey to learn about Core Data, we are going to use an original iPhone recipe application. We'll create the application in this appendix. While the application itself is fairly complex and contains a large number of views, the concepts behind these views are standard and will be familiar to anyone who has done work in Objective-C. If you have not yet mastered Objective-C and Cocoa, then I highly suggest you review Tim Isted's *Beginning Mac Programming [Ist10]* and Bill Dudney and Chris Adamson's *iOS SDK Development [AD12]*, both published by the Pragmatic Bookshelf.

Our goal in this appendix is to establish a baseline application from which to work. Core Data is a supporting framework, and we need something for it to support in order to explore and demonstrate its features and characteristics. We've placed the details of the application in this appendix so you can follow along if you want. This recipe application is the foundation used in the book. You can use this appendix as a reference of the overall picture of the application as we're exploring the inner workings of Core Data in the rest of the chapters.

If you are already comfortable with storyboards and the creation of iOS applications, feel free to skim the provided code sample and jump to Chapter 2, *iOS: NSFetchedResultsController*, on page 23, in which we'll begin to dive into the substance of Core Data.

## A1.1 The Storyboard

To keep the structure of our application as simple as possible, we will use a *storyboard* to design the entire UI of our iPhone application. As you will recall from your reading or experience, a storyboard allows us to view the entire application interaction in one place. We can also control a greater portion of the UI within the storyboard and thus allow for even less boilerplate code to be introduced to our project. If you are not familiar with the storyboard feature of Xcode, take a look at the WWDC videos from 2011 and 2012, which discuss this component in detail. You can see a zoomed-out version of our storyboard in Figure 43, *Our application storyboard*, on page 210.

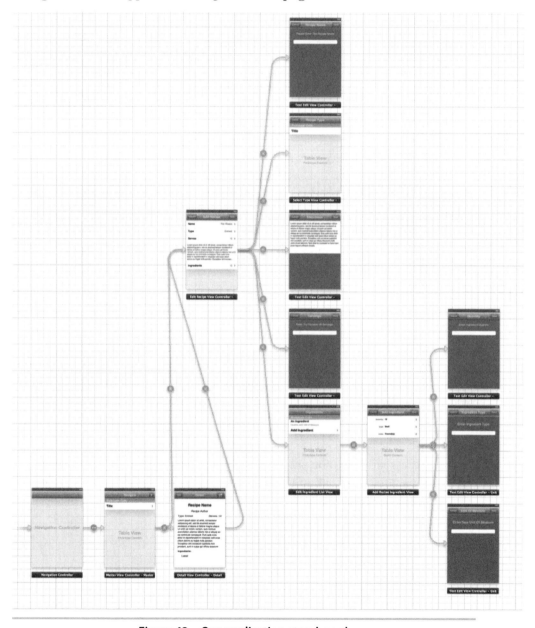

**Figure 43—Our application storyboard**

This storyboard may seem complex. It is, a bit. However, most of the code needed to support these views is minimal, and there's even a fair amount of view controller reuse that will make the application easier to develop and maintain.

There are three primary elements to this application: a list of recipes, a detailed view of a single recipe, and the ability to add/edit recipes. The add/edit feature is the most complex, so we'll save it for last.

## A1.2 The Recipe List

When users launch our application, they are immediately presented with a list of recipes. The list is represented in the storyboard as a UITableView with a prototype cell. We are using a basic cell in the prototype, as shown in Figure 44, *The beginning of our application*, on page 211.

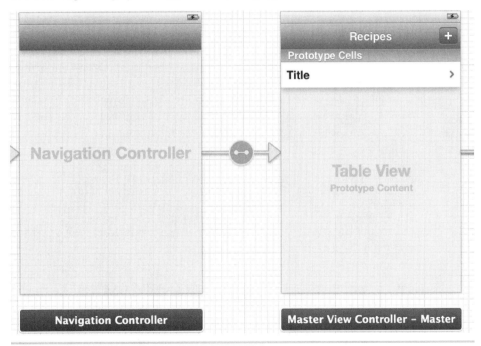

**Figure 44—The beginning of our application**

Associated with this UI element in the storyboard, we also have a UIViewController named PPRMasterViewController. The data for this UITableViewController is driven by an NSFetchedResultsController (which we explore in detail in Chapter 2, *iOS: NSFetchedResultsController*, on page 23). Right now we are concerned with the seques of this UIViewController. The segues describe the transition that our application uses when going from one view controller to another. A segue can happen when we select a row in a table, a button in the navigation bar, a button on the tab bar, or virtually anything that causes the UI to move to another view controller.

RecipesV1/PPRecipes/PPRMasterViewController.m
```
- (void)prepareForSegue:(UIStoryboardSegue *)segue sender:(id)sender
{
  if ([[segue identifier] isEqualToString:@"showRecipe"]) {
    [self prepareForDetailSegue:segue sender:sender];
    return;
  } else if ([[segue identifier] isEqualToString:@"addRecipe"]) {
    [self prepareForAddRecipeSegue:segue sender:sender];
    return;
  }
  ALog(@"Unknown segue: %@", [segue identifier]);
}
```

When a segue is activated, the current UIViewController receives a call to -prepareForSegue: sender:. That is our opportunity to prepare the next UIViewController for display. It's a good idea to use this method as a branching point for each potential segue. Taking this step aids with code clarity and maintenance. With one or two segues, this method is fairly easy to maintain. However, when we have many possible segues, the code quickly becomes unwieldy. Instead of waiting for the code to become unwieldy and refactoring it, we start off by using this method as a branching point.

RecipesV1/PPRecipes/PPRMasterViewController.m
```
- (void)prepareForDetailSegue:(UIStoryboardSegue*)segue sender:(id)sender
{
  NSIndexPath *indexPath = [self.tableView indexPathForSelectedRow];
  id object = [[self fetchedResultsController] objectAtIndexPath:indexPath];
  [[segue destinationViewController] setRecipeMO:object];
}
```

The first segue brings in the PPRDetailViewController and displays a single recipe in detail. The method -prepareForDetailSegue: sender: demonstrates the *dependency injection pattern*. We obtain a reference to the about-to-be exposed UIViewController, and we *inject* the information that it needs. We'll use this pattern extensively throughout the book.

RecipesV1/PPRecipes/PPRMasterViewController.m
```
- (void)prepareForAddRecipeSegue:(UIStoryboardSegue*)segue sender:(id)sender
{
  NSManagedObjectContext *context = nil;
  NSEntityDescription *entity = nil;
  NSManagedObject *newMO = nil;
  context = [[self fetchedResultsController] managedObjectContext];
  entity = [[[self fetchedResultsController] fetchRequest] entity];
```

```
newMO = [NSEntityDescription insertNewObjectForEntityForName:[entity name]
                            inManagedObjectContext:context];
[[segue destinationViewController] setRecipeMO:newMO];
}
```

The second segue branches us into the editing capabilities of our application. This is our first bit of code reuse.

Instead of having an "add" logic path and an "edit" logic path, the paths are combined. In fact, their functionality is 99 percent identical. The 1 percent difference between them concerns whether an object is being created or an existing object is being edited. By again using dependency injection, we pull that 1 percent difference out of the logic path and let the parent UIViewController make the decision. As far as the rest of our editing workflow is concerned, there is no difference. It is being handed a data object, and it does not matter whether the object has been created anew or whether it previously existed.

## A1.3 The Recipe Detail

When users select a recipe in our application, we want to display everything about the recipe in one screen so they can easily absorb the information and prepare the recipe. We'll need one fairly complex UIViewController in order to give them that one-screen access. Take a look at Figure 45, *The recipe detail view*, on page 214 for a sample of the view.

In our UIViewController, we'll take the data object that was passed to us and display it in one (potentially) lengthy UIScrollView.

The edit button in the UINavigationBar is the interesting part of this view controller. When the edit button is clicked, we enter the edit workflow (we'll discuss this further in the next section). This process is identical to the add workflow we discussed in Section A1.2, *The Recipe List*, on page 211. With this code reuse, we can now enter the same workflow from the view controller that allows us to view a recipe as we did from the list recipes view controller. Both of these produce the same effect: we can edit a recipe, and it does not matter if that recipe is new or existing.

RecipesV1/PPRecipes/PPRDetailViewController.m
```
- (void)prepareForEditSegue:(UIStoryboardSegue *)segue sender:(id)sender
{
  id controller = [segue destinationViewController];
  [controller setRecipeMO:[self recipeMO]];
}
```

Note the subtle difference in this reuse. In the previous version of the edit workflow, we created a new data object. In this version, we take our existing reference to the data object and hand it off to the edit workflow.

Figure 45—The recipe detail view

## A1.4 The Edit Workflow

The complexity of our application really lives in the edit workflow shown in Figure 46, *Starting the edit workflow*, on page 215. It is in this workflow that we edit, delete, and change data objects.

The bulk of the complexity of the edit workflow is in the very first UIViewController. To begin with, this UITable ViewController uses static cells, as opposed to prototype cells. In this design, we have a known quantity of cells, and each cell displays a different piece of information.

By utilizing static cells, we do a significant portion of the work of the edit workflow directly in the storyboard. We avoid handling a large amount of complexity in our application when a user selects a cell. In other words, instead of having to figure out which cell was selected, determine the view controller to build, populate that view controller, present it, and so on, we can have the storyboard do the bulk of that work for us. Each cell in this UITableViewController has a segue to another UIViewController. Each of those segues is named, and we can therefore do away with a large portion of code. Our UITableViewController subclass needs to look only at the identifier of the segue and inject the right dependencies.

Figure 46—Starting the edit workflow

RecipesV1/PPRecipes/PPREditRecipeViewController.m

```objc
- (void)prepareForSegue:(UIStoryboardSegue *)segue sender:(id)sender
{
  if ([[segue identifier] isEqualToString:@"editRecipeName"]) {
    [self prepareForEditRecipeNameSegue:segue sender:sender];
  } else if ([[segue identifier] isEqualToString:@"selectRecipeType"]) {
    [self prepareForSelectTypeSegue:segue sender:sender];
  } else if ([[segue identifier] isEqualToString:@"selectNumberOfServings"]) {
    [self prepareForSetServingsSegue:segue sender:sender];
  } else if ([[segue identifier] isEqualToString:@"selectIngredients"]) {
    [self prepareForSelectIngredientsSegue:segue sender:sender];
  } else if ([[segue identifier] isEqualToString:@"editDescription"]) {
    [self prepareForDirectionsSegue:segue sender:sender];
  } else {
    ALog(@"Unknown segue: %@", [segue identifier]);
  }
}
```

Here we see the value of using the -prepareForSegue: sender: method only for branching. Had we put all of the flow logic into this one method, it would easily be 100 lines of code or more and be a mess to maintain.

All of the UIViewController instances that are accessed from the edit UITableViewController fall into one of two categories: edit something or select something. Let's look at an example of both kinds of instance. See Figure 47, *Reused text edit view controller*, on page 217.

## Text Edit View Controller

The PPRTextEditViewController is easily the most reused UIViewController. The bulk of a recipe is text, and the text is probably going to need to be edited. As a result, the process of editing in our application must be highly reusable. This is also a great opportunity to use a block callback to assist in the reusability of the PPRTextEditViewController.

RecipesV1/PPRecipes/PPREditRecipeViewController.m
```
- (void)prepareForEditRecipeNameSegue:(UIStoryboardSegue *)segue
                               sender:(id)sender
{
  id editRecipeNameViewController = [segue destinationViewController];
  NSString *name = [[self recipeMO] valueForKey:@"name"];
  [[editRecipeNameViewController textField] setText:name];

  [editRecipeNameViewController setTextChangedBlock:^ BOOL (NSString *text,
                                                           NSError **error) {
    NSIndexPath *path = [NSIndexPath indexPathForRow:0 inSection:0];
    UITableViewCell *cell = [[self tableView] cellForRowAtIndexPath:path];
    [[cell detailTextLabel] setText:text];
    [[self recipeMO] setValue:text forKey:@"name"];

    return YES;
  }];
}
```

The most interesting part of this segue preparation is the callback. The PPRTextEditViewController is actually quite dumb. Its entire job is to consume the text entered into a text field and listen for either the Done button to be clicked or the Return key to be tapped. When either of those things happens, it takes the text from the UITextField (or the UITextView) and passes it to the callback block.

Note that the block accepts both an NSString and an NSError *pointer*. The parent, which defines the block, then validates the text and sets the error if there is a problem. The PPRTextEditViewController receives a pass/fail from the block. In the event of a failure, it displays the error.

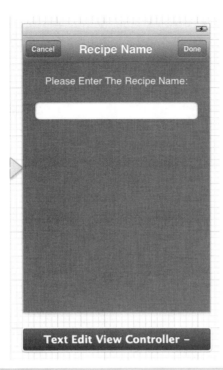

**Figure 47—Reused text edit view controller**

If the block returns a pass, the text view controller pops back to its parent.

With this design, we can use the PPRTextEditViewController to edit any piece of text we choose, and it does not need any custom or special handling code. The only thing we need to do for each instance is set up its view in the storyboard and pass in the text that it needs to start with. By customizing the view, we also gain access to which keyboard is appropriate for each text edit, thereby making it easy to reuse this UIViewController for numeric text, email addresses, or virtually any data we can think of.

The second function of the callback block is to update the data object and the edit view. Since we are using static cells, we must grab a reference to the existing cell and refresh it based on the text being passed into the block.

### List Ingredients View Controller

While there are a couple of "select something" items in the PPREditRecipeViewController, the ingredients selection is by far the most interesting. First, we want to display all of the existing ingredients. To do this, we need a selection view controller. Next, we want to add ingredients, which means we need to add an

Add Ingredient row when the user taps the Edit button. When the users select the Add Ingredient row, we then need to put them into another view controller that allows them to edit the individual components of an ingredient. In the Add Ingredient view, we then need to allow the user to set the quantity, type of ingredient, and unit of measure. The end result can be seen here:

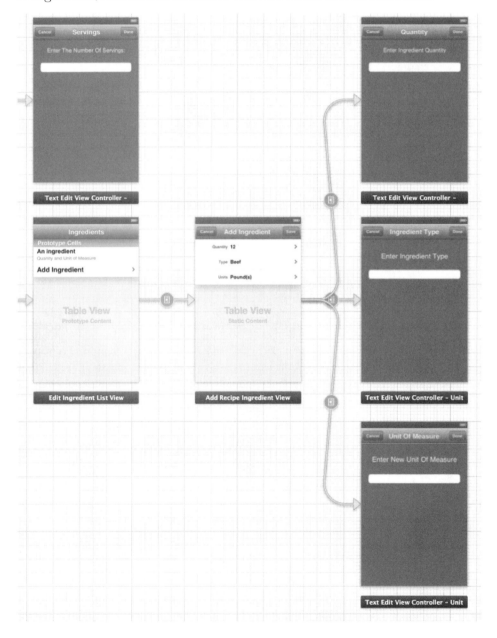

Later, as we update and enhance our application, this workflow becomes even longer and more complicated. Fortunately, the code stays quite sane with the reuse of view controllers and the use of the storyboard.

Unfortunately, we need to build two specific view controllers for this workflow. We need one to handle listing the ingredients (including adding and deleting) and one for adding an ingredient. Fortunately, we can get a lot of reuse from our text edit view controller in this part of the application.

## A1.5  Ready for Core Data

I have intentionally glossed over the Core Data portions of the application in this appendix. This is the foundation we will use as we learn and work with Core Data. In Chapter 1, *Under the Hood of Core Data*, on page 1, we step through the components of the Core Data structure of this application and discuss each in detail. At the end of that chapter, you will have a firm understanding of the Core Data stack and how to access it. From there we will begin to utilize some of the more advanced concepts behind Core Data to improve upon our application. You can use this appendix as a reference of the overall picture of the application as we delve deeply into the inner workings of Core Data.

# Macros in the Precompiled Header

As you read this book, you may wonder what I was thinking when I was formatting the code. While I have tried to keep it as "natural" as possible, the code examples throughout the book have been clarified as much as they can be within the limitations of print formatting. If you are reading the dead-tree version of this book, the formatting avoids line wrapping and lines running off the page. If you are reading an electronic copy of this book using iBooks, Kindle, or another reader, be aware that all of the code is formatted to be less than 80 characters wide. If you adjust the font size of your reader (or the orientation) to allow 80 characters in text width, the code should be legible.

In addition to general line wrapping, I frequently declare a variable on one line and then set it on a following line, with the goal of keeping within 80 characters and maintaining legibility. Please do not feel obligated to duplicate this code style while working through the code samples. I adopted the style simply for the sake of clarity within the limitations of print, and your code has no such limitation.

I've made some other adjustments of which you should be aware. Over the years, I have created several pieces of code to assist me in my daily development. Some of those come in the form of macros, and these macros make an appearance in this text. To avoid discussing them in bits and pieces, I'll lay them out here in order to provide a reference.

## A2.1 Where Are the Macros?

All the macros that I use are placed in the Prefix.pch file. In recent versions of Xcode, this file has changed names to ${ProjectName}_Prefix.pch. Actually, I dislike that naming convention very much; I'm of the strong opinion that consistent naming of files and consistent placement of those files promotes efficiency. Therefore, in all of my projects, I rename the precompiled header *back to*

Prefix.pch. It's what I am used to, and I always know where to look for it. You will find a similar consistency in some other files such as Info.plist and AppDelegate.[m|h]. Whenever you see a reference to one of these files in this book and you cannot find it in your project, try prepending ${ProjectName}_ to the front, and I suspect you will locate it.

```
#ifdef DEBUG
  #define DLog(...) NSLog(@"%s(%p) %@", __PRETTY_FUNCTION__, self,      \
    [NSString stringWithFormat:__VA_ARGS__])
  #define ALog(...) {                                                   \
    NSLog(@"%s(%p) %@", __PRETTY_FUNCTION__, self,                      \
      [NSString stringWithFormat:__VA_ARGS__]);                        \
    [[NSAssertionHandler currentHandler] handleFailureInFunction:[NSString \
      stringWithCString:__PRETTY_FUNCTION__ encoding:NSUTF8StringEncoding] \
      file:[NSString stringWithCString:__FILE__ encoding:NSUTF8StringEncoding]\
      lineNumber:__LINE__ description:__VA_ARGS__];                    \
    }
#else
  #define DLog(...) do { } while (0)
  #ifndef NS_BLOCK_ASSERTIONS
    #define NS_BLOCK_ASSERTIONS
  #endif
  #define ALog(...) NSLog(@"%s(%p) %@", __PRETTY_FUNCTION__, self,      \
    [NSString stringWithFormat:__VA_ARGS__])
#endif

#define ZAssert(condition, ...) do {                                    \
        if (!(condition)) {                                            \
          ALog(__VA_ARGS__);                                          \
        }                                                             \
      } while(0)                                                      \
```

## A2.2 What Do They Do?

At the core of this collection of macro code are three functions: DLog, ALog, and ZAssert.

DLog is designed to be a debug version of NSLog. It has the same syntax as NSLog, with one very important difference. If there is no DEBUG compiler flag set, DLog will compile down into a no-op. This allows us to add as many DLog statements to our code as we think is appropriate without worrying about them degrading the performance of the production application.

The second of these macros is the ALog. ALog is very similar to NSLog; in fact, it has the same syntax—but it performs a very different function. ALog, when the DEBUG compiler flag is set, will throw an NSAssertion whenever it is hit. In addition, when the DEBUG compiler flag *is not set*, it will still print its results out to the console, just like a default NSLog would. This functionality is ideal for those coding situations in which I tell myself "This will never happen." Now, instead of a comment that causes me to smack my head later, I get an NSAssertion immediately.

The third of these commonly used macros is the ZAssert. ZAssert is designed as a replacement to the venerable NSAssert. When the DEBUG compiler flag is set, this will perform in a similar way as NSAssert. It will throw an NSAssertion if the condition fails. However, in production, when assertions have been turned off, it will still function but will spit out its results to the console only on a failure. This allows us to actually roll functionality into the ZAssert, which we were not able to do previously because the NSAssert would not perform the conditional check at all if assertions were turned off.

# Bibliography

[AD12]    Chris Adamson and Bill Dudney. *iOS SDK Development*. The Pragmatic
          Bookshelf, Raleigh, NC and Dallas, TX, 2012.

[Ist10]   Tim Isted. *Beginning Mac Programming: Develop with Objective-C and Cocoa*.
          The Pragmatic Bookshelf, Raleigh, NC and Dallas, TX, 2010.

# Index

## A

-action: method, 81

Adamson, Chris, *iOS SDK Development*, xi

-addEntityToWatch: withPredicate: method, 33–34

-addObserver:for-KeyPath:options:context: method, 142

addPersistentStore WithType:configuration:URL:options:error: method, 41–42

adding property to retrieve relationship, on NSManagedObject, 14

allKeys method, 166

-allObjects method, 195, 205

-allParameterNames method, 186

-allParameters method, 185–186

ALog macro, 39, 222

AppDelegate
    adding -save: method to, 157–158
    adding to xib file, 124
    binding NSApplication delegate outlet to, 200
    updating, 132–133

-application: openURL: sourceApplication: annotation: method, 87

-applicationDidFinishLaunching: method, 193, 200

arrangedObjects controller key, 127, 131, 143

asynchronous
    adding NSPersistentStore to NSPersistentStoreCoordinator, 108–109
    saving, 94–97
    tracking of changes in iCloud, 109–110

atomic stores, 61–62

attribute mappings, in mapping model view, 45–46

automatic data migration, turning on, 41–42

-awakeFromFetch method, 14, 16–17

-awakeFromInsert method, 14, 16

## B

baseline application
    about, 209
    edit workflow, 214–219
    recipe detail, 213
    recipe list, 211–213
    storyboard, 209–211

*Beginning Mac Programming* (Isted), xi

binary data, storing, 63–65

binary repository, 61

binding
    Cocoa, 137, 143–147
    NSApplication delegate outlet to AppDelegate, 200
    NSArrayController, 127, 133, 143
    table column, 144
    values of columns to NSTableView, 131–132

Bonjour (zero-configuration networking)
    about, 189
    building client, 199
    building server, 192, 194
    in peer environment, 207
    in testing networking code, 204

broadcasting service using Bonjour, 192–193

## C

cache, warming up the, 69, 73

cacheName, NS-FetchedResultsController building up data cache on disk using, 25–26

calculated values, storing, 66

child-parent NSManagedObjectContext instances, features of, 92–98

cleaning, project, 40

client
    building, 199–202
    distributed user interface, 199–200
    receiving requests from, 195–199

Cocoa bindings, 137, 143–147

concurrency types, 94

-consumeIncomingFileURL: method, 87

-contextDidSave: method, 80

-contextInitialized, 87

-contextUpdated: method, 34–36

-controller: didChangeObject: atIndexPath: for-ChangeType: newIndex-Path: method, 29–30

-controller: didChangeSection: atIndex: for-ChangeType: method, 28–29

-controller: sectionIndexTitle-ForSectionName: method, 30

-controllerDidChangeContent: method, 31

-controllerWillChangeContent: method, 28

Core Data, about, ix–x, 2

Core Data Document-based Application template, 181

Core Data stack
    adding iCloud to, 101–102
    caution on using iOS 5.0, 77
    integrating iCloud to, 106–107
    model of, 9
    NSManagedObjectContext, 8–9
    NSManagedObjectModel, 1–5
    NSPersistentStoreCoordinator, 5–8

-createChildForObject: method, 198, 205

createDestinationInstances-ForSourceInstance: method, 49–51

-createObject: method, 196

-createParameter: method, 185

createRelationshipsForDestinationInstance: method, 51

cross-thread communication, 79–80

D

data, sharing between iOS and OS X iCloud, 119–120

data migration
    in iCloud, 112
    progressive, 54–59
    turning on automatic, 41–42

data model
    about, 2
    creating versioned, 39–42

distributed server, 190
editing data model, 3
grid view of, 3
loading, 4–5
optimizing, 63–67
relationships in, 67
sharing, 122–123

data quantity thresholds, iCloud, 118

database normalization, levels of, 66

-dealloc method, releasing resources using, 16

debugging
    dumping logs into contents of objects during, 15
    output from iCloud, 110–111

default model issue dialog box, error message for, 38

#define settings, 200, 205

-deleteObject: method, 197, 205

deletedObjects variable, 159

deleting objects, as performance issue, 73–74

denormalizing data, improving performance by, 66

desktop foundation, adding, 121–135
    adding custom code, 132–135
    application design, 122
    building controller layer, 123–126
    building user interface, 126–132
    list view tree, 128
    manual data entry for combo box, 131
    recipe application, 122–123, 127
    sharing data model, 122–123

desktop iCloud integration, 116–118

-didChangeValueForKey: method, 185

-didTurnIntoFault method
    overriding in NSManagedObject, 16
    releasing resources using, 16

-disconnect method, 203

disk access
    faulting and, 75
    vs. memory access, 72

disk persistence, 5

distributed client user interface, 199–200

distributed objects protocol, 191

DLog macro, 222

document-style application parameters or settings for, 179–187
    Spotlight and Quick Look in writing, 177

DocumentPreferences, 181–186

Dudney, Bill, iOS SDK Development, xi

duplication of all data, preventing in recursive relationships, 85

@dynamic keyword, 140–141

E

edit workflow, 214–219

Editor Style control, 2

entity hashes, 52–54

entity inheritance, 65

entity mappings, in mapping model view, 45

+entityForName:inManagedObjectContext: class method, 18

-executeFetchRequest:error:, calling on NSManagedObjectContext, 18

exporting recipes, in demonstrating multithreading, 81–87

external record flag, turning on, 63–64

F

faulted state, retrieving NSManagedObject in, 69

faulting, 71–75

faults, about, 15, 71

-fetchRequestTemplateForName: method, calling on NSManagedObjectModel, 20

fetched properties, 21

fetching, 67–71

file URL, determining for iCloud, 100–101

file rename strategy, for determining whether migration is required in iCloud, 113–116

filter predicate
    instantiating instances of NSEntityMigrationPolicy, 48–51
    in Mapping Model inspector, 46–47

-finalize method, releasing resources using, 16

-findParameter: method, 183

Finder, Quick Look thumbnail used by, 169

## G

GoFetch application, 68

## H

-hasChanges method, 93

hashes, entity, 52–54

heavy migrations
    about, 44
    completed mapping model, 45–46
    creating mapping model, 44–46
    customizing, 46–48
    in iCloud, 112
    instantiating instances of NSEntityMigrationPolicy, 48–51
    mapping model template, 45
    vs. light migrations, 42–44

HTML page, setting up options for Quick Look preview, 171–175

## I

iCloud
    about, 99–100
    configuring, 101–102, 106–107
    consuming changes from, 109–110
    data migration in, 112
    data quantity thresholds, 118
    desktop integration, 116–118
    directing NSManagedObjectContext to, 106–109

functioning through transaction logs, 111
    migrating existing application in, 113–116
    ordered relationships working in, 112
    sharing data between iOS and OS X in, 119–120
    turning off, 112
    turning on debugging, 110–111
    under hood of, 110–113
    using UIManagedDocument for iCloud, 100–105

iCloud URL
    determining file for, 100–101
    requesting, 114

iOS
    Cocoa Bindings and, 137
    sharing iCloud data between OS X and, 119–120

iOS 4.x, caution on using, Core Data APIs, 77

iOS 5.0, x–xi, 77

*iOS SDK Development* (Dudley and Adamson), xi

images
    displaying in application, 132–135
    sorting with Quick Look, 168

in-memory repository, 61

inheritance tree, building object-like, 65

-initWithConcurrencyType: initializer, 94

-initWithManagedObjectContext: method, 33

-initXXX methods of NSManagedObject, overriding in NSManagedObject, 14

-initializeCoreDataStack method, 39

intelligent relationships, 67

Interface Builder
    about, ix–x
    configuring NSArrayController using, 133, 145
    configuring Xcode project in building client, 200

Isted, Tim *Beginning Mac Programming*, xi

## J

JSON structure, NSManagedObject converting into dictionary for, 84–87

## K

KVO (Key Value Coding), 137–141

KVO (Key Value Observing), 142–143
    showing and testing across distributed objects, 205

KVO methods, overriding in NSManagedObject, 15

## L

large binary data, storing, 65

light migrations
    in iCloud, 112
    vs. heavy migrations, 42–44

local area sharing, setting up, 189–207
    building client, 199–202
    building server, 190–198
    testing networking code, 202–206

-logError: method, 194

## M

Mac OS X, *see* OS X

macros, in precompiled header, 221–222

-mailRecipe method, 83

MAIN, 100

-main method, 78–79, 86, 88

manipulating object model, 1–2

manual/heavy migrations, 44–51

many-to-many relationships, creating relationships for, 67

Mapping Model inspector, setting filter predicate in, 46–47

mapping models, 54
    completed, 45–46
    creating, 44–46
    template, 45

medium binary data, storing, 64

memory access vs. disk access, 72

-mergeChangesFromContext-DidSaveNotification: method, 79

metadata file, retrieving and loading into NSDictionary, 171

metadata files
accepting, 167
creating, 155–156
decreasing size of, 176–177
generating and updating, 157–162

metadata method, implementing, 156

metadataFilename method, 160

-metadataFolder method, 161–162

metadataname method, 157

methods, overriding in NS-ManagedObject, 14–17

migrations
data, 51–54
demonstrating simple, 39–42
of existing applications in iCloud, 113–116
heavy/manual, 44–51
light vs. heavy, 42–44
progressive data, 54–59

model version, setting current, 39, 41

MOM
changes inside, 53–54
ignoring child classes defined in, 52
migrating data from old to new, 54
objects, 51, 54

.mom files, 2

multithreading
about, 77–79
creating multiple contexts, 78–80
exporting recipes in demonstrating, 81–87
features of parent-child NSManagedObjectContext instances, 92–98
importing recipes in demonstrating, 87–92

-mutableSetValueForKey: method, 13

**N**

-netServiceBrowser:didFind-Service: method, 201

-netServiceDidResolveAddress: method, 201–202

network, distributing Core Data on, 189–207
building client, 199–202
building server, 190–198
testing networking code, 202–206

normalized databases, 66

NSApplication, 193

NSApplication delegate outlet, binding to AppDelegate, 200

NSApplicationDelegate, 186

NSArray
of entities returned matching search criteria, 18
fetched property returned as, 21
in importing recipe process, 89
NSSortDescriptor objects placed within, 20
of NSString, loading relationships by passing, 71
reducing complexity of underlying SQL using, 75
responding to NS-FetchedResultsSection-Info protocol, 27
returning NSManagedObject objects as, 69
in -testChildInsertion testing networking code implementation, 205
in -testObjectDeletion testing networking code implementation, 205
in -testobjectfetch testing networking code implementation, 204–205

NSArrayController
about KVO and KVC and, 145–146
adding to AppDelegate header, 133
adding to xib file, 124–126
associating pop-up boxes to, 129–132
binding, 127, 143

configuring within Interface Builder, 145
connecting buttons to, 128

NSAttributedString, Rich Text setting and, 129

NSCompoundPredicate, 34

NSConfinementConcurrency-Type, 94

NSConnection
in -disconnect testing networking code implementation, 203
-rootProxy of, 202

NSData, 83, 88–89

NSDictionary
in importing recipe process, 89
NSManagedObject converting into, 84–87
in NSMigrationManager, 50
retrieving and loading metadata file into, 171

NSEntityDescription, 17–20, 86, 90, 138

NSEntityMigrationPolicy, 48–51

NSEnumerator, 204

NSError, 83, 159–161
passing NSFetchRequest to, 20

NSFetchedResultsController
building ZSContextWatcher, 32–36
initializing, 25–26
listening to, 28–31
populating with data, 26
under hood of, 31–32
using, 23–31
wiring to UITableView, 26–28

NSFetchedResultsControllerDelegate protocol, 28–31

NSFetchedResultsSectionInfo protocol, 27

NSFetchRequest
in -allObjects server implementation, 195–196
creating, 17–20, 24–25
disk access and, 71

in -objectsOfName:with-
Predicate: server imple-
mentation, 199
returning NSArray of NS-
ManagedObject objects,
69
NSFileManager, requesting
cloudUR from, 114
NSFormatter, 146–147
NSInferMappingModelAuto-
maticallyOption, 42
NSJSONSerialization, 86
NSJSONSerializer, 89
NSMainQueueConcurrency-
Type, 94
NSManagedObject
accessing attributes, 10–
11
accessing relationships,
12–14
converting into dictionary
for JSON structure,
84–87
in -createChildForObject:
method, 199
in -deleteObject server
implementation, 197
overriding methods in,
14–17
passing into -populateM-
anagedObject: fromDic-
tionary:, 89–91
prefetch objects property
values, 69
primitive access, 11
queryable via KVC proto-
col, 139
resolving from repository
of, 67
retrieving faulted, 69
retrieving from parame-
ters table, 184–185
retrieving only objects
property values, 69
subclassing, 14
NSManagedObjectContext
accessing and initializing,
8–9
in -allObjects server im-
plementation, 195–196
asynchronous saving us-
ing parent-child in-
stances, 94–97
calling -executeFetchRe-
quest:error: on, 18
constructing in -main lo-
cal, 88

in -createObject server
implementation, 196
creating separate in-
stances for threads,
78–79
-deleteObject server implementation, 197
directing to iCloud, 106–
109
initializing using -
initWithConcurrency-
Type: initializer, 94
notifying of changes to
iCloud, 109–110
NSFetchedResultsCon-
troller requiring, 25
NSMigrationManager
tracking associations
of, 51
passing around, 199
passing by reference, 197
refreshing metadata files
when saving, 157–158
saving using parent-child
instances, 93
scheduling autosave of,
193
sharing across distribut-
ed objects, 207
syncing instances of
threads, 79–80
in -testobjectfetch testing
networking code imple-
mentation, 204
NSManagedObjectContextDid-
SaveNotification, 32, 80
NSManagedObjectContextOb-
jectsDidChangeNotification,
31
NSManagedObjectContextWill-
SaveNotification, 31
NSManagedObjectID objects
loading only, 68
loading property values
and, 69
retrieving, 68–69
NSManagedObjectModel
about, 1–5
calling -fetchRequestTem-
plateForName: method
on, 20
NSMigratePersistentStore-
sAutomaticallyOption, 42
NSMigrationManager, NSDictionary in, 50
NSMutableDictionary, 84–87

NSNetServiceBrowser, 200–
201
NSNumberFormatter, 146–
147
NSObject, KVC implemented
through, 138
NSObjectController, 147–148
NSOperation, naming issue
using, 78
NSOperationQueue, issue
calling -start method, 78
NSOutlineView, 148–149
NSPersistentDocument, subclass in desktop iCloud integration, 116–118
NSPersistentStore, adding to
NSPersistentStoreCoordinator, 6–7, 39, 101–102, 106–
109, 114–115
NSPersistentStoreCoordinator
adding iCloud to Core
Data Stack, 101–102
asynchronous saving us-
ing, 94–95
holding data as part of
cache, 73
initializing, 5–8
integrating iCloud to Core
Data Stack, 106–109
saving using, 93
NSPersistentStoreDidImpor-
tUbiquitousCon-
tentChangesNotification,
110
NSPersistentStoreUbiquitous-
ContentNameKey, 119
NSPredicate
filtering results on NS-
ManagedObject, 18–19
passing around, 199
passing in -testobject-
fetch testing networking
code implementa-
tion, 204
NSPrivateQueueConcurrency-
Type, 94
NSRemoveTemplate, 128
NSSearchField, 149–151
NSSet
accessing to-many rela-
tionship using KVC
and getting back, 13
immutable, 13
looping through, 160
passing to metadata-
building method, 161

NSSocketPort, 192, 202

NSSortDescriptor, 20–21

NSString
loading relationships by
passing NSArray of, 71
Rich Text setting and,
129

NSTableColumn, 127

NSTableView
binding values of
columns, 131–132,
143–145
for recipe source list,
127–128

NSTimer, 199

NSTreeController, 149

NSUnderlyingErrorKey, 194

NSUnderlyingException, 194

NSURL, 87

NSUserDefaults, 186

-numberOfSectionsInTable-
View: method, 26

### O

object inheritance, treating
entity inheritance as, 65

object model, manipulating,
1–2

-objectWithID: method, 84

Objective-C, changing file extension to compile in, 166

-objectsOfName:withPredi-
cate: method, 199

-observeValueForKey-
Path:ofObject:change:con-
text: method, 142–143

one-to-many relationships,
creating relationships for,
67

order of logic, impacting
search performance, 75

ordered relationships, working in iCloud, 112

OS X, 121
adding custom code,
132–135
adding desktop founda-
tion, 121–135
application design, 122
building controller layer,
123–126
building user interface,
126–132
Cocoa bindings, 143–147

functionality meeting
quality developing for,
153
KVC on, 137–141
KVO on, 142–143
list view tree, 128
manual data entry for
combo box, 131
NSArrayController, 145–
146
NSFormatter, 146–147
NSObjectController, 147–
148
NSOutlineView, 148–149
NSSearchField, 149–151
NSTreeController, 149–
151
recipe application, 122–
123, 127
sharing data model, 122–
123
sharing iCloud data be-
tween iOS and, 119–
120

OS X 10.7 Lion, x–xi, 77

### P

parent-child NSManagedOb-
jectContext instances, features of, 92–98

passing objects by reference,
197

-performBlock:, 92

-performBlockAndWait:, 92

performance tuning
about, 61
access patterns in, 75
faulting in, 71–75
fetching in, 67–71
optimizing data model,
63–67
persistent store types,
61–62

pictures, displaying in application, 132–135

-ping method, 195, 204

pop-up boxes, setting, 129–
131

-populateManagedObject:
fromDictionary:, 89

PPRExportOperation
comparison to PPRImpor-
tOperation, 88–92
constructing, 83–87

PPRImportOperation
comparison to PPRExpor-
tOperation, 88–92

constructing, 87
impact of parent-child
NSManagedObjectCon-
text instances in updat-
ing, 97–98

precompiled header, macros
in, 221–222

prefetching, 69, 72

preview, Quick Look, 171–176

-primitiveValueForKey:
method, 11, 14

project, cleaning, 40

@property keyword, 139–141

### Q

queries, searching across relationships by limiting, 75

Quick Look
about, 154
generator, 169–177
integrating with, 168–175
preview, 171–176
thumbnail, 169–171
writing application that
uses document model,
177

### R

recipe detail, 213

recipe list, 211–213

recipes
exporting in demonstrat-
ing multithreading, 81–
87
importing in demonstrat-
ing multithreading, 87–
92

reference, passing objects by,
197

regular expressions, impacting search performance, 75

relationship mappings, in
mapping model view, 46–47

relationships
intelligent, 67
loading, 70–71

-removeObserver:forKeyPath:
method, 142

reusable storage system,
reusable storage system,
179–187

Rich Text setting, turning off,
129–130

-rootProxy of NSConnection,
202

## S

-save: method, 93, 157–158

-saveAction: method, 193

saving to disk, in batches, 73

scalability, 189, 207

searching
  impacting performance, 75
  within properties, 66

sectionNameKeyPath, 25–26

segues, about, 211–213

-setContent: method, 148

-setName: method, 139

-setPrimitiveValue:forKey: method, 11

-setValue:forKey: method, 139, 187

-setValue:forUndefinedKey: method, 183–186

-setValuesForKeysWithDictionary: method, 90

sharing iCloud data between iOS and OS X, 119–120

Simmons, Brent, 61

small binary data, storing, 64

Spotlight
  about, 153–155
  accepting metadata files, 167–168
  creating metadata files, 155–156
  decreasing size of metadata files, 176–177
  generating and updating metadata files, 157–162
  implementing metadata method, 156–157
  implementing metadataname method, 157
  importer, 162–167, 176
  integrating with, 154–168
  template, 164, 166
  writing application that uses document model, 177

SQL, reducing complexity of underlying, 75

SQLite persistent store
  about, 62
  for resolving NSManagedObject from repository, 68

storing medium binary data, 64

table layout, 65

SQLite repository, 61

stack, Core Data
  adding iCloud to, 101–102
  caution on using iOS 5.0, 77
  integrating iCloud to, 106–107
  model of, 9
  NSManagedObjectContext, 8–9
  NSManagedObjectModel, 1–5
  NSPersistentStoreCoordinator, 5–8

-start method, 78

-startBroadcasting method, 192

-startTestTimers method, 202–203

storyboard, 209–211

subclassing, NSManagedObject, 14

@synthesize keyword, 140–141

## T

-tableView: cellForRowAtIndexPath: method, 27–28

tableView: numberOfRowsInSection: method, 27

-testChildDeletion method, 206

-testChildInsertion method, 205

-testObjectDeletion method, 205

-testObjectFetch method, 204–205

-testObjectInsertion method, 205

-testPing method, 204

thread blocking, 94

threading
  about, 77–79
  creating multiple contexts, 78–80
  in distributed user interface, 190
  exporting recipes in demonstrating, 81–87

features of parent-child NSManagedObjectContext instances, 92–98

importing recipes in demonstrating, 87–92

thumbnail, Quick Look, 169–171

to-many relationship, accessing on NSManagedObject, 13

to-one relationship, accessing on NSManagedObject, 12

transaction logs, iCloud functioning through, 111, 118

## U

UIActionSheet, constructing, 81

UIAlertView, 39

UIApplicationDelegate, 87, 116

UIManagedDocument, using for iCloud, 100–105

UINavigationBar edit button, 213

UITableView
  about, 23
  NSFetchedResultsController wiring to, 26–28

UITableViewDatasource methods, 26

Unicode text, impacting search performance, 75

URL, iCloud
  determining file for, 100–101
  requesting, 114

user interface, building, 126–132

UTIs (Uniform Type Identifiers), 162–164, 176

## V

-valueForKey: method, 13, 138–139, 187

-valueForUndefinedKey: method, 139, 182–183, 186

version error on iOS, 39–40

versioning
  about, 52
  creating versioned data model, 39–42
  fundamentals of, 51–54
  mapping model, 44

## W

warming up the cache, 69, 73

-willTurnIntoFault method,
overriding in NSManagedObject, 16

WithType: configuration: URL:
options: error: method, 7–8

## X

.xcdatamodel files, 2, 122

.xcdatamodeld files, 40

## Xcode

compiling .xcdatamodel
file in, 2
handling Spotlight importer, 163–164
project tree, 170
subproject for Quick Look
generator, 169–175
subproject for Spotlight
importer, 163–164

.xcodeproj file, 122

xib file, adding objects to,
123–126

XML repository, 61

## Z

ZAssert macro, 223

zero-configuration networking
(Bonjour)
about, 189
building client, 199
building server, 192, 194
in peer environment, 207
in testing networking
code, 204

ZSContextWatcher, building,
32–36

# More Mac

More for Mac power users, and Ruby on iOS!

Squeeze every drop of juice from OS X with over 400 quick and easy tips, tricks, hints and hacks in *Mac Kung Fu: Second Edition* . Exploit secret settings and hidden apps, push built-in tools to the limit, radically personalize your Mac experience, and make "it just works" even better. In addition to core OS X technologies, this significantly revised and expanded update to the best-selling first edition dissects new OS X Mountain Lion tools such as iCloud, Notifications, Reminders, and Calendar.

Keir Thomas
(424 pages) ISBN: 9781937785079. $39
*http://pragprog.com/book/ktmack2*

Make beautiful apps with beautiful code: use the elegant and concise Ruby programming language with RubyMotion to write truly native iOS apps with less code while having more fun. You'll learn the essentials of creating great apps, and by the end of this book, you'll have built a fully functional API-driven app. Whether you're a newcomer looking for an alternative to Objective-C or a hardened Rails veteran, RubyMotion allows you to create gorgeous apps with no compromise in performance or developer happiness.

Clay Allsopp
(112 pages) ISBN: 9781937785284. $17
*http://pragprog.com/book/carubym*

# Learn iOS Programming

Ready to learn how to program on iOS? We've got you covered.

Welcome to the new state of the art development for iOS, with the radically overhauled Xcode 4 toolchain and iOS 5 SDK. With this book you'll accelerate your development for iPhone, iPad and iPod Touch. You will learn the new tools like Storyboards, practice on new APIs like the Twitter framework and use the latest features of the Objective-C 2.0 programming language.

Chris Adamson and Bill Dudney
(300 pages) ISBN: 9781934356944. $35
*http://pragprog.com/book/adios*

Take your iPhone and iPad apps to the next level. You've seen cool features and tricks in other apps, but haven't had the time to really look into how they're done. We've got the answers for you. This book walks you through clean, reusable solutions to a wide variety of problems and patterns common to iOS development with Cocoa Touch and Objective-C. With these recipes in your arsenal, your next apps will be more polished and more maintainable than ever.

Paul Warren and Matt Drance
(200 pages) ISBN: 9781934356746. $33
*http://pragprog.com/book/cdirec*

# Welcome to the New Web

You need a better JavaScript and better recipes that professional web developers use every day. Start here.

CoffeeScript is JavaScript done right. It provides all of JavaScript's functionality wrapped in a cleaner, more succinct syntax. In the first book on this exciting new language, CoffeeScript guru Trevor Burnham shows you how to hold onto all the power and flexibility of JavaScript while writing clearer, cleaner, and safer code.

Trevor Burnham
(160 pages) ISBN: 9781934356784. $29
*http://pragprog.com/book/tbcoffee*

Modern web development takes more than just HTML and CSS with a little JavaScript mixed in. Clients want more responsive sites with faster interfaces that work on multiple devices, and you need the latest tools and techniques to make that happen. This book gives you more than 40 concise, tried-and-true solutions to today's web development problems, and introduces new workflows that will expand your skillset.

Brian P. Hogan, Chris Warren, Mike Weber, Chris Johnson, Aaron Godin
(344 pages) ISBN: 9781934356838. $35
*http://pragprog.com/book/wbdev*

# Career++

Ready to kick your career up to the next level? Start by growing a significant online presence, and then reinvigorate your job itself.

*Technical Blogging* is the first book to specifically teach programmers, technical people, and technically-oriented entrepreneurs how to become successful bloggers. There is no magic to successful blogging; with this book you'll learn the techniques to attract and keep a large audience of loyal, regular readers and leverage this popularity to achieve your goals.

Antonio Cangiano
(304 pages) ISBN: 9781934356883. $33
*http://pragprog.com/book/actb*

You're already a great coder, but awesome coding chops aren't always enough to get you through your toughest projects. You need these 50+ nuggets of wisdom. Veteran programmers: reinvigorate your passion for developing web applications. New programmers: here's the guidance you need to get started. With this book, you'll think about your job in new and enlightened ways.

Ka Wai Cheung
(250 pages) ISBN: 9781934356791. $29
*http://pragprog.com/book/kcdc*

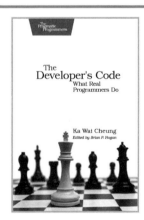

# Seven Databases, Seven Languages

There's so much new to learn with the latest crop of NoSQL databases. And instead of learning a language a year, how about seven?

Data is getting bigger and more complex by the day, and so are your choices in handling it. From traditional RDBMS to newer NoSQL approaches, *Seven Databases in Seven Weeks* takes you on a tour of some of the hottest open source databases today. In the tradition of Bruce A. Tate's *Seven Languages in Seven Weeks*, this book goes beyond a basic tutorial to explore the essential concepts at the core of each technology.

Eric Redmond and Jim Wilson
(330 pages) ISBN: 9781934356920. $35
*http://pragprog.com/book/rwdata*

You should learn a programming language every year, as recommended by *The Pragmatic Programmer*. But if one per year is good, how about *Seven Languages in Seven Weeks*? In this book you'll get a hands-on tour of Clojure, Haskell, Io, Prolog, Scala, Erlang, and Ruby. Whether or not your favorite language is on that list, you'll broaden your perspective of programming by examining these languages side-by-side. You'll learn something new from each, and best of all, you'll learn how to learn a language quickly.

Bruce A. Tate
(328 pages) ISBN: 9781934356593. $34.95
*http://pragprog.com/book/btlang*

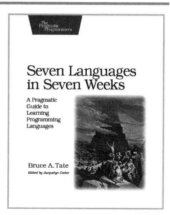

# Deal with the Real World

From exploratory testing to outsourcing, see how to get it done.

Uncover surprises, risks, and potentially serious bugs with exploratory testing. Rather than designing all tests in advance, explorers design and execute small, rapid experiments, using what they learned from the last little experiment to inform the next. Learn essential skills of a master explorer, including how to analyze software to discover key points of vulnerability, how to design experiments on the fly, how to hone your observation skills, and how to focus your efforts.

Elisabeth Hendrickson
(160 pages) ISBN: 9781937785024. $29
*http://pragprog.com/book/ehxta*

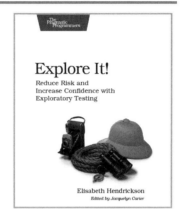

If you need to expand your business but not your budget, if your group has an intense but short-term project, if you don't have the skill set to get a job done- it's time to think about outsourcing. Starting from the first step (should you outsource part of your tech work?) to the last (how can you protect your intellectual property?), you'll learn everything about setting up projects overseas.

Nick Krym
(264 pages) ISBN: 9781937785055. $35
*http://pragprog.com/book/nkout*

# Be Agile

Don't just "do" agile; you want to *be* agile. We'll show you how.

The best agile book isn't a book: *Agile in a Flash* is a unique deck of index cards that fit neatly in your pocket. You can tape them to the wall. Spread them out on your project table. Get stains on them over lunch. These cards are meant to be used, not just read.

Jeff Langr and Tim Ottinger
(110 pages) ISBN: 9781934356715. $15
*http://pragprog.com/book/olag*

You know the Agile and Lean development buzzwords, you've read the books. But when systems need a serious overhaul, you need to see how it works in real life, with real situations and people. *Lean from the Trenches* is all about actual practice. Every key point is illustrated with a photo or diagram, and anecdotes bring you inside the project as you discover why and how one organization modernized its workplace in record time.

Henrik Kniberg
(176 pages) ISBN: 9781934356852. $30
*http://pragprog.com/book/hklean*

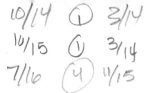

# The Pragmatic Bookshelf

The Pragmatic Bookshelf features books written by developers for developers. The titles continue the well-known Pragmatic Programmer style and continue to garner awards and rave reviews. As development gets more and more difficult, the Pragmatic Programmers will be there with more titles and products to help you stay on top of your game.

# Visit Us Online

### This Book's Home Page
*http://pragprog.com/book/mzcd2*
Source code from this book, errata, and other resources. Come give us feedback, too!

### Register for Updates
*http://pragprog.com/updates*
Be notified when updates and new books become available.

### Join the Community
*http://pragprog.com/community*
Read our weblogs, join our online discussions, participate in our mailing list, interact with our wiki, and benefit from the experience of other Pragmatic Programmers.

### New and Noteworthy
*http://pragprog.com/news*
Check out the latest pragmatic developments, new titles and other offerings.

# Save on the eBook

Save on the eBook versions of this title. Owning the paper version of this book entitles you to purchase the electronic versions at a terrific discount.

PDFs are great for carrying around on your laptop—they are hyperlinked, have color, and are fully searchable. Most titles are also available for the iPhone and iPod touch, Amazon Kindle, and other popular e-book readers.

Buy now at *http://pragprog.com/coupon*

# Contact Us

| | |
|---|---|
| Online Orders: | *http://pragprog.com/catalog* |
| Customer Service: | *support@pragprog.com* |
| International Rights: | *translations@pragprog.com* |
| Academic Use: | *academic@pragprog.com* |
| Write for Us: | *http://pragprog.com/write-for-us* |
| Or Call: | +1 800-699-7764 |